THOMAS
WELCOME ROYS

America's Pioneer of
Modern Whaling

CAPT. THOMAS WELCOME ROYS (ca. 1816–77)
(Courtesy Suffolk County Whaling Museum, Sag Harbor, N.Y.)

THOMAS WELCOME ROYS

America's Pioneer of Modern Whaling

FREDERICK P. SCHMITT

CORNELIS DE JONG

FRANK H. WINTER

PUBLISHED FOR

The Mariners Museum

NEWPORT NEWS, VIRGINIA

BY

The University Press of Virginia
CHARLOTTESVILLE

Property of Library
Cape Fear Technical Institute
Wilmington, N. C.

THE UNIVERSITY PRESS OF VIRGINIA

Copyright © 1980 by The Mariners Museum, Newport News, Virginia

Mariners Museum Publication no. 38

First published 1980

Library of Congress Cataloging in Publication Data
Schmitt, Frederick P.
  Thomas Welcome Roys, America's pioneer of modern whaling.
  (Mariners Museum publication ; no. 38)
  Includes index.
  1. Whaling—United States—History.   2. Roys, Thomas Welcome.
3. Whalemen—United States—Biography.   I. De Jong, Cornelis, joint
                                                 author.
II. Winter, Frank H., joint author.   III. Title.
IV. Series: Mariners' Museum, Newport News, Va.
Museum publication ; no. 38.
SH383.2.S35   639'.28'0924 [B]   79-12612

Library of Congress Cataloging in Publication Data
ISBN 0-917376-33-1

PRINTED IN THE UNITED STATES OF AMERICA

Contents

List of Illustrations

Preface

It is one of those peculiar ironies of history that Capt. Thomas Welcome Roys, who was well-known to virtually every other skipper in the Yankee whaling trade in the 1850s and 1860s and who contributed more toward the advancement of his industry than any other nineteenth-century American whaleman, should have lapsed into the obscurity of perhaps a mere line or two in most whaling source books. Even his name has been misspelled—"Royce"—in all save a few such references. Yet Roys's achievements were truly myriad. He was the first to dare to push beyond the feared Bering Strait into the lavish Arctic whaling grounds, preserving the whaling trade from rapid decline by the discovery of whole new herds of timid bowhead whales to slaughter. Roys ventured into every ocean in search of these leviathans, ranging from Iceland to the fringes of the Antarctic and from the northernmost navigable wastes of Russia to the lush atolls of the South Pacific. He became more than a mere hunter, for he observed and recorded everything he encountered. In time, Roys realized that the mighty rorquals—the largest of all cetaceans, but neglected—for the most part, because of their immense size and strength—offered promise of a whole new resource to exploit.

To pursue the rorquals, Roys developed a radically new weapon: the rocket-powered harpoon, fired from a bazookalike launcher resting on the operator's shoulder. Its sophistication amazes military men to this day. Unfortunately, he was never able to perfect the weapon completely, but other methods which evolved in the course of its development became Roys's contribution to modern whaling. He was among the first to apply methods of the machine age to the whaling trade. Roys originated the concept of a remote shore station, near the whaling grounds, from which fast iron steamers could be dispatched quickly to the scene of action. Rocket-fired bomb-harpoons struck their marks, and the victims were towed to the shore base to be processed for their precious oil. Nothing was wasted, not even the bones, flesh, and entrails, which had previously been discarded by old-time whalers. Roys's methods and basic ideas are used to this day.

Much of Roys's crisp, vivid writing is preserved in a number of museums and archives, and it reflects a probing, alert intellect that overshadowed virtually all those of his American contemporaries. Indeed, he was interested in every aspect of cetaceans, from their natural history and habits to the mechanized harvesting of their numbers. No doubt Roys might be criticized by conservationists today, but even he—the total pragmatist—realized that not all whale populations were infinite.

Roys remained in practically total obscurity until 1940, when the Norwegian historian Dr. Arne Odd Johnsen wrote to Mr. William H. Tripp, curator of the Old Dartmouth Historical Society Whaling Museum at New Bedford, Massachusetts, asking for any information "about the Americans, Lilliendahl and Roys' experiments of catching finwhales at Island [Iceland] in the years 1859-1867." Dr. Johnsen was writing a book on modern whaling for the Norwegian Whaling Association at Sandefjord. Mr. Tripp, it seems, knew very little about Roys and his partner in the Iceland venture, Gustavus A. Lilliendahl, and was only able to find references to them after carefully searching through old newspapers and numerous manuscripts in the museum's collections. Dr. Johnsen's book, *Finnmarks fangstens historie, 1864-1905*, the first volume of the monumental *Den moderne hvalfangsts historie* [The modern whaling history], was published in 1959. In it, he notes that "Roys' adventurous life and his important achievements in American whaling are almost forgotten. He belongs however undoubtedly to the most interesting and important persons in American whaling and therefore it is to be hoped that he will sooner or later find his biographer."[1]

Preface

The groundwork of our book was laid in the mid-1960s. Interestingly enough, the authors began their research independently, not even knowing each other. Dr. Cornelis de Jong, a Dutch economist now of the University of South Africa, discovered Roys in the course of writing a paper on Capt. C. J. Bottemanne, who had copied Roys's rocket-harpoon whaling methods. Dr. de Jong was introduced to the other authors by Mr. Mitchell Sharpe, space writer, of the Marshall Space Flight Center, Huntsville, Alabama. Mr. Frank H. Winter came across Roys in his work as historian of the National Air and Space Museum of the Smithsonian Institution. I myself found Roys quite by accident while writing *Mark Well the Whale!* the story of Cold Spring Harbor, Long Island, whaling. Mr. Sharpe had contacted me for information on Roys's rocket-harpoons while I was assistant curator of the Cold Spring Harbor Whaling Museum. Eventually he led me to Mr. Winter and then to Dr. de Jong.

Mitchell Sharpe, under pressure of other projects, was unable to continue the biography of Captain Roys, but he contributed immensely to the research, especially the material dealing with the later years of Roys's life. He rediscovered the most important single manuscript we have: Roys's personal memoirs, which were written in the twilight of his life. Mr. Sharpe obtained a handwritten transcript of the memoirs from one of the captain's descendants and was told that the original could be found in the Suffolk County Whaling Museum at Sag Harbor, Long Island. Letters to the curator of that museum and several cursory searches turned up nothing. Then, Frank Winter and I spent the better part of one bitter cold St. Valentine's Day searching the museum from cellar to attic, shivering because there was no heat. Almost ready to give up, we finally found the treasured original buried among a batch of papers in an old peck basket. Excitedly, we squinted at the faded and water-stained pages in the faint light, surrounded by stacks of books and papers and mounds of bric-a-brac and watched over—no jesting!—by a brace of shrunken human heads.

In the main, our book has been fashioned around Roys's

memoirs, fleshed out with thousands of pages of research material culled from reports, documents, logs, books, and newspapers uncovered halfway across the globe. Many of these sources are in languages foreign to the American authors—such as Danish, Norwegian, Icelandic, French, and Dutch—and without the translation talents of Cornelis de Jong, these crucial accounts might not have yielded their secrets.

At last—Dr. Arne Odd Johnsen take note—Roys has found his biographers; now may all historians know of his contributions and accomplishments.

F. P. S.

Cold Spring Harbor, Long Island, New York

August 1979

Acknowledgments

THE FOLLOWING PERSONS AND ORGANIZATIONS generously permitted the authors access to their research materials. They have our sincere appreciation for their cooperation and assistance, without which this book could not have been written.

University of Alaska Library, College, Alaska
The Bancroft Library, University of California, Berkeley
Banner Press Publishing Co., David City, Nebraska
Mr. John Bockstoce, West Hartford, Connecticut
Brown University Library, Providence, Rhode Island
Mrs. David M. Byington, Aurora, Colorado
California Historical Society, San Francisco, California
Commander Chr. Christensen's Whaling Museum, Sandefjord, Norway
Cork City Library, Cork, Ireland
Mrs. Fred Cornwall, Pultneyville, New York
David City Public Library, David City, Nebraska
Fiske Icelandic Collection, Cornell University Library, Ithaca, New York
Mr. Norman Hacking, West Vancouver, British Columbia
Dr. David A. Henderson, Northridge, California
University of Hong Kong Library, Victoria, Hong Kong
Huntington Historical Society, Huntington, New York
International Marine Archives, Nantucket, Massachusetts
Jersey City Public Library, Jersey City, New Jersey
Kendall Whaling Museum, Sharon, Massachusetts
Library of Congress, Washington, D.C.
Long Island Collection, Queens Borough Public Library, Jamaica, New York
Mr. Thomas G. Lytle, Norwalk, Connecticut

Mariners Museum, Newport News, Virginia
Maritime Museum, Vancouver, British Columbia
Maritime Museum of British Columbia, Victoria
Melville Whaling Room, New Bedford Free Public Library, New
    Bedford, Massachusetts
Mr. Seigo Motoki, Hokodate, Hokkaido, Japan
National Archives, Washington, D.C.
National Library of Iceland, Reykjavik
National Maritime Museum, Greenwich, England
Old Dartmouth Historical Society Whaling Museum, New
    Bedford, Massachusetts
Patent Office, Orpington, Kent, England
Pennypacker Long Island Collection, East Hampton Free
    Library, East Hampton, New York
Mr. Donald LeMar Poole, Chilmark, Massachusetts
Provincial Archives, Victoria, British Columbia
Public Archives, State of Hawaii, Honolulu
Public Record Office, London, England
The Royal Library, Copenhagen, Denmark
San Francisco Historical Records, San Francisco, California
Smithsonian Institution, Washington, D.C.
Southold Free Library, Southold, New York
Mr. Edouard A. Stackpole, Nantucket, Massachusetts
Mrs. Willa Hall Stafford, David City, Nebraska
Suffolk County Whaling Museum, Sag Harbor, New York
U.S. Census Office, Washington, D.C.
U.S. Patent Office, Washington, D.C.
Mr. Andrus T. Valentine, Cold Spring Harbor, New York
County of Wayne, County Clerk and Department of History,
    Lyons, New York
Whaling Museum Society, Inc., Cold Spring Harbor, New York
G. W. Blunt White Library, Mystic Seaport, Mystic, Connecticut

THOMAS
WELCOME ROYS

America's Pioneer of

Modern Whaling

1

Learning the Ropes

IN their literature on whaling, the Dutch respect Willem Barendsz; the British, the Scoresby and Enderby families; and the Norwegians their Svend Foyn. But an archetypal hero never seems to have emerged from the lusty nineteenth-century Yankee whaling industry, save perhaps for the mythical Ahab of *Moby-Dick*. There was one American, however—still highly regarded in Norway and the Netherlands as the bridge between ancient and modern whaling methods—who had a dynamic impact on that vital trade of more than a century ago, which employed thousands of men and generated fortunes, large and small. In fact, at one long moment during the last of the flush days of the industry, this man is credited with almost single-handedly having rescued American whaling from imminent collapse.

"I commenced whaling . . . at 17 years of age," he once wrote a friend, "and it has been the whole study of my life ever since. . . ."[1] Later, he recalled—not without an obvious measure of pride—that "My knowledge is merely practical, not scientific, as I came to sea too young to acquire any thing more of an education than is taught in the common school. . . . I have neglected and forgotten the most of that and there has been no one at sea . . . to teach me. Every thing gives place on a whale voyage to the obtaining of oil, consequently there is little else attended to."[2]

Roys was thought to have been born on a farmstead in the tiny village of Pultneyville in Wayne County, New York, not far from Lake Ontario, about 1816,[3] to an old-line Yankee family that could trace its lineage seven generations back to one Robert Roys, who, legend had it, was driven out of Boston in 1634 with twenty-one others for their religious beliefs.[4] Thomas's father, Philander, was an original settler of Pultneyville, having arrived there from Connecticut about 1814, and in time he became a prominent citizen known for his "sterling integrity."[5] Thomas Roys was born to a large family. Tamimer, his mother, bore at least half a dozen children before passing away in 1818 at age forty-one.[6] His father later remarried—choosing a Massachusetts girl, Orpha Warner, some sixteen years his junior—and they too had at least half a dozen offspring.[7] It appears, however, that Thomas and his brothers and half brothers had little patience with the mundane, humdrum life of the farm, for all of them but one eventually shipped for some time in their lives, either in whalers or aboard ships that plied the Great Lakes.[8] And so it was that Thomas Welcome Roys left his upstate home and signed aboard the Sag Harbor, Long Island, whaler *Hudson* in July 1833, where he matured quickly, learning and absorbing the rudiments of his life's trade and earning the appellation "whaleman," instead of being considered a hayseed 'lubber.[9]

Years afterward, putting his memoirs to paper, Roys remembered those first, miserable days as a greenhand under Capt. Henry Green with remarkable clarity.

. . . We touched at Fayal, one of the Western Islands [Azores], to procure vegetables. I had been seasick from the first, lying on the deck, utterly regardless of the men running over me, and when I went below, lying down with coat, hat and boots all on, and perfectly indifferent to all around me and entirely regardless of my fate. Many of the Portuguese came on board, with baskets of fruit for sale and quantities were bought by the sailors, and when we were tacking ship, the sailors would try to run over and upset the boats and appropriate some fruit to themselves; after eating some . . . I began to feel better, and took my turn at the helm for the first time.

A coil of rope was on the deck and I was ordered by the mate to stop it up, not knowing the meaning of the word, I stood still, when he abused me, in all kind of terms, wondering that I should be such a fool, as not to know, what stop a rope meant; at last he told me to tie it up, which I did; but I never forgot what "stop" meant; at the same time he asked me some questions, to which I answered "yes," and he wanted to know if I was reared among savages, that I could not say "Yes Sir."

After having sighted the Cape Verde islands we saw the island of Tristan D'Acunha where we began to see whales, and I shall never forget my first chase after them. I did not know how to row and made bad work of it, and the mate found fault with every stroke I pulled, and made me believe I scared the whales away, to the great disadvantage of every one.[10]

Gradually, young Tom Roys adapted to the life and customs of the sea. Although a whaling cruise involved wearisome toil under the sharp eyes of uncompromising mates and long, monotonous periods of hunting for the elusive leviathans, it could also be adventurous, romantic, and definitely unforgettable, especially for a young greenhand. Roys never forgot, for instance, when *Hudson* hove into Saint-Augustin Bay, Madagascar, for wood and water: "Here we found a finely formed native race with straight black hair and copper complexion, ruled by Kings and under the most despotic government, for when the prince had bought a gun, he amused himself by firing it right among his people, wounding several, but treating them with indifference, himself in high glee at the effect it gave."[11]

After touching at the island of Bassas da India, between Madagascar and the east coast of Africa—where the crew replenished *Hudson*'s larders with hefty and savory green sea turtles—they had a fine run of "greasy luck" in the nearby Mozambique Channel, taking 350 barrels of desirable

sperm-whale oil, then prized for illumination and candlemak-
ing. They put in briefly at the Cape of Good Hope, then filled
the ship with oil out east of Tristan da Cunha. Captain Green
sailed *Hudson* home into Sag Harbor in January 1835, with a
full cargo of oil and whalebone.[12] It was a good voyage all right,
gauging out to 350 barrels of sperm-whale oil and 2,350 of
less-valuable whale oil, worth upwards of $37,000. The ship's
agent, Luther D. Cook, was well pleased with this old London
packet on her maiden voyage as a whaler, as were the officers
and men with their shares, or "lays" as they called them, in so
successful a voyage.[13]

Satisfied that whaling should be his life's work, Roys sailed
again that summer under Captain Green in the 368-ton
Hudson for the coast of Patagonia and the Falklands. They
returned the following July, their holds bursting with a valuable cargo worth perhaps $35,000.[14] By now Roys knew the
ropes, and he sailed again with Captain Green in *Hudson* in
August 1836, this time as a petty officer—harpooner, or
boatsteerer to use the correct parlance—for the whaling
grounds west of Tristan da Cunha. There they filled the ship in
an incredibly short cruise of seven months and thirteen days,
without ever having seen a glimpse of land![15] Successful
again, they put into Sag Harbor on April 9, 1837, with $30,000
worth of oil.[16] Call such easy money luck of the novice, but
with this early success, Roys was hooked for life on the sea.
Always when he came ashore, Roys wasted no time returning
to sea, and that summer he signed aboard as boatsteerer in the
Sag Harbor ship *Gem,* under Capt. Isaac Ludlow, on a very
profitable nine months' voyage to the South Atlantic.[17] They
brought home 180 barrels of sperm-whale oil and 1,350 of
whale oil.[18]

In September 1839, Roys signed on as chief officer of
Gem, Capt. Theron B. Worth, which sailed for the sub-Antarctic Crozet Islands grounds by way of the Cape of Good Hope,
touching at Saint Helena, then home again in nine months
with a full catch. The following August—by now filled with
enthusiasm and spurred on by success—he sailed again in the

same ship under the same captain. They cruised the same grounds, returning in ten months with about $25,000 in oil.[19] Surely Thomas Welcome Roys seemed to have the Midas touch.

Finally, Roys earned his own command. It was late summer 1841 when he became master of the Sag Harbor ship *Crescent,* and from every indication, the voyage initially showed promise of being another fabulous one, for he took 400 barrels of oil south of the Cape of Good Hope and another 600 barrels at the Crozet ground. But then his luck changed. While transiting the Strait of Djailolo in the East Indies, *Crescent* ran hard aground onto a reef. Roys and his men were frantic, for—in addition to their immediate dilemma—a number of ominous-looking natives had gathered their canoes nearby, "waiting to see the ship a hopeless wreck, then make us their prey." Roys had some 600 barrels of water thrown overboard to lighten ship, then tried to kedge off sternfirst with the bower anchors, but she would not budge. By the grace of Providence a gale blew up, so Roys had all sails set. The spars and masts wavered wildly, then suddenly the 340-ton whaler shot like an arrow clear across the stubborn reef, leaving part of her false keel behind. Fortunately, the damage was only superficial, so the captain anchored for the night off Gebe Island, some six miles from the reef. The following day he returned in the boats to the site of the near mishap and gingerly retrieved the chains and anchors left behind in their haste.[20]

At Gebe, Roys and a dozen armed men from *Crescent* threaded their way through twelve miles of jungle to the native king. The little chief lived in a large compound, where he royally entertained the whalemen on a dinner of rice and fowl with honey, served from crockery but without knives, forks, or spoons. Well pleased with the hospitality, Roys—upon leaving—presented the chief with a musket. The captain then laid his course northward up past the Mariana and Bonin islands and the coast of Japan to Kamchatka—that massive, 800-mile-long peninsula jutting down from eastern Siberia. Here he filled his ship with the oil of the North Pacific right whale, taking what he claimed was the first cargo of oil and whalebone ever brought to the United States from the eastern side of Kamchatka. Roys was fascinated with everything relating to whales and their capture, but nothing mystified and intrigued him more than their migratory habits, especially in the North Pacific. Referring to eastern Kamchatka, he wrote:

> ... While on this coast about 800 miles from land, whales were seen going a direct course west northwest day and night without varying. I steered on with the ship, keeping the same course until I found them 8oo miles from where I started. Thus whales without any apparent guide keep steady on their courses in midocean for thousands of miles and evidently possess knowledge or ability of some kind of which we have no idea.[21]

The northern whaling season over, Roys headed for the Hawaiian Islands for a refit and a deserved rest. But this plan failed, for his chronometer had stopped. Unable to obtain any satisfactory navigational fix, *Crescent* sailed clear past Hawaii. Then, only to worsen their quandary, the majority of the crew came down with the dreaded sailors' disease, scurvy. Something had to be done, and quickly, for the classic signs—lassitude, yellowish pallor, swollen extremities, and bleeding gums—began to appear. Unless Roys could secure medical aid for his ailing men, without question they would be unable to run the ship. So he continued south, hoping for a landfall. At Palmyra Island, in the Line Islands, he could find no assistance. Sailing southwestward to Fiji, he attempted to land in two of the whaleboats at Amargura in the Vava'u Island group.[22]

Rather than risk both boats, in the treacherous, fuming surf, Roys sent in one. It was promptly splintered and cast violently upon the beach by the pounding breakers, leaving one man injured and rendering their guns and powder wet and useless against the cannibals that they believed inhabited the island. Standing offshore in the other boat, Roys shouted over the roaring seas that they should attempt to cross the island, where he would try to get them off at another bay. He arrived at

FIG. 1.   A TYPICAL SAG HARBOR WHALESHIP

Roys spent a good portion of his long career in Sag Harbor, L.I., whaleships, serving in *Hudson, Gem, Crescent, Josephine, Superior,* and *William F. Safford.* He became a captain in 1841.

(Courtesy of Library, Nassau County Historical Society, East Meadow, N.Y.)

the appointed rendezvous and waited about three hours, but no one was to be seen. Impatient, the pugnacious captain tucked a few pistols and some ammunition into his hat, grabbed a boat hatchet, leaped into the water, and swam right through the perilous swells directly for the shore. Wet to the skin and near exhaustion, he was shocked to find himself confronted by a towering precipice. It must have been at least three hundred feet high.[23]

Undaunted, Captain Roys began hacking a series of steps to the top of the cliff with his hatchet. Finally, he reached the crest, but he was stymied again, this time by a thick, impenetrable jungle. Now he knew why his men had been unable to meet him here. Fearing the worst for them, perhaps at the hands of grisly savages, he was beside himself. Then, as he turned to descend the sheer bluff, he suddenly realized, to his sorrow, that the steps he had cut coming up were too far apart for him to get down safely. Confronted with this new hazard, he saw his only hope in a bush which projected halfway down the cliff. Slowly, he inched down the steep face, then suddenly he lost his footing, his fall being broken only through that fortunately located bush. From there he was able to tumble to the ground, where he picked himself up—all torn, scraped, and bleeding from head to toe.[24]

Again Roys dove into the breakers, then swam back to the boat and ordered it to the point where his men had last been seen. And there they were, but none among them was willing to attempt to swim through the frighteningly powerful surf. Then, quite by accident, Roys discovered a fishing line and sinker in the floorboards of the boat. He cast the lead ashore, bent a heavy rope to the end of the fishing line, then had the stranded men draw it slowly ashore, where they secured it to a tree. With its other end fast to the boat, the rope was kept taut by constant rowing, producing in effect a jury-rigged breeches buoy. One by one, the frightened men hauled themselves over the raging, billowing combers, and all were accounted for save the cooper, who was nowhere in sight.[25]

After they had pulled at the oars for about half a mile to

return to the ship, however, lo and behold, they saw the cooper brazenly standing on shore, wildly waving a handkerchief. Roys was furious: "I returned and in no very gentle terms accused him of the folly of being away from the others and I now saw no way but to leave him on the island." Panicking, the cooper sprang into the breakers, only to be rolled up senseless onto the beach. One of the boatsteerers, wanting no more of this nonsense, fastened a line to himself and, lashed to an oar, fought his way to shore. He revived the cooper, tied him to the oar, then the boat crew hauled both in with all their might. They could not see him in the boiling waters until he was right alongside. When they pulled him aboard, the cooper was again unconscious, but was revived quickly. In a masterful under-statement Roys said, "I returned to the ship with the opinion that I had had enough of this island." Unfortunately, he still had not found help for the scurvy that was ravaging his crew.[26]

Roys charted a course for New Zealand next. Meanwhile, his crew increasingly began to show the more unpleasant symptoms of scurvy. There was no question that Roys was sympathetic to his crew, but upon falling in with a pod of sperm whales, he could not resist the temptation to take four of them. He searched in vain but could find no more, so he pressed on, seeking help for his ailing men. Suddenly one night, a ship's light appeared from the inky darkness. Could they help? Roys hailed the stranger and shouted across that he had sick men aboard, but all he received in response was a request for the longitude in which they were sailing. Enraged by this obvious indifference, Roys roared back, "we did not use longitude [in the whaling trade]," and broke away. By the time New Zealand was sighted, there were some twenty men down with the disease, and several were in convulsions. Yet strangely enough, one of the men, who had helped cut in the sperm whales and had then bound his scurvy-afflicted hands in the animal's flesh, was recovering nicely. On reaching port, Roys rented an entire building for a temporary hospital, and within a month all of his men were well enough to return to sea.[27]

This had been a grueling and miserable voyage, but there

was joy in the thought the ship was full and it was time now to head for home. *Crescent* touched at the Chatham Islands, east of New Zealand, rounded the Horn, stopping at Santa Catarina Island on the coast of Brazil and then at Rio de Janeiro, where Roys sold off 1,500 barrels of whale oil at a favorable price.[28] At last, after having sailed clear around the world in twenty-three months, *Crescent* entered Sag Harbor in August 1843, her captain triumphant and delighting the ship's agents, owners, officers, and crew alike, for when the cargo was tallied, they learned that they had brought home 300 barrels of sperm-whale oil, 1,200 of whale oil, and 18,000 pounds of bone—all worth an astounding $40,000.[29] No doubt about it, Roys had earned the grudging respect and admiration of his contemporaries for this smashingly successful voyage as master of his own whaler. He also seems to have captivated the heart of a daughter of a crusty old mentor, Capt. Henry Green, under whom he had formerly served, for he married Ann Eliza Green soon after he arrived home, on August 24, 1843, at Southampton, Long Island.[30]

2

The Rise to Success

Roys was beginning to enjoy a deserved reputation as a skillful mariner and whaler when he assumed command of the Sag Harbor ship *Josephine* and sailed from that port in the 397-ton whaler on October 29, 1843.[1] He wasted no time, but beat around Cape Horn, touched briefly at Hawaii, then went off for a season on the coast of Kamchatka, taking about 2,400 barrels of oil. According to Roys's own description, here happened "one of the most extraordinary circumstances ever . . . in the killing of whales." As the story goes, the first mate, Charles Ludlow, had harpooned and fastened to one whale from a pod of five. Suddenly the animals dispersed in fear, and one, completely confused, struck the boat in the stern, knocking it clean over and spilling the surprised crew into the frigid waters. Fortunately, the men only received a good dousing for their trouble and were rescued by the fast and neat work of another boat crew. Soon afterward, they were returning to *Josephine* for a change into dry clothing and, surely, a tot of rum.[2]

In the meantime, Roys saw an opportunity for himself to knock off a spouter or two. He maneuvered his boat right into the pod, where he harpooned one whale, then thrust his long, razor-sharp killing lance into another. The lance struck a bone, however, and a loop of rope at the end of the wooden shaft caught the captain's shoulder pulling him overboard among the thrashing beasts. The rest, while perhaps true in the main, is such a rich sea tale, rivaling Jonah's famous Biblical ride, it can be told only in the captain's words:

[The moment I struck the water] a whale buoyed up under me and I was sitting on his back. Thinking this a poor place to rest I sprang

FIG. 2.   A "REAL-LIFE" JOHN TABOR

An old woodcut of "John Tabor's Ride," based on an old sea story of a whaleman who traveled halfway around the world on the back of a spouter. Roys took a brief, unexpected ride on a whale himself as skipper of the whaleship *Josephine*.
(From the private collection of Frederick P. Schmitt.)

up and jumped as far as I could from him, apparently into the water, but right upon the head of another whale. I tumbled off this whale's head and was thrown by the flukes of a third whale back into the boat again entirely unharmed, and catching up my lance I killed 3 of them at a single lance each so dead that we saved them.[3]

Roys put into Hawaii at the end of the season to refit, and no doubt this incredible sea story was repeated again and again at every gam, or gathering of whalemen. From Hawaii he cruised the South Pacific along the line out as far as the Bonins, then proceeded north for a summer on the Russian whaling grounds in the vicinity of Kamchatka. It was between here and the Northwest Coast Grounds off Alaska that his boat was cut right in two by the flukes of an especially rambunctious prey, dumping Roys and his boat crew into the chill waters, where they remained for some time before another boat could rescue them. Injured in the cheek and with two ribs broken—by the flukes of this ornery whale or by a large fragment of the boat—the captain was clearly suffering from exposure as well, and he ordered *Josephine* into Petropavlovsk-Kamchatskiy, Siberia, so that he might recover while the ship went out again under his first mate, Charles Ludlow.[4]

At that time Petropavlovsk was little more than a small military post of about a thousand inhabitants. When he arrived there, Roys was suffering terribly from what might well have been dysentery and tetanus, so the governor and other residents suggested he go inland some forty miles to a mineral spring, where he could bathe in and drink the healing waters. Taking with him eight Kamchadals (men of mixed Russian and Chukchi blood), Roys crossed the Bay of Avacha in a canoe and was then carried in a litter on the shoulders of those men, four men at a time. It took two days for them to reach an immense mountain, some 16,000 feet high. At the base was a large lake, its center boiling wildly in very large bubbles. This turbulence gradually died away toward the edges, where the water was about 100° F. A rivulet flowed from the lake and passed a small spa a short distance away. As soon as Roys entered the stream, he felt relief, and alternately bathing in and drinking the water, he began to improve rapidly within a week.[5]

As he regained his health, Captain Roys really began to enjoy this remote and interesting place. He lived well here in a log cabin, with the ship's steward to care and cook for him, and the natives, using his guns, to bring in a bountiful supply of duck, venison, and bear meat for his table. He sent for more amenities—flour, tea, and sugar—and mended quickly on this hearty diet. A practical man, Roys quickly learned that money was of no use here, for everything was bartered for tea, sugar, rum, gunpowder, and lead. He noted that his hosts were inveterate tea drinkers, with every family having a charcoal-heated samovar of the beverage always at hand. "To economize," he wrote in true Yankee admiration, "they put a lump [of sugar] in their mouth and then drink several cups of tea until the lump is dissolved." Approving of such thrift, he commented, "This answers very well as I have often tried it."[6]

Once on his feet, Roys enjoyed hunting and fishing with the natives. The people there relied heavily on salmon for food throughout the year. What was left over was fed, after being dried, to cattle when there was no hay. Being a man of the sea himself, Roys was especially fascinated by their method of catching the tasty, rich local salmon. It seems that the natives had developed an ingenious trapping system utilizing two parallel rows of stakes driven across a stream opening. The fish swam past the specially positioned first row and became trapped between it and the second; all the natives had to do was stand on the bank with a pitchfork and heave out as many fish as they pleased.[7]

But when he had almost recovered, Roys wanted to attempt something more adventurous. He was anxious to hunt one of the huge brown bears of that locality. Numerous and bold, they throve in summer on the plentiful salmon. Quite wisely, the natives refused to let Roys shoot the bear himself, knowing the danger, so he allowed one of them to take his double-barreled gun, loaded with two-ounce slugs, while he stood about a quarter of a mile away to watch. The native located, then began to stalk, one of the bears, and when about thirty feet from it, he fired, striking the bear just behind the foreleg. The shot went clear through, and with blood streaming from both sides of the wound, the ferocious bear growled angrily and sprang at the hunter, narrowly missing him. Realizing that he was in a most difficult spot, the Kamchadal hurriedly slung the gun across his shoulders, then turned and ran furiously, with the bear snapping close to his heels. They were heading straight for

Roys and his party, so it was imperative that the raging bear be stopped with the second shot in the double-barreled gun. For one moment they appeared to be safe when the animal staggered and fell, but it rose again almost immediately and continued the chase. By now the native was able to far outdistance his pursuer, however, and it stumbled several times more, then fell dead. Everyone was so thoroughly alarmed they dared not go near the animal that night. The following day, however, a party cautiously ventured out, and when they determined that the bear was dead, dressed it and brought it in. The animal weighed an amazing 1,400 pounds; the forepaw alone being 23 pounds.[8]

A short time later Roys returned to Petropavlovsk to await the return of his ship. Soon enough *Josephine* arrived, and after a short cruise, during which he took a few hundred barrels of oil, Roys sailed for Ocean Island, in the Gilbert and Ellice group. Here he discharged a crewman at his own request, for the hand did not wish to go home. He said that he preferred to live out the remainder of his life on that island. Roys left him some supplies, including cooking implements, and being short of cash, he paid him his share in the voyage with a gold watch and chain.[9]

Coincidentally, a native decided to ship in the man's place, and although it was rather incongruous at first to see him standing there almost entirely nude, with only a string of beads around his neck, seemingly he was happy to have the opportunity to join the ship's crew. When he had learned enough English to communicate, he revealed in halting phrases that he was the son of a king on an island that was overpopulated. Concerned for his subjects' eventual fate, the young chief and a group of his people had put to sea in an open boat in search of a new home. After drifting for weeks, they finally were rescued by a passing ship and landed at Ocean Island, only to be treated as slaves by the inhabitants there.[10]

The crew later learned that the young man had hoped that *Josephine* would be able to bring him home, but such was not the case, and he was brought to Sag Harbor. From there, he

Fig. 3   Sag Harbor in the 1840s

Located out on Long Island's east end, Sag Harbor was a major
nineteenth-century whaling port. Active from 1784 to 1871, 574
whaling voyages originated from this village.

*(Courtesy of Long Island Collection, Queens Borough Public
Library, Jamaica, N.Y.)*

shipped aboard *Josephine* again in 1846, and her new captain, Hiram Hedges, was able this time to return the man to Hope (Kusaie) Island—speaking good English after three years in the fo'c'sle. At home he was welcomed, for he had become king during his long absence. In gratitude to his Yankee benefactors, their former shipmate loaded *Josephine* to the gunwales with island produce before sending his friends on their way.

Roys himself had other experiences with the romantic, mystical, yet sometimes fierce South Seas peoples during his own voyage in *Josephine*. After taking the young chief aboard, he had passed near Pitts (Makin) Island, where the natives came off in many canoes. One bore the king himself, who bravely came alongside while his more timid subjects remained at a respectful distance. These men were completely naked also, save for ominous-looking strings of sharks' teeth about their necks. Taking no chances, the captain offered them bread, but they pushed it aside, not knowing what it was. The same thing happened with tobacco, which was proffered next. Finally, they accepted some small pieces of iron hoop.[11]

Sensing that these men were probably curious and meant no great harm, Captain Roys invited the king aboard. He was quite willing, but when he had climbed part way up the ladder, his companions pulled him back into the boat. Roys passed him a small bottle of whiskey instead. The chief put the bottle to his mouth, and the whalers watched intently as he tested the strong alcohol. He liked it! So much so, in fact, that he took another nip, then guzzled the entire bottle down in a single draught. As might be expected, he passed out and lay in the bottom of the canoe, "his eyes so far shut you could only see the white, the most comical looking mortal I have ever seen. . . ." At this, the tiny flotilla retreated to their island.[12]

It was almost time to head for home. When *Josephine* touched at Sydney, Australia, on December 20, 1845, she had a respectable cargo of 3,000 barrels of whale oil and 50 barrels of sperm-whale oil.[13] With the touch of inquisitiveness so typical of a restless soul, Roys took his ship down along the Antarctic pack ice as far south as he dared to sail in waters where few explorers, let alone whalers, had ever ventured. He cruised eastward until he reached the approximate longitude of Cape Horn, then turned his keel north.[14] After a dramatic and dangerous thirty-four months and fifteen days at sea, Roys reached Sag Harbor on September 14, 1846—his second whaling voyage in command of a vessel another complete success.[15]

Roys seems to have been unique in his desire to find new whale grounds, such as those of the Antarctic, for the American desire to find and exploit new hunting grounds had evolved only gradually over two centuries. Colonists had first ventured off the shores of Long Island and New England during the mid-seventeenth century. Then, as the demand for oil burgeoned and the offshore whale populations correspondingly dwindled, the Yankee whalemen began to work deeper waters. Gradually, this pelagic fishery expanded, first into the North Atlantic and Davis Strait, then to the South Atlantic, Indian, and finally South Pacific oceans. By the 1840s American catchers were routinely driving north into the Pacific as far as the Bering Sea, but no whaleman—no matter how headstrong—had the temerity to sail through the Bering Strait itself—considered by some in the trade to be equivalent to the River Styx.[16]

While master of *Josephine,* Roys fell in with the Danish whaleship *Neptun* in 1845. While he and Capt. Thomas Jensen Södring of that ship were gamming, conversation turned to a most unusual whale that the Dane had taken off Petropavlovsk a short time before. His ship had taken three of this strange new species, and at Roys's insistence, the Danish captain sketched the animals as best he could, noting distinctive features. Roys found these whales very puzzling, for they seemed different from any he had ever seen. Instinctively, he surmised that more of these whales might be found even further to the north. A short time after that meeting, he suffered the unfortunate accident that sent him into Petropavlovsk to recuperate. During his sojourn there, he chanced to meet a Russian naval officer, who had sailed through the

Bering Strait. The man spoke good English, so both had a pleasant chat about the Arctic regions. While recounting his experiences, the Russian mentioned having seen large numbers of whales far to the north, but he did not know what kind they were.[17]

Naturally, all this talk set Roys to thinking. After questioning and cross-questioning the officer, and examining a sketch drawn by him, Roys was able to determine that these whales were identical to those taken by Captain Södring. Knowing he was on the brink of an important discovery, Roys readily plunked down $100 for some Russian naval charts, deciding to keep secret what he had learned so far. After recuperating and returning to *Josephine*, he gammed with Capt. Eli White of the Cold Spring Harbor, Long Island, whaleship *Sheffield* and was able to accumulate more information about the mysterious new whale. As soon as he reached home, Roys pored through narratives of polar exploration, and all confirmed that there were numerous unmolested herds of whales in the Arctic, waiting for someone with nerve to take them. But it was a passage in Captain F. W. Beechey's *Voyage of Discovery towards the North Pole* that really whetted Roys's interest. Roys quoted: "Off [Icy Cape, Arctic Ocean] . . . we saw a great many black whales, more than I remember ever to have seen, even in Baffin's Bay." Only one major question remained to be answered: could these whales be caught economically at a place so desolate and forbidding?[18] Roys was determined to know the answer.

FIG. 4.   AN 1846 MAP OF EASTERN SIBERIA
In the mid-1840s, as captain of the Sag Harbor, L.I., whaleship *Josephine*, Roys concentrated on whaling in the Sea of Okhotsk and in the vicinity of the Kamchatka Peninsula, Russia. He was injured during an especially dangerous chase, and while recuperating at Petropavlovsk-Kamchatskiy, he learned that numerous whales lived north of the Bering Strait. In 1848, returning in the Sag Harbor whaler *Superior*, he crossed into the Arctic Ocean, over the protests of his crew, discovering one of the greatest whaling grounds of all time.

(*Courtesy of the Whaling Museum, Cold Spring Harbor, N.Y.*)

3

A Bold Voyage into
the Unknown

RოYS gained his opportunity to search for the "new fangled monsters" beyond the Bering Strait within a year after returning home, when he assumed command of the scant, 275-ton Sag Harbor bark *Superior* in July 1847.[1] He had, however, specific orders from the owners to work the relatively safe whaling grounds in the South Atlantic and was fully expected to return with a full cargo in eight to ten months. Covertly though—spurred by what he had learned at Petropavlovsk and from his own research—Roys longed to fit out for the Arctic Ocean. He dared not even broach the subject with the ship's conservative owners, Grinnell, Minturn & Co., for if they knew his true intent, they surely would not let him go. He sensibly realized also that he would have to use the greatest diplomacy in convincing a crew to sail there.[2]

At first, following the owners' wishes, Roys worked the sub-Antarctic Crozet and Desolation islands grounds, taking only seven whales—poor ones at that—for his trouble. When—by either design or circumstance—it appeared that the ship would not be able to fill in the time allotted for the voyage, the crew became disgruntled. Captain Roys then proposed to cruise into the Pacific—secretly, of course, setting his mind's course for the rich, untapped grounds he just knew must lie to the north. Vainly he tried to persuade several other captains, including Thomas Long of *Charles Carrol* out of New London, Connecticut, and Freeman Smith of the Cold Spring Harbor whaler *Huntsville,* to accompany him, but none would agree, and some even ridiculed the entire idea. Determined, Roys ". . . then resolved to go it alone."[3] It is quite possible that while Roys was on these grounds, he learned from an arriving ship of the death at Southhampton of his young wife, Ann Eliza, on August 3, 1847, soon after giving birth to their son Philander.[4] Although such a melancholy event is only conjectural, its occurrence could well have had a strong influence on his decision to sail through the Bering Strait.

Superior arrived at Hobart, Tasmania, on March 7, 1848, with a paltry 120 barrels of oil; a poor catch indeed for seven and a half months' hard work at sea. Because of ice conditions, it was too early to head for the Arctic, so Roys sailed on a short, lackluster cruise through the South Seas.[5] Returning to Hobart, he elected to ship his oil to England for a favorable market and to refit for a year's cruise. Writing the owners (whom he knew full well would not be pleased) that he was taking *Superior* through the Bering Strait, he added that, almost as a postscript, ". . . if no tidings came from me they would know where I went."[6]

Roys finally cleared Hobart on May 20 and cut a course northward, but he could only sail past the Fox Islands in the Aleutian chain and as far as Saint Matthew Island in the Bering Sea by early May, being unable to penetrate farther north because of ice.[7] Since he had had no previous experience pushing a ship through such perilous waters, Roys wisely decided to work the area below the Strait, from the Aleutians to the Kamchatka Peninsula, for a month, searching for right whales.[8]

He continued, however, to be drawn to the waters beyond the Strait—those very gates of hell. The captain had managed to work *Superior* up to 60°N when Jim Eldredge, his chief officer, became very excited and communicated his premonitions of imminent disaster to the entire crew. After all, these polar seas had hitherto been visited only by explorers, who told lurid tales of the dual threat of ice and natives. Everyone aboard griped so much that Roys was forced to return to the fifty-seventh parallel, where he remained for the month of June. By July he had had enough of these 'lubbers' nonsense, and he told the officers that he fully intended to sail right through the Bering Strait and into the Arctic Ocean, despite the crew's belief that no new whales existed and their anxious feeling that they would never see home again.[9] Brushing their pleas aside, Roys "started in dead earnest to go [in mid-July] if not stopped by impossibility."[10]

July 15 arrived, and his men's premonitions seemed realized, for—just as *Superior* rounded the eastern end of Saint Lawrence Island and entered the forbidding passage—they saw seven native umiaks standing off nearby (each bearing approximately forty men), crossing from the Alaskan to the Siberian coasts. Roys cautiously decided not to signal them, since his armament consisted of a single revolver. Through a stroke of good luck, the wind picked up, and the ship slipped away before the Eskimos could reveal their intentions.[11]

On first entering the Arctic Ocean, the ship was encumbered greatly by thick blankets of fog and pelting rain.[12] When the sun eventually peeked through, Roys and the first mate took a navigational sight. Jim Eldredge was very confused. Either his quadrant or the nautical books were incorrect, for the latitude appeared to be 65°N. "Something must be wrong," he exclaimed, but the captain assured him that the instrument was indeed correct, for he had personally been keeping a rigid dead-reckoning track all the while.[13]

"Great God," Eldredge shrieked in horror, "where are you going with the ship? I never heard of a whale ship in that latitude before! We shall all be lost!" Dashing down to his stateroom, the mate collapsed on his bunk, where he burst into tears. Instantly word of Roys's madness raced through the ship—and all kinds of ruses were attempted—short of open mutiny—to force the "old man" to change his mind and to turn back.[14]

Pods of gray whales began to gambol nearby, but these fast swimmers generally could not be taken with hand harpoons from open boats.[15] Soon afterward, the ship was surrounded by more whales—odd whales. Roys took a careful bead through his spyglass and was elated to discover that these were the mysterious new species he had been seeking.[16] They looked, he said, "as I fancied a polar whale should. . . ."[17] Roys passed the glass to the mate, asking for his opinion, but to his chagrin, Jim Eldredge said that they were probably just ordinary humpbacks, and the second officer agreed.[18]

"Clear away the boats," Roys bellowed impatiently, and "we will see what he is!" The captain's boat was the first to approach the creature, and when it rose to the surface to breathe, he buried two irons deep into its side. Startled, the whale sounded and then ran along the bottom for a full fifty minutes. His red hair bristling, Roys swore—although knowing better—that he "was fast to something that breathed water instead of air, and might remain down a week if he liked." Eventually the whale surfaced and was killed. Although Roys had never seen one before, he knew that this was the elusive "polar whale," but his officers steadfastly maintained that it was nothing more than a common humpback. Despite some thick weather, Roys was able to anchor *Superior* right there in the midst of the Arctic Ocean because the chill waters, surprisingly, were only twenty-five fathoms deep. When his men began to cut in and process the confusing behemoth, it was quickly apparent from the length of the whalebone, or baleen, in its mouth that it was not a humpback after all, but was indeed a polar whale—one that yielded slabs of valuable baleen averaging twelve feet in length.[19]

The first whale was taken at midnight, and it was possible to continue working after that, since even at that hour there was enough light to read in the cabin. In fact, it was possible to whale twenty-four hours a day. And the leviathans in this strange and novel place, Roys later noted with glee, were easily caught, this polar species being almost "tame." Actually, he took three distinct species there: right whales, polar whales, known more commonly as bowheads by whalers because of their large bowlike mouths, filled with baleen; and "a small whale peculiar to that ocean," probably the beluga, or white, whale.[20] One distinctive subspecies of the bowhead, which Roys first recognized, is named in his honor.[21]

It is only equitable to mention here that there is some controversy concerning when the first successful catch of Pacific bowheads occurred. Alexander Starbuck, in his authoritative *History of the American Whale Fishery* (1878), claimed that these animals had been killed initially as early as 1843 by the New Bedford whaleships *Hercules* and *Janus* off the coast of Kamchatka. And, he adds, the French claim that same honor for their ship *Asia,* which sailed the Sea of Okhotsk off Russia under an American skipper. In any event, even if they knew what bowheads were, most whalemen had foolishly ignored them previously, thinking the species to be worthless. Often the name of Capt. George A. Covill of the whaleship *Mount Vernon* of New Bedford comes to the fore, but there is some question concerning the validity of his claim. The story goes that after searching for sperm whales with no luck, he sailed for the Okhotsk sometime about 1846. There he spotted a strange whale and "with little trouble killed him." Covill thought his catch would yield a mere 70 barrels at most and was surprised to turn out a pleasing 150 instead, with a substantial quantity of whalebone.[22] Thomas Roys, who was well aware of these conflicting claims, insisted that the distinction of having first recognized them rested with Capt. Freeman H. Smith, who had commanded the Cold Spring Harbor, Long Island, whaleship *Huntsville* on a whaling cruise to the North Pacific in 1848[23]—even though Roys knew, of course, that the Danish ship *Neptun* had taken bowheads in 1845.

The waters become even more turbid if we consider seriously the boasts of Capt. Frederick W. Manter of the Vineyard Haven, Massachusetts, ship *Ocmulgee,* who maintained that his ship had accompanied Roys and *Superior* on the epic voyage to the Arctic. He said that he had sailed with Roys as far as the Bering Strait, where they encountered thick weather and became separated. Here, he claimed, his ship had caught the fattest whales ever seen, and soon even the deck space was filled with casks of oil, for lack of space below.[24] *Ocmulgee* returned in April 1850 with a fine catch of some 60 barrels of sperm-whale oil, 3,000 barrels of whale oil, and 30,000 pounds of bone,[25] and Martha's Vineyard people griped for years that Roys's was the success story that was told everywhere, and that for some time afterward bowheads were called Roys's whales in his honor.[26] Unfortunately for natives of the Vineyard, further research reveals that Manter was actually guilty of a tall "sea story," for according to the record of his own log, he had been sailing off Kamchatka and the Okhotsk Sea while Roys was up in the Arctic Ocean. Covill probably did not learn of Roys's discovery until *Ocmulgee* put into Honolulu in October 1848.[27]

Rather than attempting to arbitrate, we may simply say that—no matter who was first—the discovery was most important because these whales proved especially attractive and valuable. They are slow moving and easily captured, and they have thick coats of blubber and yield good quantities of oil and of long, heavy whalebone, their only drawback being that they inhabit only icy, dangerous waters.

According to the noted Soviet whaling expert A. G. Tomilin, bowheads that live in the Pacific will winter in the Bering Sea and may range as far south as the coast of Kamchatka, the Aleutians, and even the Sea of Okhotsk. In the spring, as the ice recedes, they migrate through the Bering Strait into the Chukchi Sea and from there along the coast of Alaska to the Beaufort Sea. These same animals are called Greenland whales in two areas of the North Atlantic—West Greenland and Spitsbergen—and Tomilin believes there is some evidence that the three stocks intermingle, perhaps by the Northwest Passage. He cites, for example, a report by a Dutch captain who saw a whale with a European-marked harpoon in the Far East in 1643 and a mention in 1714 of a whale found on the coast of

the Sea of Okhotsk which supposedly bore a European harpoon with Latin markings.[28]

While Roys concerned himself with filling the ship, the
officers and crew continued to live in hourly expectation of
some calamity.[29] Their fears, however, proved to be ill founded,
because weather and sea conditions were generally pleasant.
There was no ice to speak of, and the climate was so pleasant
the men were able to work in light clothing. Then too, the
Arctic Ocean was so shallow, that most of the while *Superior*
lay at anchor in from fourteen to thirty-five fathoms.[30]

Legend says that Jim Eldredge, Roys's mate, after he had
regained his courage at home, used to tell about some whales
up there that were so large the crew was afraid to tackle them
without specially lengthened killing lances.[31] To support this
tale, Captain Roys claimed that one monster was so large he
would not attempt to cut it in, because he was afraid the terrific
strain on the tackle would drive the ship's mast clear through
her hull. This leviathan was the largest either Roys or his crew
had ever seen, and if taken aboard, it would probably have
yielded 300 barrels. They had had no choice, however, but to
permit this "King of the Arctic Ocean" to quietly go his way.[32]

Superior cruised from continent to continent, traveling
north past the seventieth parallel and filling to her capacity of
1,800 barrels in only thirty-five days, a feat which it usually
required two seasons—at least—to accomplish.[33] Roys put into
Honolulu on October 4, 1848, and received a hearty welcome
in light of his discovery. He arrived home at Sag Harbor on May
5, 1849, after twenty-one months and twenty-one days of sailing clear around the world.[34] True to human nature, the crew
forgot their original misgivings during the return voyage, and
by the time they were safely home, everyone was touting the
new ground as "the greatest place for [whale] oil in the
world."[35]

Roys's daring and accomplishment were the talk of the
entire whale fishery, but there is substantial evidence that he
was disappointed at never having received any official recognition from the Sag Harbor townspeople or the United States

government for his discovery. He later asked, rather acidly, "where is the master of a whaleship firm and dauntless who will have the crushing power of his owners, the hostilities of his officers and crews in case of failure and encounter all the dangers and difficulties which may obstruct his passage through the ice, yielding only to impossibilities and if successfully returned, the whole whaling community receives the benefit and he from envious fools receives only the name of liar for his pains."[36]

Many years later, in his memoirs, Roys again gave vent to his feelings:

> . . . The oil and whalebone taken from Behring Straits since that time [of the discovery] amounts to more than two hundred millions of dollars. For many years I had been firm in the opinion the polar whale existed through Behring Straits and had gained every knowledge within my power and at last feeling sure I acted upon it and this is the result. But at the same time had I told them in Sag Harbor I was going there I should have been considered a madman and turned out of the ship. Thus it is dangerous to possess a knowledge greater than a community, if you are obliged to let them know what you are doing before it is fully proved in public.[37]

Save for some contemporary newspaper articles and a few lines in dusty whaling histories, Roys's only tribute emanated from, of all places, the British Lords of the Admiralty, who sent him copies of the latest charts of the Arctic regions with their compliments on "the valuable information you have given relative to the first whaling grounds in the Arctic Seas. . . ."[38] But Roys did have the rather hollow satisfaction of having anonymously bolstered the whaling industry, which soon became locked in an intense competition for ships, capital, and men following the discovery of gold in California. And so, despite warnings of smothering fog, mysterious currents, and crushing ice, coupled with erroneous charts and a paucity of piloting data, entire fleets headed for the Arctic Ocean whaling grounds.

The impact of the discovery is astounding: in 1849, 154

Cape East.   The Diamedes.

ie abandoned, Crushed by Ice Towing Blasted Whale to Ship Trying out at Anchor. Blubber Logged. Bow Head Whales Pursued.

RIGHT WHALING IN BEHERING STR

FIG. 5.   THE ARCTIC OCEAN WHALE FISHERY

In 1848 when Roys opened the whaling grounds beyond the Bering Strait, he saved the whale fishery from impending decline. Heralding a whole new era, he claimed his discovery brought $200,000,000 in oil and bone for the ships that followed in his wake.

(Courtesy of Kendall Whaling Museum, Sharon, Mass.)

ships sailing in Roys's wake returned with 206,850 barrels of whale oil and 2,481,600 pounds of bone, and the following year 144 ships took 243,680 barrels of oil and 3,654,000 pounds of bone. In those two years alone the Arctic whalers returned with over $8 million in cargo. And so it continued for several decades, and an obscure whaling master from Sag Harbor was responsible for it all.[39]

4

Return to

Whalers' Utopia

A T the time that the Arctic whaling ground was discovered, the size of Captain Roys's catch had been limited only by *Superior*'s cramped holds. Returning home, he sought a much larger ship for his next voyage north.[1] Meanwhile, word of his accomplishments had reached New York City. There, marine-insurance magnate Walter Restored Jones and some friends determined to invite Roys to command their whaler *Sheffield* of Cold Spring Harbor, Long Island.[2] Roys was delighted, for here was the ideal ship he had been seeking for Arctic whale hunting. Retired as a record-breaking transatlantic packet, *Sheffield* at 579 tons was the largest whaleship ever to sail from Long Island and the third largest to fly the American ensign.[3] But before Roys could begin whaling, the owners had one condition: because gold fever was rampant in California, Roys must agree to first sail half-loaded with a cargo of lumber and prefabricated houses to San Francisco on charter. Then he would be free to return to beyond the Bering Strait. So he stowed his try-pots below decks with the cargo, put the whaleboats on their davits, took on a load of cask shooks,[4] and cleared New York Harbor on August 17, 1849, with a crew of thirty-one. Remembering well his experience with the emotional crew of *Superior*, this time Roys took men he knew could be trusted; his brothers-in-law, Henry J. Green and Barney G. Green, went as first mate and a greenhand, while half brothers Samuel and William Henry Roys filled billets as second mate and seaman, respectively.[5] There is also a strong belief that other crew members were in-laws, friends, or neighbors.

Isaac M. Jessup, who had dabbled previously in school teaching, farming, and fishing for a living out on eastern Long Island, shipped on this cruise as a boatsteerer, and he vividly describes the departure day in his personal journal. Upon sailing, he wrote, most of the crew "probably felt high hopes . . . of success . . . and a safe return to their father land enriched with ocean's treasure. . . ." The day following, however, such optimism waned, for, "Pale faces and heads distended over the bulwarks show the commencement of sea sickness. . . ." After about a week of longing for the land they had left behind them, the initial effects of mal de mer subsided, and there was apparently a jolly, contented crew, working literally day and night till they learned the ropes.[6]

Old-time whaling—more often than not—was one of the most boring, monotonous industries of all time. Days, weeks, months could pass without taking a spouter—or even a chance of sighting one. Jessup mentions humbugging—engaging in busywork—of shifting casks of water and barrel shooks; of tending sails and halyards endlessly; of practicing rowing the whaleboats; or of lolling around (only on rare occasions, to be sure) doing nothing but eating, reading, sleeping, or, perhaps, fishing and ship-modeling. Captain Roys was a degree more tolerant than most skippers, for Jessup noted that "on board most ships . . . there is no Sunday off soundings [at sea], at least I was told so . . . by one who has followed the sea many years. Still, I believe there is plainly a Sabbath . . . here . . . [although it is not observed the same] as on land. Better fare and less work mark the Sabbath kept on ship board. . . ."[7]

Let there be no mistake though, Roys and his crusty mates ran a mighty tight ship, for on October 14, Jessup noted that

"This day is a memorable one in the annals of our voyage by reason of flaggelation, expulsion, exaltation, commiseration and fulmination. . . ." But 'lubbers learned quickly and became transformed into greenhands, the apt name for neophyte whalemen, and within another fortnight they were working as a crew. Spirits were high. The food here, it should be mentioned, was a good cut above that in other whalers, what with thick soup, chicken, roast pork, and occasionally a fresh-caught fish or porpoise, "which eats very well indeed," said Jessup. Still, he made it clear that he preferred pork. Apparently he had found his place among the whalers, boasting that, "I was never better contented with my lot in my life. . . ."[8]

It is no wonder there was a certain esprit de corps building within his officer ranks, for Roys was stable, fair, and just. They knew he wanted a well-run ship. Totally dedicated to his trade—unfortunately, to the exclusion of friends and family—he was a most serious man who, by his own personal tenacity and leadership became a hero figure for many of the men who served under him. A number, in fact, rejoined him in later voyages, so powerful was his charisma. In this respect and numerous others he differed widely from his contemporaries. Perceptive yet daring, Roys was unwilling to accept without question the timeworn habits of others. Rather than stick rigidly to proven hunting grounds he had the great courage and innovative spirit—the sheer guts—to chance it all, to gamble with fate. He was determined to find the whalemen's utopia—if there really was one—and was undeterred by the possibility of defeat. He insisted there were many more whales far to the north and south reaches of the globe, and he was determined to take his share. Many species—the rorquals, for instance—remained untouched by old-timers, because of their sheer, massive size.

Roys was fascinated by the sea and all of its creatures. Often he would heave his ship to and examine a sunfish or observe a pod of whales feeding. He carefully noted all he witnessed. Roys was intellectual far beyond the limits of his admittedly meager education. He was a paradox: a complex man within a group of narrow conservatives. Naturally a spirit so strong could antagonize others, and Roys was the first to acknowledge that he received little recognition from his brother whalemen for all his accomplishment. Quite often he was written off as boastful and vain—when he was not ignored altogether as a fool. Yet never did his stamina or staunch determination waver, for he was a professional through and through.

Sheffield passed the Falkland Islands in the remote South Atlantic toward late November 1849, then rounded the Horn, and ran up the Pacific coast of South America bound for California. "Happy go lucky is a sailor's creed," said Jessup, and this portion of the voyage was enjoyable, save for the accidental drowning of a likable young lad, Justin Pratt, son of one of Roys's neighbors upstate. "Esteemed by all his comrades," Jessup intoned, "he was nevertheless the chosen one to remind us that in the midst of life we are in death." Roys said that he was the first man he had ever lost by accident; only two in his previous ships had died of sickness. Sailing northward, they caught a glimpse of the Andes from sea, then put into Valparaiso, Chile, just before Christmas for fresh provisions. A pretty little port, surrounded by mountains which were barren save for some small, yet highly cultivated fields, it was a favorite respite for whalers weary from beating around treacherous Cape Horn.[9]

Despite relatively good treatment on the voyage outbound, discontentment began to fester in some corners of the fo'c'sle. Outward signs appeared on December 23, when the first mate, Henry Green, began preparations to get underway while the captain was still ashore. The majority of the crew refused duty, griping that they wanted more liberty in port or to attend church services. Green gave them time to reconsider, but when a dozen of them stood firm, he had no choice but to place the lot in irons and send them below. When Roys returned aboard that night and learned what had happened, he was outraged. Some of the "discontented ones," wisely sensing the depth of his wrath, agreed to return to duty at once. The day following—Christmas Eve no less—Roys called all hands aft and had the remaining "malcontents" dragged on deck. Before the entire crew, John Dalton, surely the ringleader, took a terrific beating—some twenty-six flesh-tearing lashes of the cat-o'-nine-tails. Six of his brother conspirators also received thrashings, then all were sent forward to their bunks.[10] This was whaleship justice at its worst.

Soon December was almost over, and the year 1849 was ebbing fast. In a pensive mood Jessup remarked, "Still as the moments fly I must own that I am quite as contented and more happy than when on shore." The mood aboard ship seemed relaxed. The carpenter was busily mending and painting the stove, while the crew were sorting the ship's potatoes, some of which—as usual—had rotted. The weather was warm and pleasant, so there was even time for a swim and lots of fun especially when the cooper fell overboard. It seemed that the near mutiny of just a few days before was almost forgotten, for the next day, Sunday, everyone was either reading, sleeping, washing clothes, barbering or tending the ship, and all appeared to be normal and quiet. It remained so throughout January, and even "The captain displayed his clemency by letting a man go unpunished who had broken a rule of the ship." By February, six months at sea had passed; everyone in old *Sheffield* seemed peaceful and content, but there were first undercurrents of unrest, and then the tranquil spell was broken altogether. A handful of the sailors who had been punished after leaving Valparaiso began threatening and vowing vengeance in public and private; "A conspiracy deep and diabolical," said Jessup, was underway. Rumors were rampant. Taking no more chances, Roys ordered the rascals placed in irons on the afternoon of February 8 and planned to keep them there until the ship reached California.[11]

One of the culprits, who had been threatening to murder someone for at least a month, snarled in defiance that he could break his bonds. He was taken at his word, and another pair of manacles was specially riveted, which Jessup said could resist the strength of ten men. In a few days the extent of the foiled plot became known—the mutineers had planned to murder any of the officers and crew who had displeased them and promised "to string some to the yard arm and drink the heart's blood of others." Jessup was shaken to learn that they would have knocked him unconscious at Valparaiso, if given a chance. Then they would have seized the ship and killed all who had not joined them.[12] Roys, realizing the seriousness of the charges he would have to level when the ship reached San Francisco, began to take depositions from the men who had remained loyal.[13].

Roys and several of the mates were shocked by what they learned while composing a statement.

After some days upon our passage . . . [the six men who had been flogged after leaving Valparaiso] were observed at night to be conversing in whispers . . . and warnings were given by some of the other men forward to be on our guard. . . . On . . . the . . . 6th of Jan between the hours of 10 & 2 o clock, the night being very dark, I got out of my cabin window and went forward outside of the rails and concealed myself under the bowsprit, where I heard the planning of my own death, all my officers and all my crew excepting these six. . . . I took all the precaution I could to prevent these wretches from committing this crime and let them still go at large. They still continued making threats of firing the ship and murdering men until I became convinced that ere long some bloody tragedy must be enacted if these men went at large and accordingly . . . they were put in irons. . . .

Their plan of operations was to get two men at the wheel. They could come in at the after cabin door, knife myself and [the] 1st Officer and blow out the cabin light as a signal. The 4 others to come in forward, kill the boatsteerers and they would then have charge of the cabin and seizing the arms of the officers take the ship, use the remainder of the crew while they would be of service to them, then kill them, run the ship ashore or burn her, take our revolvers, rifles and side arms and rob and plunder in California's mines. . . .[14]

When *Sheffield* finally made San Francisco on February 21, Roys found the harbor choked with over 400 ships. The Gold Rush was on in all its glitter. On the morning of the twenty-third the six prisoners were transferred to U.S.S. *Warren*. Her captain, disgusted by Roys's lurid tale of near mutiny, thought "he ought to have left the fellows on some barren island which would have saved farther trouble." Everyone was glad to see them go.[15] Considering the comparatively minor problems Roys had had with the men in *Superior*, it is ironic that he should have had serious difficulties with this, a handpicked crew.

California during those freewheeling days was filled with excitement. Carpenters were earning an astounding $12 to $14 per diem, and room and board was going for an unheard of $3 per day. Letters from relatives of shipmates boasted of having cleared $600 in just seven weeks' time. Roys went ashore to see all this hubbub for himself and was surprised to find his father-in-law, Capt. Henry Green,[16] who had come out from Sag Harbor in the old whaler *Sabina* with a crew of nineteen whaling master mariners, seeking their turn at the gold placers.[17] Captain Green came aboard *Sheffield* and visited for the night, giving an account of the gold digging that was anything but favorable; in fact he claimed to have lost about $3,000 himself in that pursuit.[18]

It took ten days to off-load the cargo, so Isaac Jessup had plenty of liberty to take seeing the sights of San Francisco, which he described as the "muddiest hole I ever saw." Joining some of the officers and boatsteerers ashore, he witnessed firsthand practically all the wonders of the town. He reported:

The gaming tables are better attended than the churches . . . oranges are 50 cts. apiece, cigars 12½ and a glass of liquor 25. . . . The streets are so muddy that an ox will go to the knees almost every step in the middle of them. It is very difficult to walk here owing to the mud on the steep side[d] hills which are very common. The gambling houses are thronged at almost all hours of the

day. They have 8 or 10 tables in a single room, each with banks of
from 1 to 20,000$ and often 500 persons are in one of these rooms,
some at the bar drinking, some playing, some betting and a far
greater number gratifying their curiosity as spectators. . . .[19]

On April 1, the crew was at last bending sails and getting
ready for sea. *Sheffield* cleared for Honolulu on April 2, 1850,
partially fitted for whaling,[20] with Roys and his crew boasting
that they expected to take 5,000 barrels of oil in ninety days.
One local—a former Sag Harbor man—suspecting a bit of
exaggeration in their vow, mused, "I hope they will do it but
sha'nt be disappointed if they don't."[21] Early out there was no
wind, so the captain decided to come to anchor and wait for a
breeze. Just as the "hook" (anchor) was let go, someone
noticed that two large rocks were within a few fathoms of the
stern. To make matters worse, there was a treacherous tidal
current running. Nearby, the royal mast of a ship which had
been wrecked only a few days before was sticking ominously a
few feet out of the water. The anchor dragged. More chain was
paid out until there was little more than room enough for the
ship to swing clear of the threatening rocks. Most of the crew
were ready to seize their valuables at a moment's notice. They
had the boats ready to abandon ship. "Oldest to youngest
expected to go on the rocks unless the tide slacked. . . ." At
noon—by good fortune—it did, and at 1:30 P.M. *Sheffield* was
out of danger. Jessup was breathing easier: "So far well and
good and we were under way and on the deep blue sea by
3 P.M."[22]

Once out of sight of San Francisco Bay, preparations for
whaling began. Harpoons and lances were honed razor-sharp;
the whaleboats were painted and repaired; and the oil casks
were assembled from the shooks, heads, and hoops stored
between decks. On April 23 *Sheffield* called at Honolulu for
liberty, fresh food, and water and to complete fitting out for
Arctic whaling. "Not a man in the watch has been intoxicated
yet," Jessup commented proudly, knowing well sailors' vices.
They sailed on May 4 to one of the Hawaiian out islands and

traded calico for melons, sweet potatoes, bananas, pigs, goats, and fowl. Then it was "Adieu to the pleasant skies of Sandwich Islands till next fall," as the captain shaped a course for the Bering Strait. By the time that the ship was squared away for hunting, Roys had raised the Fox Islands off Alaska. There were plenty of whales there, and he took a few while waiting for a clear passage in the continuous barrier of ice facing him to the north.[23]

In time the pack ice broke, and Roys began to beat up to the Strait. Remembering the close call he had had in *Superior* with natives in that vicinity, he had armed for this trip with one large cannon, four swivel guns, and twenty-four muskets.[24] The whaling season began about mid-July, when bowheads began to migrate close to shore throughout the entire Sea of Okhotsk, the Bering Strait, and the Arctic coasts of Siberia. In these golden days of whaling, there were hundreds of ships in every bay and in the mouths of rivers all along the Russian shore. Boat crews signaled ships to come in for the harvest, while others freely roamed the land, killing bear, reindeer, and other game. With an obvious note of pride, Roys crowed that "the indefatigable Yankee is already on shore among the natives . . . raising potatoes, etc. and supplying his countrymen with vegetation and amalgamating his race with the natives and Russians. . . ." Some were even engaged in mining rich deposits of coal and iron. But all of this relaxed, open commerce frightened Roys also, for it did not have the czar's approval. He felt that it could have led to seizure of any whaling vessel less than nine miles from shore, or possibly even to war. In a report to Matthew Maury, America's first oceanographer, Roys wisely asserted that the matter ". . . deserves the quick consideration of the American government."[25] No agreement was ever negotiated with the Russians, but no confrontation materialized.

The 1850 Arctic season was excellent. Roys took about 3,000 barrels of oil and 45,000 pounds of whalebone in the area of the Bering Strait alone.[26] Although this may appear to have been an easy task, these northern waters were a good match for even the most skillful captains. In the Okhotsk Sea, for example, Roys tells of forty- and fifty-foot tides, totally irregular in frequency and "utterly defying all calculations." His description of these climes is none too appealing. "Winds . . . and a great deal of thick weather . . . sometimes blowing strong for days together [and accompanied by] . . . a heavy swell makes the place inconceivably annoying and not a little dangerous [even] when it is calm. Your anchors are your only hopes." Even in calm weather, Roys said, *Sheffield* once dragged her 3000-pound bowers ahead of her in ninety fathoms at the rate of six miles per hour. When the anchors finally were raised, one had its massive stock sheared right off, and both were "as bright as silver."[27]

In late August, while the ship was lying at anchor in the Arctic Ocean, a very stiff wind sprang up suddenly. As the ship was getting underway to beat offshore, its windlass literally disintegrated, forcing the captain to abandon the grounds earlier than he had intended.[28] Then there was more misfortune. On the return passage to Honolulu, the ship had a close call, missing near destruction "and instant death to all of us by . . . only 100 ft." It appears that Roys was about to transit a narrow passage among the Fox Islands—in the central Aleutian chain—when he encountered some very heavy weather, with still gales and thick, gloomy fog. Visibility was near zero, causing him to overshoot the tricky channel. Instead, *Sheffield* ran straight for a horseshoe-shaped bay, which was surrounded by a sheer hundred-foot cliff. The sea was so rough, that the violent surf was billowing to within the very crest of the precipice. The situation was grave, for it seemed impossible to tack or to wear ship in time to avoid wrecking her on the treacherous rocks. Roys reasoned that only a heavier press of sail could save her.[29]

Let Roys narrate the situation firsthand.

With great exertion we got the mainsail upon her. All was done that man could do to save the ship with every man at his post, two men at the helm. Some are weeping, some are praying, some in sullen silence look upon the all exciting scene and calmly wait the

Fig. 6. Whaleship *SHEFFIELD* of Cold Spring Harbor, L.I.

In 1849 Roys signed on as master of the 579-ton whaleship *Sheffield*, which was the third-largest vessel to sail in the Yankee whaling fleet. Driving far north into the Arctic Ocean, Roys returned with over $100,000 in oil and bone for the ecstatic owners.

(Painting by Commander E. C. Tufnell, R.N. (Ret.), courtesy of The Whaling Museum, Cold Spring Harbor, N.Y.)

stroke of death. At this critical moment the gale increases. The tremendous weight of sail is making the ship . . . groan throughout her extreme length. The sea is breaking over her, throwing the spray upon her topsails and wetting down the men at her helm, her leerails are under water. No word is spoken, for the proud ship is laboring with destiny and with fearful speed she staggers on, bearing all on board to safety or instant death. Onward she drives, until only one wave is between us and the rocky bottom, here at a distance of about 100 feet [from shore]. Then the memories of years go flying through the brain, the cheek turns pale, the heart beats thick and the boldest hold their breath. In another moment she is free and a shout of joy resounds through the ship. The rocks are passed and orders to reduce sail are obeyed with alacrity and she runs in safety o'er the sea.[30]

What Roys had accomplished in this daring maneuver was to increase his speed by hauling as close to the wind as possible, enabling the ship to run along the rocky shore and to clear one of the promontories at the entrance of the bay by a hair's breadth. Had he been there, the hero of Roys's youth, old Capt. Henry Green, certainly would have been proud at this moment.

Sheffield entered Honolulu in early October for a refit and a well-deserved liberty for her exhausted crew.[31] Relaxed and rested, they got underway again for Hong Kong. During this cruise fortune again betrayed them. On November 26 *Sheffield* took a terrible beating in a typhoon off the Mariana group in the eastern Pacific. There had been little warning, except that Roys had been awakened during the previous night by a strange, unusual motion of the sea. When he reached the main deck, however, he found the weather calm, with no appreciable wind. He returned to his cabin, but the peculiar rocking did not permit any sleep. Restless, he again went on deck; a small puff of wind passed over the ship, then it fell dead calm. "I knew the meaning of this," he said abruptly, and with a shout, "All hands were called by those imperious orders that are well known to bide no delay." Half sleepy, the crew scrambled on deck.

It is clew down and clew up everything. The orders are obeyed with utmost speed. Every man works with all his strength. It was too late. The typhoon was upon us in all its withering power. Sails, masts, yards, boats, bulwarks, all are flying in wild confusion over the lee, while the ship broaches and defies the helm. So great is the power of the wind that men standing side by side cannot speak anything to each other. The helm is lashed and the forecastle closed up and all hands go down in the cabin and shut the door and leave the good ship to ride it out alone or perish.[32]

After eight torturous hours, the storm finally abated.[33] The ship was a muddle. Three boats—gear, davits, and all—and a suit of sails were lost, but aside from the battering of their ship, they had been lucky indeed,[34] for Roys himself admitted that "The power of the wind in these tempests is entirely inconceivable to anyone who has never witnessed them."[35] *Sheffield* limped into Hong Kong on December 6 and lay over, refitting and repairing, until February 20, 1851.[36] Clearing his holds for another season up north, Captain Roys shipped some 2,000 barrels of oil and 46,000 pounds of whalebone from there to London, a more favorable market.[37]

In the spring of 1851 Roys cruised north again. In March *Sheffield* cleared the Diomede Islands in the Bering Strait, in company with a large fleet of whalers. Here Roys encountered an unbroken line of pack ice sweeping across the horizon, much farther south than it normally occurred.[38] Although this generally was dubbed the icy season, when growlers and small bergs could be encountered anyway, it appeared that *Sheffield* would be taking no bowheads that summer.[39] In July the anxiety and monotony slackened momentarily, for Roys chanced upon H.M.S. *Plover* in Port Clarence, Alaska, just south of the strait. He had an interesting gam with her commander, and they discussed the search for the missing British polar expedition of Sir John Franklin, as well as various species of whales each had observed off the Arctic coast of North America.[40]

During his stay in Port Clarence, Roys visited the captain of H.M.S. *Enterprise,* another ship in the search party, which was being prepared to embark for the fabled Northwest Passage on one more leg of the quest.[41] In fact, Roys himself had orders from his owners to assist in this search where possible. Walter Restored Jones, out of compassion for Lady Jane Franklin, had written to her in July 1849, offering the services of his small fleet of ships out of Cold Spring Harbor, Long Island, in the hunt for her husband. He even suggested that the British government dispatch a small exploring party with Captain Roys, which could come aboard *Sheffield* when she put into San Francisco. The ship, Jones pointed out, was due to be "in the vicinity of the waters expected to be crossed by Sir John and his companions," so the searchers could be transported, "to some place convenient for the ship to land them on the shores of the Icy [Arctic] Ocean. . . ." "I have thought it proper," Jones continued, "to give you this information so that you and your friends can judge the benefits, if any, in a cause so dear, not only to you and to every British subject, but to the whole civilized world."[42]

In response, Lady Jane sent Walter Jones a packet of official reports, which she believed might be helpful to Captain Roys in the search for her husband. Jones, in turn, discussed the papers with two of his captains who were sailing for the Arctic, then promised to forward them overland to Roys at San Francisco. The suggestion of a party to accompany Roys was dropped, presumably because intensive search efforts were already underway by the British government. In his reply, Jones sought to console her: "I hope your efforts will be crowned with all of that success to which they are so eminently entitled."[43] Although he encountered ships of the Royal Navy at Port Clarence, there is no indication that Roys had a direct hand in the rescue mission. Sad to say, rumors which reached England in 1854 were highly discouraging. Evidence showed that Sir John and his men might have perished in the winter of

1850–51. Still unconvinced, Lady Franklin urged on the search with continued determination until 1859, when she received positive proof that her husband had died on June 11, 1847, following the death of twenty-four of his officers and men.

The 1851 whaling season on the Arctic grounds was a disaster. Fifteen ships were lost to the ice. Roys remained until the latter part of August, but he found no opportunity to work the fleet through the pack ice, and he decided to square away and seek a more promising ground. In September he sailed into the Sea of Okhotsk, and there he was able to stow down 1,600 barrels of oil by mid-October. Sailing south for the winter, Roys touched at Ocean Island in the Gilbert and Ellice group, near the equator. There he recruited wood and water, then continued southward to San Cristobal, one of the Solomons, which was known to be the haunt of cannibals and headhunters. Imagine the Yankees' trepidation when upon their arrival, they were confronted by approximately a hundred canoes, each containing two men. These people were strongly built and had black skin and pearly teeth. Their appearance was somewhat strange, however, for their kinky hair was as white as snow. The Americans bartered some scraps of iron hoop for fruit, but when Roys insisted on getting underway again, the natives screamed "like demons" and shot arrows into the ship's canvas, seemingly enraged at the whalers' departure. One simple soul, however, sitting alone in his canoe, grabbed a line trailing from *Sheffield*'s stern and sang cheerily as he was towed out to sea. Finally, when about ten miles off, he released the line and calmly paddled home.[44]

Roys was lucky to have had only a light encounter with these fierce people, for just a few days before, Benjamin Boyd, an Australian freewheeler, and one of his men had vanished on nearby Guadalcanal.[45] Boyd was an entrepreneur par excellence. Scotch by birth, he initially became a successful stockbroker in Great Britain, then set out for Australia to fulfill his destiny at age forty-five. No humble, obscure immigrant was he, however, and Ben Boyd arrived with a flourish off Sydney in 1842, commanding his splendid yacht *Wanderer,* which flew the prestigious burgee of the Royal Yacht Squadron. Eighty-four tons, boasting thirteen guns, she was a magnificent ship, fitting well the character of her flamboyant owner. In jig time Boyd established an empire down under, including vast tracts of sheep-grazing lands, two seaport towns—one, appropriately, named for himself—and a fleet of nine sperm whalers. In addition, he maintained several extensive shore whaling stations. Boyd was riding high. But it was all short-lived, for just six years after his arrival, his realm began to crumble. Fortunes waned rapidly, so in October 1849, in disgrace, he sailed off again in *Wanderer* to the gold fields of California. Apparently his run of bad luck continued, for he returned to the South Pacific, reportedly full of dreams of his own self-declared republic on the island of New Guinea. He sailed no further than Guadalcanal, however, where he disappeared on October 15, 1851.[46]

According to Roys, soon after Boyd and his aide went ashore, the natives attacked the yacht and she fired into them, killing hundreds. On they came in great hordes, however, and nothing, it appeared, could stop them, so *Wanderer* slipped her cables and beat a hasty retreat.[47] Boyd and his man were never found, and to compound the tragedy the schooner was wrecked on the return passage to Australia. Three years after Boyd's disappearance, two ships were dispatched to lay the mystery to rest. The story is told that a skull, said to have been that of Ben Boyd, was recovered, having been traded from the natives for twenty tomahawks![48]

In March 1852, *Sheffield* touched at Sydney to recruit, then turned north to the Okhotsk Sea for the summer, where she took about 1,600 barrels of oil. With winter setting in, Roys dropped down again to the warmer latitudes. He put in at Ocean Island in the Gilberts, where he unexpectedly found the New Bedford whaling brig *Inga*, in which his brother Sam was mate. In private, Sam revealed that he was concerned for his safety, for Capt. Thomas D. Barnes of *Inga* was trading freely with the natives and allowing them to board in great numbers,

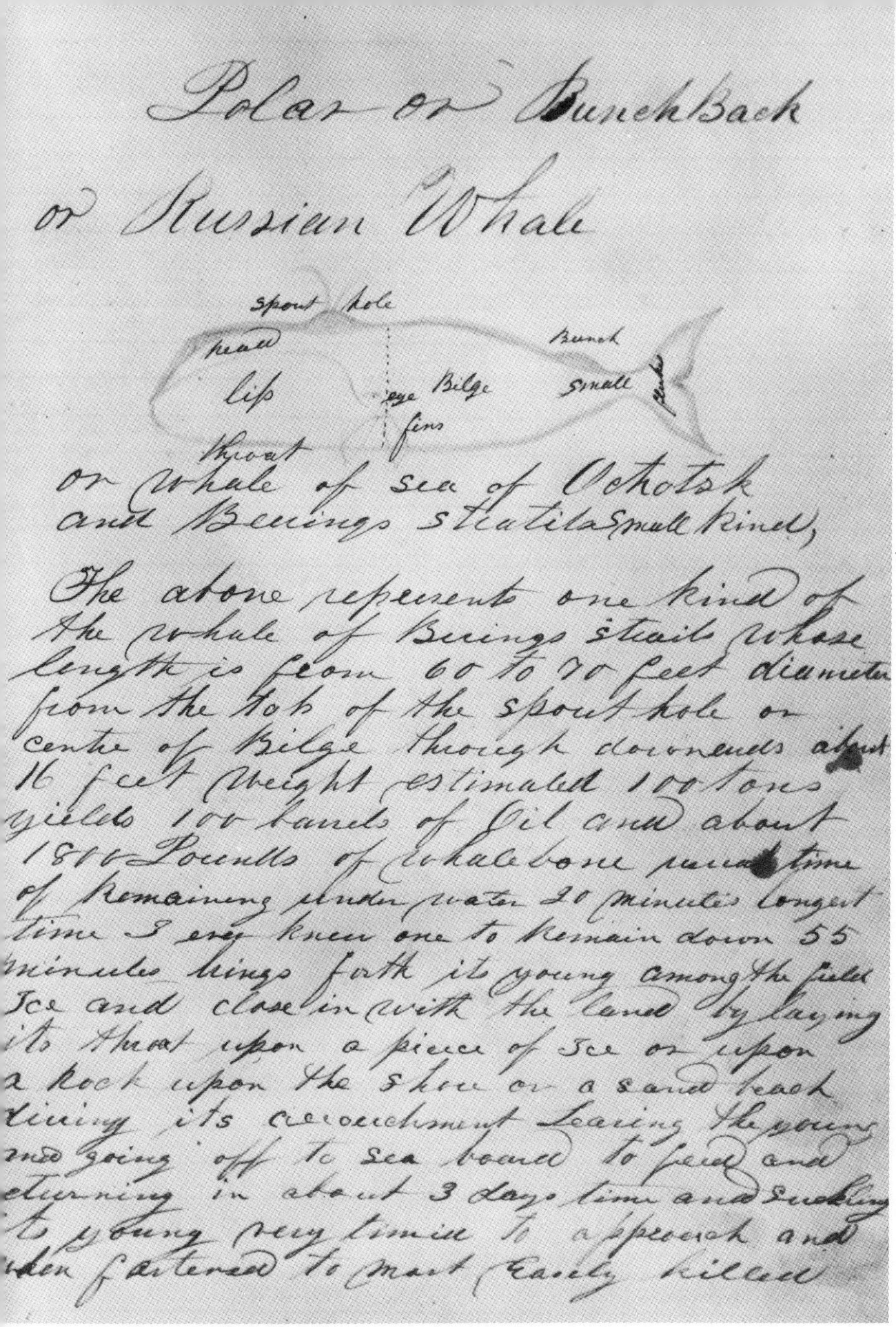

Polar or BunchBack
or Russian Whale

[handwritten labels on diagram: spout hole, head, lip, eye, Bilge, Bunch, small, fins, throat]

*or Whale of sea of Ochotsk
and Beerings straits (small kind)*

*The above represents one kind of
the whale of Beerings straits (whose
length is from 60 to 70 feet diameter
from the top of the spout hole or
centre of Bilge through downwards about
16 feet) weight estimated 100 tons
yields 100 barrels of Oil and about
1800 Pounds of whalebone. mean time
of remaining under water 20 minutes longest
time I ever knew one to remain down 55
minutes brings forth its young among the field
Ice and close in with the land by laying
its throat upon a piece of Ice or upon
a rock upon the shore or a sand beach
during its accouchment leaving the young
and going off to sea board to feed and
returning in about 3 days time and suckling
its young very timid to approach and
when fastened to meat (easily killed*

FIG. 7. A PAGE FROM ROYS'S "DESCRIPTIONS OF WHALES"

Penned aboard the whaleship *Sheffield* in 1854, this twenty-nine
page manuscript represented all that Thomas Roys knew of the
natural history of whales. It included pencil drawings and descriptions of species he had encountered in his twenty-one years of
wandering at sea.

(Courtesy of The Mariners Museum, Newport News, Va.)

foolishly taking no precautions. Clearly remembering what had happened to Ben Boyd and *Wanderer*, Roys induced his brother to join him. Lo and behold, his fears were justified, for no sooner had *Inga* touched at another island than she was boarded and everyone was killed save for a crewman, James Blair, and a South Seas island Kanaka, who somehow jumped overboard undetected. The savages, meanwhile, plundered the ship, and after setting a fire on board, abandoned her. After fourteen hours in the water, Blair and the Kanaka slipped aboard, extinguished the flames, and stole out of sight, bound on a course for Sydney. Two men were no match for a 160-ton ship, and she soon snapped her masts. They drifted aimlessly for six weeks more, until they were picked up by a passing ship and landed at Honolulu.[49]

Sheffield put into Wellington, New Zealand, toward the end of December 1852, where she was refitted for another northern cruise. By early July Roys had filled the remainder of his casks—some 1,400 barrels—in the Okhotsk, so he left the ground early, bound for Hawaii and then home. He entered Honolulu harbor on September 9, 1853, and learned immediately that there was an epidemic of smallpox. Paying no mind to his own safety, but considering that of his crew, Roys went ashore alone for the night, and predictably, he broke out with the dread disease a week later. Wisely, he quarantined himself to his cabin, where he was attended only by his steward, who had had the sickness and was immune. For four weeks Roys remained isolated, and fortunately no one else fell ill.[50] Roys returned from this his last voyage to the North Pacific, on January 24, 1854, arriving at New York City with 2,700 barrels of whale oil and 41,000 pounds of bone aboard.[51] All in all, it was a spectacular voyage—so typical of this determined Yankee skipper—for in fifty-three months and forty-seven days he had taken approximately 8,000 barrels of oil and well over 100,000 pounds of whalebone—worth perhaps $100,000 or more![52] Roys's ability was unparalleled in the trade.

5

The Professional
Whaleman

T HE science of the sea is a relatively new discipline. Until the eighteenth century it was characterized in the main by conjectures, half-truths, and outright fabrications. Capt. James Cook, R.N., in his three major voyages of exploration from 1768 to 1779 heralded a new era, for he began to gather some of the first concrete oceanographic data. Later his steps were retraced somewhat by Comdr. Charles Wilkes, U.S.N., who led the U.S. Exploring Expedition around the globe from 1838 to 1842, generating volumes of observations on everything from anthropology, ocean currents, and meteorology to whales and whaling. In the field of biology Charles Darwin opened the door to true knowledge, courageously smashing centuries-old myths and false hypotheses. His contemporaries—marine biologists like Edward Forbes of Great Britain, Michael Sars of Norway, and Henri Milne-Edwards of France—were, like Darwin, among the first to carry studies directly into the field, in contrast to the work of their predecessors, which was characterized by casual observations of long-dead specimens and reliance on hearsay evidence. Soon hydrography was creating as much stir and interest as space technology does today. And,

of course, the culmination of all this early research was when
H.M.S. *Challenger* sailed from Portsmouth, England, in 1872,
on what was to become the greatest and most fabled oceanographic cruise ever, seeking mysteries of the seas on a
68,890-mile globe-girdling voyage during which her scientists
gathered priceless information and specimens throughout
four oceans.[1]

More than any man, Lt. Matthew Fontaine Maury, U.S.N.,
was responsible for the encouragement and development of
ocean science in the United States. Known synonymously as
the father of American oceanography and the "Pathfinder of
the Seas," Maury began his career in science in 1842, when he
was appointed superintendent of the Depot of Charts and
Instruments, the forerunner of today's U.S. Naval Observatory
and Oceanographic Office. At first he concentrated on improving astronomical observations, raising the Naval Observatory
in Washington to the best European standards by 1846. Next,
he turned his talents to preparing wind and current charts of
the world's oceans, using old, discarded Navy logbooks for his
statistical bases. His charts substantially reduced the sailing
times for clippers, and heartened by the success of this project,
Maury embarked on an even more ambitious endeavor: a plan
for systematic observations at sea. Maury wrote letters to hundreds of ship owners and whaling-ship, Navy, and clipper-ship
masters and received many letters from them in return; in
short order, he had a network of more than a thousand vessels
gathering information for him in every sea. His methodology
was not unlike that of Benjamin Franklin, who had consulted
with Nantucket whaling captains before charting the Gulf
Stream almost a century before. The product of Maury's
studies was his *Explanations and Sailing Directions to Ac
company the Wind and Current Charts* (1851 ff.) and *The
Physical Geography of the Sea* (1855 ff.)[2]

Almost simultaneously, Roys was experiencing a somewhat mystical transformation of his own life's goals. He literally abandoned a soaring career as an accomplished and
financially successful whaling captain—after all, he could have

FIG. 8. LT. MATTHEW FONTAINE MAURY, U.S.N. (1806–1873)

Known as the "Father of Oceanography" and "Pathfinder of the
Seas," Maury led the American nineteenth-century marine science effort. Roys gave Maury much data for his charts and sailing
directions and met with him several times. He considered Maury
his friend. This painting, by E. Sophonisba Hergesheimer, hangs
in Maury Hall, U.S. Naval Academy.

(Courtesy of U.S. Navy Academy Museum, Annapolis, Md.)

had his pick of ships, writing his own terms—and chose instead to pursue more tenuous and nebulous goals such as the study of the biological aspects of whales and their ecology and the development of radically new methods of whaling, which were to form the foundations of the mechanized trade of later years. "Whaling," Roys boasted, had become ". . . the whole study of my life. . . ."[3] This period began, very likely, with a letter he received from Matthew Maury. Surely it was the crystallizing factor in his already penetrating interest in cetacea, bringing scientist and professional whaleman into a friendship that spanned a decade. It read:

> National Observatory
> Washington, D.C.
> Oct. 3rd, 1849

Dear Sir:

In the course of my investigations as to the habits and places of resort of the whale, it has become a matter of exceeding interest to ascertain whether the [bowhead] whale of Behrings Strait [in the North Pacific] and of Davis Strait [in the North Atlantic] be the same. Not only this; but to obtain answers to the following questions: How many kinds of whale are there in the [Arctic] Ocean beyond Behrings Strait? What are the leading characteristics and most striking peculiarities of each kind? The same, as to Baffins Bay and Davis Strait—the kind and characteristics.

Do these Arctic [bowhead] whale ever sound under icebergs? If so—how high and broad is the largest iceberg you have ever known a whale to go under? How far do they go without coming to the surface to breathe. Do they hybrinate under the ice. May I ask of you the kindness to bring me some part, at least, of the skull bone and teeth of each kind of whale found up Behrings or Davis Straits also: the horn of a "hog" or horned whale [narwhal], with drawings and descriptions of each kind of whale; together with any facts in relation to their habits, places of resort &c, in your possession.

The Professional Whaleman

In truth any information that you may find time and inclination to give, touching this animal, will be most thankfully received.

> Wishing you all manner of
> good luck. I remain very
> truly yours,
> M. F. Maury

To Capt.
Thomas B. Roys
  Ship *Sheffield* . . .
Care of Walter R. Jones Esq.
  New York[4]

These were tough questions indeed, but true to form, Roys sensed another challenge and replied enthusiastically.

> Ship *Sheffield*
> Hong Kong, January 19, 1851

I received your favor with pleasure, and am very willing to communicate any knowledge I possess respecting the whaling business. The whales of Behring's Straits and Baffin's Bay are the same; yet they differ very much from the Kamtschatka or northeast whale, or the right whale of the South Seas. I have known a whale to sound deep enough to take one thousand and fifty fathoms of line from the boat; yet I never knew a whale to remain longer under water than 35 minutes, of the right whale species; and one hour and 30 minutes for the sperm whale kind. I have never known them to sound under ice, that is, [ice]more than 30 feet above the water's surface, which was in the South Seas [probably referring to the Antarctic Ocean]. I have never seen any ice to the northward of Behring's Straits more than 30 feet high. The right whale feeds upon a small animal substance, which seems to vegetate and come to maturity every year, and perish like the vegetation upon the land. And it is in only one state that the whale will eat it; consequently, in the northern hemisphere, in the month of January, the food is to be found from 30° to 35° north; and in February it is ripe for the whale; a little further in March; still further, and so on, until August, when it is as far north as the Kamtschatka whales go, which is 60°; while the feed from 35° to 40° becomes dead and unfit to nourish the whale; consequently, the whale cannot live at that season in those latitudes; while the humpback and fin-back take possession, and seem to enjoy and revel in the food, after it has passed its stage for the right whale. The polar whale's feed differs a little from the others; and in January, may be found in 50° north, and in August, from 70° to the pole. I am firm in the opinion that the south is the same; but as no one has ever yet seen a right whale, the opposite of the arctic whales, in the antarctic, the matter still remains in doubt; and it is a lamentable truth, that the ships of war who have visited those seas are not able to tell us for certainty the kind of whales they saw there. It is not the easiest thing in the world to distinguish the different kinds of whales, even to those who have been in the whaling business, and a ship must be brought close by a whale to tell for certain his kind.

The sperm whale is found in all climates, and in every sea; he feeds upon an inanimate animal substance called a squid, which grows upon the bottom of the sea, and is never seen upon the surface, except when torn up by the whale. I have seen it in large pieces floating upon the surface. I have seen a dying whale vomit it up. I have opened the stomach of a whale and seen it there in pieces; which convinces me that the animal is very large, also, as well as small; and that the sperm whale almost always, when in want of food, goes to the ocean's bed.

I do not know as I shall be able to procure for you a whale's horn, as they are difficult to take; but, if no ill betide me, I will bring you the under and upper jaw of a Russian whale, which will be about 24 feet long by 16 diameter, which will serve to show the magnitude of this animal, and, perhaps, we may obtain the horn and something more.

. . . I am writing a book, with all the knowledge I possess, giving particular description of all kinds of whales, with all my opinions, &c., which I will forward unto you upon my return to the States. I shall sail from here the 10th of February, and expect to be in 60° north on the 20th of March. It would require too much paper to send, by mail, full answers to your inquiries, and I can only say that I heartily rejoice that we have one man in our Government who will condescend to take notice of a business, the annual income of which is millions, and at the present time has broken down all competition of other nations, and is supplying the markets of the world with oil. I shall also be able to give you some of my opinions of ocean currents, &c. I have a set of your Wind and Current Charts, which, I am happy to say, I consider very useful, and have found them so. When I arrive at home, you will hear from me soon.

Thomas W. Roys[5]

The fruit of Roys's efforts, a 29 page, illustrated manu-script, entitled "Descriptions of Whales," would be judged somewhat naive by today's scientific standards, yet Lieutenant Maury thought it a "very interesting paper," and he even wrote Roys a short series of letters during 1854—soon after he had received the manuscript—asking him to amplify certain points.[6] Somewhat apologetically, Maury stressed that, "I ask these questions not for any idle notice, but for the sake of information, hoping that you will find it convenient to answer them, and to tell me whatever else may occur to you concern-ing the habits of the whale. . . . "[7] Roys's book, incidentally, contains illustrations of some eighteen species—with detailed descriptions, natural history data, distribution patterns, and feeding habits for sixteen of them.[8] In his correspondence Maury implies that he might have made copies of the little book, thus sharing Roys's findings and observations with other scientists.[9] It was here, for instance, that he found the first description of the "Bunch Back" whale, a subspecies of the bowhead that was later named for Roys.[10] This particular animal received its curious name from the small "bunch," or hump, near the base of its spine, where the usual bowhead has

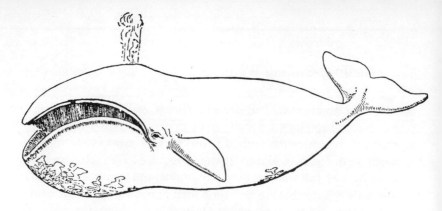

FIG. 9.   BOWHEAD WHALE

These slow-moving, docile whales became a staple for the whaling industry after Captain Roys found them in vast numbers beyond the Bering Strait in 1848. Overkill has brought these creatures practically to the brink of extinction. They are completely protected from whalers, save for native Eskimos, now. Compare this drawing with Roy's "bunch back," Fig. 10.

(From Alexander Starbuck, History of the American Whale Fishery *[Washington, D.C., 1876], p. 771, courtesy of The Whaling Museum, Cold Spring Harbor, N.Y.)*

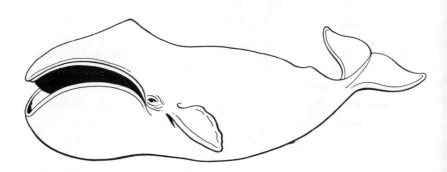

FIG. 10.   ROYS'S "BUNCH BACK" WHALE

Captain Roys was the first person to describe the "bunch back" whale—a subspecies of bowhead—later named for him *(Balaena mysticetus Roysii* Dall, 1874). It supposedly differs from the true bowhead in that it has a "trigger" or "bunch," on the small of its back, about six feet forward of the flukes. Scientists now dispute that it is a true subspecies, but since the bowheads are so gravely endangered, no one can be sure.

(From Charles M. Scammon, Marine Mammals of the Northwestern Coast of North America *[San Francisco and New York, 1874], p. 56, in the private collection of Frederick P. Schmitt.)*

none. It was first described for the scientific community by Capt. Charles M. Scammon and E. D. Cope—using material from Roys's natural history writings—in the lofty and respected *Proceedings* of the Academy of Natural Sciences of Philadelphia in 1869.[11] Roys likewise received credit for this discovery in Scammon's classic, *The Marine Mammals of the Northwestern Coast of North America* (1874).[12]

Roys also was responsible for generating scientific interest in the killer whale, or orca, of which little was then known by Americans, save for a few scholarly papers in some dusty old European journals. At the 1855 meeting of the American Association of Scientific Discovery in Washington, Lieutenant Maury presented a paper on orcas in which he mentioned that Roys's manuscript included details on a strange whale, "which the lieutenant did not find in any of the books. The captain [Roys] called him the 'killer whale,' and described him as thirty feet long, yielding about five barrels of oil, having sharp, strong teeth, and on the middle of the back a fin, very stout, and about four feet long. The 'killer' is an exceedingly pugnacious fellow. . . . The captain sent a drawing of the 'killer,' which was exhibited. . . ."[13]

About 1871 Roys wrote this terrifying and brutal account of the killer whale and its behavior:

. . . They are found in all oceans where other whales exist and they kill and feed upon other species of whales except sperm whales. They go in packs of 20 or 30 together and attack the right whale by biting his throat on the outside. This causes the whale to open his mouth. Another killer runs his head into the whale's mouth and seizes his tongue. Then another does the same thing and finally when enough of them is hold they drag the whale under water and keep him there until drowned, as they possess the power to remain under water much longer than the whale. Thus these small animals destroy the mightiest of whales; even the mighty rorqual cannot escape them.

I saw near Nova Zemla [Novaya Zemlya islands, Russia] a pack of these animals tugging at the mighty rorqual. They were biting his throat and the sea all around him was purple with his blood. The whale seemed to know that to go down was death and remained upon the surface striking with his enormous flukes most vicious and powerful blows that made the ocean all around them one white foam. But it did not seem of any use to him as they seem to defend themselves with this hard backfin which is yielding substance and seems to be formed purposely to protect them from the blows of the whale. Whales seem to be in most abject fear of these animals and sometimes after the whalemen have killed a whale the killers seize the whale and take it down. An instance is known of a whale being attacked by killers in a calm, fleeing to a ship for protection, running its throat high up on the sides of the ship. Here the poor whale was pierced by the lances of the whaleship until it yielded unto death. It did not seem to dread the lance that took its life blood so much as it did the biting of the killers.[14]

Roys was so pleased with Maury's attention to his writings, he journeyed to Washington in 1855 and visited the lieutenant's home, binding an acquaintance that was to last until the Civil War.[15] That same year Maury began to encounter difficulties in his navy career. Jealous rivals supposedly had his name placed on the "reserved list," so he was given an involuntary leave of absence. After three years of persistent effort, he finally was restored to his original billet with the rank of commander. While he had suffered humiliation in his own country, Maury had received recognition and acclaim for his accomplishments throughout Europe. But Maury was a Southerner—a Virginian by birth—and when his home state seceded from the Union in 1861, he resigned his commission and accepted one in the Confederate Navy. After the war he first went into exile in the West Indies and Mexico, then moved to England, where he was reduced to writing school geography books. Maury finally returned home in 1868 to accept the chair of astronomy at Virginia Military Institute. He died in 1873.[16]

Roys realized whales were not a limitless resource and from his careful observations deduced that some whale populations were declining alarmingly. He wanted the government to sup-

port his quest for yet undiscovered grounds, writing as early as
1854, in "Descriptions of Whales":

Ten years from this day the greater part of the Kamshatka and
Polar whales will be killed and what then if the opposite of these
whales is not found in high South Latitudes? It will come to this:
the Humpback, Grey and Sulphur [blue] will supply the place of
the destroyed and used up Right whales and give us wealth for
centuries to come. These whales will not generally allow a boat to
come nearer than three or four rods of them, hence the difficulty of
fastening to them which prevents our getting them at the present
time.[17]

Then seventeen years later in his memoirs, Roys lamented
that:

All the southern grounds, which a few years ago produced large
cargoes [of right whales] are now abandoned. There is no longer
whales enough upon them to make it pay to cruise there. Although
more than 20 years since these grounds were abandoned, still they
do not revive, which shows the increase of these whales to be very
slow.

. . . .

The American whaling business has never been fostered in
any manner by the United States government. It has been, when
the ships numbered over 600, a great nursery of American seamen; for each ship, when it sailed, carried from 10 to 20 landsmen,
who, in those long voyages, become good seamen before returning.

Had the government of the United States put forth its helping
hand to demonstrate the taking of the Rorqual and Finback
whales, it would have been accomplished years ago, and there
would now have been a large fleet of whaleships in successful
operation, drawing wealth from the oceans of various parts of the
globe, and greatly increasing the commercial interests of the
United States.

But nothing has ever been done to perpetuate the whaling
business except by private enterprise; and when failures have

been made for the want of a little capital to carry a voyage out, others have been deterred from parting from the regular track, and the business is consequently dying out, and can only be revived by a voyage of different organization from the ordinary one. . . .[18]

The United States government never specifically acted upon Roys's suggestions to send out ships in search of new whale populations, but in 1924, in an unrelated event, the British recommissioned the polar exploratory ship *Discovery* for exactly that purpose. Among its many signal contributions to science, the Discovery Committee aided modern whalers in locating vast new areas containing herds of Antarctic rorquals—the largest of whales—which were there, just as Roys had predicted. These latter-day whale hunters were infinitely more efficient, and have brought several species to the brink of extinction. Today, no further undiscovered stocks of whales exist for mankind to exploit. Broad-scale whaling could well be in its final phase, as the quest for economical and plentiful substitutes for whale-derived products quickens.[19]

6

Chasing the Mighty Rorquals!

By the mid-1850s Roys had set his sights toward the mighty rorquals—blues, finbacks, seis, and the like—which had been completely untouched by whalers before him, for their speed and sheer massiveness was no match for tiny thirty-foot cedar whaleboats and hand-propelled harpoons. A blue whale, for example, often outmeasured even the whaleships, for these enormous animals range upwards of 100 feet in length and 150 tons in weight at maturity, making them larger and more powerful than any dinosaur that ever roamed the earth. Roys itched for an opportunity to take these whales and wrote, about 1871: "The rorqual whales are more numerous and spread over a greater extent of surface than any other species of whales at present day.... [They can be found in virtually every ocean.] Thus it may be seen at a glance that these whales number hundreds of thousands. The average value . . . is two thousand dollars each. . . ." Roys concluded that there were hundreds of millions of dollars to be earned in the exploitation of these species.[1]

The means of their capture became apparent to him earlier in the 1850s. In "Descriptions of Whales," he wrote:

These whales [he refers here to blues as well as to humpbacks and grays]will not generally allow a boat to come nearer than three or four rods of them, hence the difficulty of fastening . . . which prevents our getting them at the present time.

No gun that can be rigged to shoot an iron with accuracy will be available for this reason: an iron must be heavy to make it convey the line any distance without destroying its aim and if heavy cannot be fired from a man's shoulder; if fired from a pivot on the [bow of the] boat, except in very smooth water, the motion of the boat destroys the aim and makes it useless.

But there is a bomb lance fired from the shoulder, enclosing a steel head with a half pound of powder which has been used this season by the ship *Daniel Wood* [of New Bedford, Massachusetts] with success. . . . It explodes in the whale, tearing his joints from their sockets and producing quick death.

These guns will soon be brought to bear upon humpback, grey and sulphur bottom [blue] and large yields of oil will be the result. If whales should be inclined to sink after being killed in this manner, there is abundance of them in shoal water that will rise again in 30 hours and still be available. So long as whale oil is worth 40 cents per gallon, so long will this business be a source of wealth and a nursery for seamen to the nation engaged in it.[2]

Soon after his visit to Matthew Maury at Washington, Roys contracted with Benjamin Brown, a wealthy shipowner of New London, Connecticut, to take command of the 441-ton-ship *Hannibal* on a voyage to Hudson Bay, Canada. Roys received Brown's permission to protect the ship against icy conditions, using his own judgment. Wisely, he journeyed to England, where he studied the heavily reinforced supply ships of the Hudson's Bay Company and consulted with Dr. William Scoresby, the respected Arctic whaler and explorer. Returning to New London, Roys instructed the owners how to prepare *Hannibal* against the pack ice he could expect to encounter in a northern voyage. The owners readily agreed to his suggestions and arranged to notify him as soon as the ship was ready, promising to allow Roys to inspect the work before she actually sailed. Roys went home to New York and waited for weeks, but no word was forthcoming. Finally, unable to stand the suspense any longer, he wrote the owners and learned that the ship awaited his scrutiny.[3]

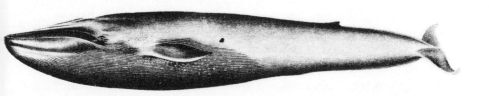

FIG. 11.   A RORQUAL WHALE

This is the blue whale, largest of the rorquals. Blues can attain a length of over 100 feet and weigh as many tons. Old-time whalers, working from small boats, avoided them because of their sheer magnitude and strength. Roys was among the first whalemen to specifically hunt these massive animals, utilizing specially developed catching methods.

(From G. O. Sars, Om "blaahvalen," *[Christiania, Norway, 1874], plate 1), in the private collection of Frederick P. Schmitt).*

Arriving at New London, Roys was enraged at what he saw. *Hannibal* was protected only at her stem by some upright timbers fastened about two feet below the waterline to about two or three feet above it. With this feeble armor she was expected to navigate through treacherous, ice-packed waters! "In vain," Roys railed, "I remonstrated against this folly. I was obliged to go as she was, or give up my cherished expedition and like a good natural fool I consented . . . in hopes a favorable season might enable me to gain Cumberland Inlet and obtain a

[65

cargo [of oil and whalebone]."[4] So on May 21, 1855, Roys sailed in the thirty-three year old ex–packet ship on the first American voyage north to the seas around Spitsbergen.[5] Three weeks out, *Hannibal* touched at Faial, in the Azores, for vegetables and supplies, before heading north in quest of leviathans.[6]

Reaching Resolution Island in Davis Strait, Roys found not the slightest hope of driving *Hannibal* through the ice-filled inlet. The owners had told him that if he lost her in the ice he would be held financially responsible. Rather than wreck the ship, he had been told to sacrifice the voyage. Roys believed that he ". . . was completely hampered by these most extraordinary instructions, which were no doubt given because no insurance was effected on the ship when I sailed."[7] On July 10, Roys had pushed as far at 66° north latitude and 58° west longitude, in the vicinity of the entrance of the Davis Strait. Dropping down to St. John's, Newfoundland, in late August,[8] he purchased fresh provisions, then drove north again, spending three weeks embedded in the ice pack. It was certain: there was no possibility of getting through.[9]

Disgusted, Roys set sail for a bay in Lapland, intending to winter there, in the vicinity of Iceland. Outbound, while a little south of Iceland, he killed a blue whale with a Brown's bomb gun.[10] This animal—the first of its species Roys had seen dead—yielded only thirty to thirty-five barrels of oil, but, he added quickly, "If I had a better weapon, these whales would assist me greatly in filling up the *Hannibal*."[11] In these same waters the ship endured a terrible beating by a heavy gale and her upper works leaked so badly Roys had to put into Lorient, France, in October for repairs. From there he wrote to one of the ship's owners, Benjamin Brown, informing him "how the defrauding me in protecting the ship from ice had prevented my reaching the destination."[12]

While at Lorient, Roys ordered "two rifles in pairs for killing [rorqual] whales," informing the owners of his plans. When they received this proposal, they brought the letter to the ship's underwriters in New York, demanding that the insurance company pay for the loss of a season because of Roys's "insanity." The captain's letter, they said, was proof enough of his instability. Benjamin Brown hopped the next packet for France and upon arriving at Lorient, discharged Roys on the spot. But the intrepid whaler remained in France long enough to see his guns nearly completed, then left for home by steamer, ordering the guns to be dispatched by way of England when finished.[13]

Sometime after he returned home, Roys was in the office of Higgins & Johnson in New York and discovered for the first time that a claim of his insanity had been filed by Benjamin Brown. Outraged, Roys telegraphed Brown, demanding that he meet him at the underwriter's office. Naturally, Brown did not show up, so the claim was abandoned the following day.[14]

The *Hannibal* interlude behind him, Roys was even more determined to take rorquals and substantiate his claims. Soon after he arrived home, in the spring of 1856, he persuaded Capt. Theron B. Worth—a friend since his greenhand days and his former skipper in the *Gem*—and another crony, Thomas Brown, a prosperous Sag Harbor whaleship owner and agent, to purchase the brig *William F. Safford*.[15] A tiny ship, barely 175-tons, she measured but eighty-seven feet from stem to stern. But she was, by whaleship standards, a comparatively new vessel, having been built at Bangor, Maine, in 1848.[16] Obviously Roys had no intention of any record voyage in *Safford:* she was, instead, his personal research ship, which would scour the seas for rorquals and enable him to test his experimental whaling guns.

About 1850, New York became the center for shady, illegal slave trading, and it is said that at least half of the slavers sailing in the decade that followed flourished under the American ensign. The slave traders were clever though, usually operating under some legitimate cover. Often they claimed to be whalers, and eastern Long Island became one of their favorite lairs. In fact, out in Sag Harbor there were strange and unaccountable rumors for years of apparently indigent whaling captains who suddenly became affluent in a single voyage.

"Black ivory," they discovered, was far more profitable than chasing whales. It was possible, for instance, to net perhaps $150,000 to $250,000 in a single six months' slaving voyage.[17]

Against this background, Roys was fitting his strange whaling ship. He equipped her with only two whaleboats, whereas the standard was four or five, and loaded aboard several kinds of bombs and guns to use against rorquals.[18] Unfortunately, the guns Roys had ordered in France were lost in the steamer *Pacific*. Roys turned to C. C. Brand of Norwich, Connecticut, to fabricate replacements.[19] In 1852 Brand had patented a "bomb lance," consisting of a heavy gun which fired an explosive missile. Instead of using an old-time hand lance, whalemen could now keep well out of range of a whale's sweeping flukes, for once the bomb had penetrated deep inside the animal, it would explode, killing the whale safely and efficiently.[20] Brand was unable to forge duplicates of the French guns in time for *Safford*'s sailing, but Roys was able to persuade him to increase his bomb missiles to three pounds, which was the greatest weight that could be fired from a shoulder gun.[21]

William F. Safford sailed May 5, 1856, bound for Spitsbergen, about 400 miles north of Norway.[22] "Gossips and fools," Roys snickered, "imagined that I was going into the slave trade or smuggling."[23] Ignoring this scuttlebutt and tavern chatter down in Sag Harbor, Roys sailed with the notion of either catching bowheads in the Barents Sea or, if none could be harvested, taking a cargo of four species "never yet available to mankind."[24] On the outbound voyage, Roys proceeded directly northeast, reaching Bjørn Island, about 150 miles south-southeast of Spitsbergen. Here he found no bowheads, but saw instead vast pods of blues, finbacks, and humpbacks. He shot about sixty of them. Some sank after dying; others limped off spouting blood—their chimneys on fire, as the whalemen used to say. Still other animals showed no effects whatsoever of having been shot. Only one animal could be saved, yielding just forty to fifty barrels of oil. This whale had floated. A monster blue, it measured ninety-two feet long.[25]

FIG. 12. DEVELOPING AN EARLY HARPOON GUN

This watercolor, by William Ladd Taylor, depicts a nineteenth-century whaling captain examining the lastest effort of a master whalecraft maker. In the mid-1850s Roys at first worked with a gunsmith in Lorient, France, and then with the famous C. C. Brand of Norwich, Conn., inventor of the bomb lance, to develop a shoulder-fired gun capable of killing the mighty rorqual whales.

(Courtesy of Kendall Whaling Museum, Sharon, Mass.)

Next, Roys plotted a course eastward toward Novaya Zemlya in search of bowheads, skirting the edge of the polar ice from latitudes 74° to 76° north until he reached the islands.[26] He cruised throughout the adjacent seas, finding no bowheads, but plenty of blues, finbacks, humpbacks, and bottle-nosed whales. He was able to capture two humpbacks using his gun, but the weapon did not seem to be powerful enough to kill rorquals.[27] *Safford* cruised past Kolguyev Island, about fifty miles off the Russian coast; south past the mouth of the White Sea; and along the coast of Norway. She crossed the Norwegian Sea and came to anchor at Queenstown (Cobh), Ireland, in September. Here, she was searched, the port officials suspecting her of being a smuggler. They tore down the cabin ceilings, but could not find the hidden cargo of silks they supposed was aboard.[28]

Roys's arrival was important news. An article in the Cork *Examiner* (which erroneously refers to whales as fish) recounts his adventures to date.

Among the numerous arrivals to our harbor from all parts of the world, it is seldom that the flag of an American whaleship floats opposite Queenstown. A whale fishing brig called the *W. F. Safford,* 174 tons register, belonging to Sag Harbor, arrived at Queenstown on Friday last from Nova Zembla. On her voyage, which was merely an experimental trip, she captured three whales, from which nearly 8 tuns [sic] of oil have been obtained. A new system has been introduced, by which it would seem that this valuable animal is more surely, safely and speedily destroyed than by the old means; and we understand that the credit of introducing the present mode belongs to the captain of the *W. F. Safford.* Instead of being harpooned as formerly—a course that was both dangerous to life and uncertain in the result—the fish [sic] are now shot, and after the ball enters the flesh it explodes in the body, on much the same principle as a shell. The effect of the explosion is to shatter that portion of the fish where it has entered, and it seldom fails to reach a vital part. Capt. Roys, the master of the whaler, is at present in Birmingham, where he is having some guns of a peculiar construction made, which he expects will be highly effective in the capture of these fish. . . . It is his intention in the summer months to fish in the North Seas and in the winter to visit the coast of Patagonia and he is anxious to ascertain whether this harbour would suit him as an intermediate port at which he might refit and replenish his stores. . . .[29]

In England, Roys set out to reconstruct his lost French-made guns. He even applied for a patent, but was refused; he found that his polygonal rifle bore was the same as one that had been patented by Sir Joseph Whitworth about the same time that Roys was developing his original guns.[30] Sir Joseph was one of England's most brilliant mechanical engineers and was an expert in all types of machinery. In 1857, after three years of experimentation, Sir Joseph produced the polygonal bore—far superior in accuracy, penetration, and range to anything previously invented.[31]

By chance, Roys happened to meet Whitworth, who agreed to manufacture some rifled whaling guns and shells for him. Roys had difficulty obtaining proper fuses, but through Sir Joseph's introduction he was able to procure some from the Royal Arsenal at Woolwich.[32] Roys then returned to his ship, and what happened next is best told in his own words.

We sailed from Queenstown [on November 26, 1856] bound south and when in the Bay of Biscay, I took up one of my guns to try the explosion under water. Standing on the main hatch, I fired the fuse, ignited the powder in the shell and it exploded, blowing up the gun and sending me backward about eight feet. I did not fall. Looking around me, I enquired who was hurt. There was no reply. I then saw lying upon the deck a finger with a ring upon it which I knew, and looking I saw my left hand was gone to the wrist, but for the moment it had given no pain, only a sensation of numbness. Walking into the cabin, I sat down and had it amputated [by Rogers Bishop, the first mate and a trusted friend] as well as we could with razors, and we now steered for Oporto [Portugal].[33]

On the inbound voyage the weather also turned against Roys. Battered by gales, the brig was forced to heave to under bare poles. Because of the heavy seas, there was no possibility of keeping Roys's wounded arm still. The passage took seventeen days, and finally, when *Safford* was within thirty miles of Oporto, the weather became calm. The captain lowered away his boat and ordered his crew to pull for port, but the authorities would not allow him to land at first, because there was no ship in sight. Roys demanded to see the American consul, but he was out of town. When he returned, the boat party was finally permitted to land. Roys's lower arm had to be amputated. The doctors told him that he could not live, but he staunchly refused to pay heed to them. The operation was successful, and after a two-month recuperation, Roys was again in England. In the interval he had sent *Safford* out again under Rogers Bishop, suggesting they meet in Liverpool, England, in April 1857. While awaiting his ship, Roys returned to Manchester, where he lost another gun, then finally developed a safe fuse.[34] He secured a British patent on the device later that year.[35]

By June Roys became anxious, for his ship still had not reached Liverpool. He was convinced that she had been lost at sea.[36] He was ready to depart for home, when his spirits were lifted by Sir Joseph Whitworth and E. R. Langworthy, who with some other leading citizens of Manchester offered to purchase another vessel for him. Naturally Roys accepted. His new ship, *Pacific*, was nearly fitted out and ready for sea, when Rogers Bishop arrived in *William F. Safford*. Two whalers would be more useful than one, so Roys left Bishop in command of the brig, and he sailed in *Pacific*. He outfitted both ships with his new guns and shells, and he was especially anxious to test some fuses which were supposed to be better than any used previously.[37]

The experimenters cleared Liverpool about mid-June. Arriving off Iceland, Roys fired into numerous rorquals, but the projectiles ricocheted off water or whale blubber upon impact. Meanwhile, Bishop, in *Safford,* had headed for Labrador and

Greenland, where he had similar luck.[38] Frustrated, yet determined to continue, Roys later griped that this voyage was ". . . a complete failure. The same shell that would pierce wrought iron and oak [in experiments ashore], would not enter the blubber of a whale. . . ." He returned to Liverpool to labor on still another projectile. Roys had the front end of the shell squared off, which enabled it to be fired directly through the water, penetrating whales without glancing off. Roys apparently was not satisfied with his powder-fired guns either. He devised an entirely new system,[39] using ideas he probably learned during his visits to the Royal Arsenal at Woolwich, for he borrowed heavily on principles developed there earlier in the century by Sir William Congreve. Congreve's rockets, of course, had been used widely by the military and for lifesaving,[40] and there is some indication that they had been utilized experimentally for whaling before.

Roys redesigned his gun to conveniently fire rocket-powered harpoons from a shoulder launcher, similar to the present-day military bazooka. Leaving *Pacific* laid up in the docks at Liverpool, he sailed again in *William F. Safford,* with forty of these novel weapons aboard.[41] This voyage was not without disappointment either. Soon after going to sea, he shot several whales with the brand-new rocket-powered harpoons, but the charge was not sufficient to penetrate the animals properly.[42]

Aside from the rocket-harpoons, Roys encountered other problems too. Going into Bantry Bay, Ireland, with plenty of the rockets and some shells and powder scattered about the decks, the brig aroused suspicions and it was again searched by government officals.[43] Naturally, they found nothing. Then Roys took *Safford* all the way down to South Georgia, on the fringes of the sub-Antarctic, but took no whales, for his weapons proved "full of difficulties and errors." Undaunted as usual, he continued to improve his rocket-harpoon, finally killing two blue whales off Zeeland. Unfortunately, they too sank and were lost. Finally, he took a ninety-five-footer and a thirty-footer, both of which yielded some oil and whalebone.[44]

Yet hard luck continued. When *Safford* put into Lisbon, Portugal, for provisions, new shells, and powder composition, she was ordered to anchor outside the harbor, while Roys and his officers, along with the ship's logbook, were summoned ashore

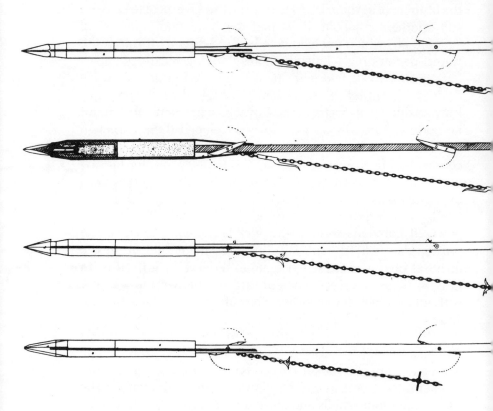

FIG. 13.   Roys's First Patented Rocket-Harpoon

Detail from British patent 2301 / 1857 for "Apparatus applicable to the Capture of Whales, &c.," issued to Thomas Welcome Roys in 1857. The rocket-harpoons illustrated were fired by a launcher tube, and the heads would explode on impact, killing the whale. The movable barbs (various positions indicated by dotted circles) would hold the harpoon in place, while the chain secured the weapon to the whaleline.

(Courtesy of The Patent Office, Orpington, Kent, England.)

and questioned by a council for at least half a day. Supposedly they were suspected of being slavers. A little later, while off the coast of Africa, the tiny brig was battered by a gale, forcing the captain to slip both anchors and cables and to beat a hasty retreat to sea. It was a good ten days before he could return to the spot and recover them.[45]

From Africa Roys set a course westward to the island of Tobago in the West Indies, where he took several humpbacks.[46] On January 10, 1859, he put into Barbados, several hundred miles to the north, where he rendezvoused with his brother Sam in the Sag Harbor whaler *Parana*. Leaking, *William F. Safford* entered Kingston, Jamaica, on April 15 with 150 barrels of oil.[47] Roys had purchased new shells and fuses at Barbados, but three guns were destroyed—incorrect loading being the cause. He finally obtained new weapons at Jamaica and cleared there in the latter days of April, bound for Iceland, where—as chance would have it—two guns exploded on the very first day.[48]

Never yielding to failure, Roys ordered additional guns fabricated while he was in Iceland, but still they were far from perfect. He shot, for instance, one finback which died instantly and sank. The harpoon shells were another problem: one bored clear through a whale, exploding harmlessly on the opposite side; another entered a right whale but did not explode; and in a third attempt, the harpoon barbs did not take hold in the animal's flesh. The difficulty, Roys believed, was insufficient power. Undeterred, however, he sailed south to Cabo de São Vicente, Portugal. There he shot two rorquals, which promptly sank. Another whale ran away with one of the whaleboats trailing behind, held fast by the harpoon line.[49]

After a brief call at Bremerhaven, Germany, *Safford* reached Liverpool in late summer of 1859.[50] In England Roys was shocked to find that liens had been filed against his ship. Reluctantly, he was forced to surrender the brig to the Admiralty Court, only avoiding a term in debtors' prison through the generosity of Sir Joseph Whitworth and another friend, who paid some of Roys's liabilities. Fortunately, *Pacific* was still at his disposal, so he fitted her with 100 harpoons and sailed for the West Indies again. While Roys was away in *Safford*, the owners had been persuaded to fit *Pacific* with zinc plating, most likely as a method of preventing fouling and penetration of her underwater planking by tropical marine organisms. It was a poor idea, for the zinc fouled so terribly that Roys had to give up an entire season on the West Indian whaling grounds. He was especially disappointed, for he had equipped *Pacific* with a newly designed forty-inch false keel, which was supposed to keep the ship steady in the fast Serpent's Mouth Strait between Trinidad and Venezuela, "where the whales were."[51]

Roys continually searched for the proper powder charges for his weapon. A composition he bought in London was no good, so he was obliged to mix a new formula, which proved more potent than any he had used before. Now the recoil from the guns was too great, causing the operators to overshoot their quarry.[52] These experiments were conducted initially, off the islands of Tobago and Trinidad in the West Indies, then across the Atlantic near the Canaries, and eventually off Cadiz, Spain.[53] Roys was determined to perfect his weapon. Coming up off Cabo de São Vicente, he fired at some rorquals. The harpoon "went right through exploding on the opposite [side] of them and they walked off with boats and lines." Roys finally arrived at a sound solution. He had a stout iron bar forged perpendicular to the harpoon shaft, preventing it from entering more than five and one-half feet into the whale's blubber. This, the captain purred, "did the business thoroughly and effectually, and every whale since has been killed instantly dead and fastened to with strength of barb and line such as has never been before." "But," he complained, "they sunk, they all sunk." He was able to retrieve three animals from shallow water, but the remaining whale pods seemed to sense danger —or so Roys believed—for they moved into deeper water, "where it was entirely useless to shoot them." Roys remained at the ground for about a month and a half, but the whales did not come back to shallow water. Again he returned to England.[54]

After clearing Cadiz, Roys and his crew saw a ship in distress. He managed to rescue her crew just in the nick of time, for she had a cargo of iron and must have sunk straight to the bottom. Her men were all exhausted—some from having thrown over iron pigs until the ends of their fingers were skinned and bleeding, while others had been working at the pumps continuously. Roys took them to Mogador (Essaouira), Morocco, landing them in the care of the French consul.[55] Roys eventually worked his way back to Liverpool. To date, Sir Joseph Whitworth and his friends had poured about $25,000 into Roys's experiments, yet they still consented to another voyage in *Pacific,* if he could raise roughly $5,000 to outfit her. This was difficult—if not impossible—for Roys had sunk all of his property and savings, some $25,000, into the experiments. Still, he hoped "to be able to find means to carry out my purpose."[56]

In a touching letter to his friend Matthew Maury, Roys recounted that for "five long, weary years I have pursued this object, sacrificing my property, my limbs, my friendships and my loves, yet the knowledge that my operations must greatly benefit mankind is a solace that my hand is not lost in vain. As for my property, that will all come back again if my patent is secured to me, which must be if I have my rights. . . ." "Through all my misfortunes," he continues, "Joseph Whitworth has stood firm my friend, bearing me on with his capital, when I had no power to go further and it is to him and his friends I have been able to get a weapon complete and perfect." Only one item was left undone: rorquals usually sank after being shot. Roys hoped that the problem could be solved with the development of special boats.[57]

Roys was planning to visit his friend Matthew Maury in Washington in November 1860, while looking after his patent applications in the capital. He wrote Maury that he intended ". . . to give you any information in my power." He regretted, however, that a little notebook he had been keeping "from the time I sailed in the *Hannibal* up to my arrival [at Liverpool in the fall of 1860]," in which he had "noted everything that

[77

might interest you with the greatest care," had been snatched from Roys's unlocked desk when he was ashore. He complained that the incident "vexes me extremely" and blamed its disappearance on a "rascally" third mate.[58]

Roys secured his fourth British patent, for "Rocket Guns," on April 16, 1859. It covered improvements to the rocket launcher, or gun, itself.[59] Roys's rocket-harpoons, as described in his letter to Maury, were fired from the shoulder without any recoil or the slightest inconvenience. The charges weighed sixteen, eighteen, and twenty-one pounds each and exploded in eight seconds. The rocket launcher, or gun, weighed sixteen pounds itself and was balanced conveniently on the shoulder for firing. With this system, Roys could now fasten to whales at a distance of 60 to 100 feet, and with four-inch line and harpoon barbs of proportionate strength could take hold of virtually any size whale. Proudly, he proclaimed that "whales of every description can now be killed and saved throughout all the vast seas." Roys is said to have been among the first to successfully take the blue whale for oil and bone, and he claimed that "there is enough of them to give full employment to all the ships now engaged in whaling for the next 20 years. . . ." It now became possible, Roys bragged with enthusiasm, to take at least four kinds of whales that previously had gone unmolested by man, "because hitherto there has been no power to take them, but now it is all over with the poor whales; the weapon cleaves them like fate, making an internal wound about 10 feet in diameter closing at once every artery of life."[60]

7

Intermezzo

Y<small>ANKEE</small> whaling was a lonely lot, a life which parted hus-
bands and wives, lovers and sweethearts, parents, sons, and
families for years. Many a youngster's only recollections of his
father were of brief periods spent at home between voyages.
True, a few captains opted to pack off with their entire families
a-whaling, but this arduous life agreed with only the strongest
and bravest women. Separations of four or five years were
common, and there is an oft-told story, of an incident that
supposedly took place in a Long Island Sound port, where a
weeping wife was frantically waving her handkerchief in a first
goodbye to her departing husband. "He didn't even kiss me!"
she sobbed, To which a crusty shipowner standing on the
wharf retorted, "What are you crying about? He's only going to
be gone a year or two!"[1]

Roys, of course, was a widower, but he continued to maintain strong ties with his in-laws on Long Island, the Greens, as
well as with his own family in upstate New York. When he
could muster enough time to tear himself away from the whaling profession, he was a sensitive man. We even find him
paying his mother-in-law's rent during difficult times.[2] In
1851, he wrote to his friend Benjamin H. Foster, "I wish you to
pay Mother [Green] 25 dollars a year more for the keeping of
my boy [Philander] and pay her house rent. . . ." Writing from
Sydney, Australia, five months later, he asks Foster to, ". . . see

that my boy has everything he needs and someday or other I will requite you."[3] Eventually, Philander settled in Pultneyville, New York, near the home of his father, and followed him by taking to the sea as a sailor.[4]

FIG. 14. MARIE SALLIORD ROYS

She was Roys's second wife. They met and married in Lorient, France, during one of his voyages, then returned to America and settled on the north fork of Long Island, where she was a music teacher. While her husband was off on one of his many long adventures, Marie Roys supposedly ran off with one of his former shipmates.

(Courtesy of Suffolk County Whaling Museum, Sag Harbor, N.Y.)

During his voyage in *William F. Safford,* Roys chanced to meet an attractive, dark-eyed brunette about twenty years old—half his age. Marie Salliord lived in Lorient, France, and no doubt she became infatuated with this brash, red-bearded Yankee, who told both fascinating and hair-raising tales of his many years at sea. They were married about 1860 and settled on Long Island on "Blubber Row" in the tiny east-end hamlet of Peconic, then—as the colorful nickname implies—a community largely inhabited by whalers and their families. Roys had many friends here, including his old shipmate and backer in the ill-fated *William F. Safford* expedition, Capt. Theron B. Worth, and Roys's former father-in-law, Capt. Henry Green, who was regarded as the commodore of Blubber Row until his death. After settling in Peconic, Marie Roys became a piano teacher to fill her time while her husband was off on further adventures.[5]

Roys had returned to a country divided between sympathies pro-North and pro-South. On December 20, 1860, South Carolina seceded from the Union, sparking the outbreak of the Civil War. Meanwhile, Roys's friend Matthew Maury became caught in an agonizing dilemma: whether to continue in oceanography in the service of the U.S. Navy or to join the cause of his fellow Southerners. As we have noted, he did join the Confederate States Navy in 1861, after his home state of Virginia broke with the Union. Roys, however, was characteristically apolitical throughout his life, and nothing—save whaling—really rallied his interest and support. To be sure, the Civil War would pose little hindrance or inconvenience to his coming plans and activities. While Confederate States Navy raiders were decimating the Yankee whaling fleets worldwide, Roys continued to work unimpeded.

Meanwhile, on January 22, 1861, Roys's first United States patent, "Improvement in Harpoon-Guns," was granted. The specification describing the invention reveals that "The chief use to which I propose to put this gun is to shoot bomb-harpoons for the purpose of killing whales. . . ." Roys then differentiates between small arms and larger ordnance, noting that the former can be shot with more control and accuracy at sea, enabling the gunner "to keep his sight bearing on the object to be struck, notwithstanding the motion of the vessel." Bigger guns, he maintains, are more difficult to aim, but are necessary to hurl larger missiles. "The firing of large rockets or shells . . . at sea," he points out, "has hitherto been attended with a great deal of uncertainty in point of effect."[6]

More specifically, he says that "To unite in a single gun the means of complete control and the capacity for throwing large rockets weighing as high as eighteen or twenty pounds with accuracy, notwithstanding the motion of the vessel, and without injury to the gunner or any one standing near him, is the chief object of my invention." He continues, "To this end I make my gun without stock or carriage, making the barrel of such shape and proportion as to balance on the shoulder of the gunner, and so arrange and combine a lock therewith as to be within his convenient reach while so balanced on his shoulder, from whence it is to be fired. By this means the gunner is enabled to shoot a much larger and heavier gun with perfect accuracy than he could if the gun were made with a stock to shoot from against his shoulder and supported by his arms, as is now the practice."[7]

The barrel of the gun, or launcher, consisted of a cylinder of sheet copper or other metal. Secured around the barrel, forward and to the rear of the gunner, were two split circular flanges. The upper halves were hinged and connected to several valves leading to the firing chamber. The top portions of the flanges were folded down before the operator took aim, and after firing they popped up by pressure escaping through the valves, protecting the man's face from backfire and gases. The bomb-harpoon was unique in that it had two movable barbs, which prevented it from boring clear through a whale or from "drawing," or pulling out.[8]

During his experimental voyages in *William F. Safford* and *Pacific*, Roys engaged in a correspondence with Thomas Nye, a New Bedford, Massachusetts, whaleship owner. While initially there was no evidence of his intention, it became obvious that Roys planned to solicit Nye's moral and financial support for a major expedition in quest of rorquals, using rocket-harpoons. He continually kept Nye abreast of his activities in the two ships, and his reports were often couched in overly optimistic and even exaggerated claims of success. He spoke of the possibility of establishing a rorqual whaling enterprise on a large scale. In time, Roys's true intentions surfaced, for he wrote that just one more cruise was needed to complete his research, which would then, ". . . place the whole whaling

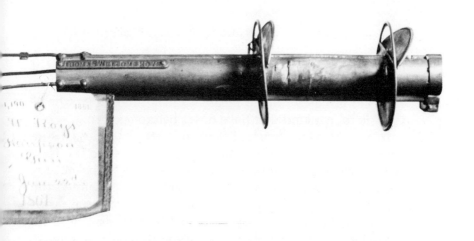

FIG. 15.   PATENT MODEL OF ROYS'S ROCKET-HARPOON GUN

Formerly, the U.S. Patent Office required that working scale models accompany all patent applications. This is the model for Roys's patent no. 31,190, "Improvement in Harpoon-Guns," issued on January 22, 1861. The long metal tube, similar to the modern-day bazooka in its operation, fired rocket-powered harpoons at whales.

(Courtesy of Suffolk County Whaling Museum, Sag Harbor, N.Y.)

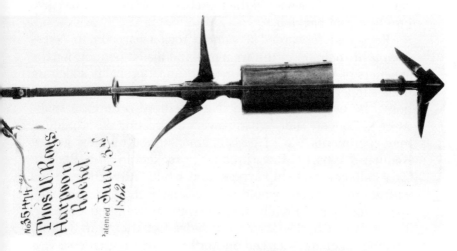

FIG. 16.   PATENT MODEL OF ROYS'S ROCKET-HARPOON

This is a working scale model of the rocket-powered harpoon which was fired from the gun illustrated above. Upon impact, it would explode, killing the whale; and the barbs at the head plus the second set of wings at the middle of the shaft would set, holding the carcass fast. Roys received U.S. patent no. 35,474, "Improved Rocket-Harpoon," on June 3, 1862.

(Courtesy of Smithsonian Institution, Washington, D.C.)

business upon a broad and sure basis and destroy all chances of
. . . [it] becoming improfitable, which will soon occur unless
some one brings forth the means to make the other whales
available to mankind that have never before been so. . . ."⁹

In one of his letters, dated December 18, 1859, Roys, being
in need of money, begged Nye to bring his case to the New
Bedford whaling community, so that he could "carry out my
experiments until the thing is complete." Roys painted the
future for rorqual whaling in overly rosy colors, for certainly his
meagre catches could not justify such enthusiasm. Yet, he
continued: "I have clearly proved three things—fastening to
them at 100 feet [away is now possible], killing them with the
explosion, and fastening hawsers to them when [the whales
sink] on the bottom to heave them up." At this juncture,
however, he finally acknowledges a remaining major problem:
"Again now, if I can make buoys to float them, the long day's
task is done, and every whale that swims the ocean is available
to mankind, and there is not the slightest need of sending any
vessel out of the Atlantic for a cargo of oil."¹⁰ As he was about to
leave England for home, Roys predicted he would have a full
cargo in sixty days should the merchants of New Bedford give
him financial backing.¹¹

Roys had forwarded a sample rocket-harpoon to Nye—
asking his opinion of the weapon—and also a petition for the
"Owners of Whaleships in America," most probably soliciting
their support of his catching methods.¹² When Roys arrived
home, he headed directly for New Bedford, where he spoke
twice at Concert Hall, "giving a very interesting description of
his experiments. . . ." He also demonstrated his new gun at
Rodman's Wharf.¹³ Roys fired three rockets in New Bedford
for whalemen and shipowners, and while "All were satisfied
with them, . . . none would buy because I charged 25 dollars
apiece for them." Finally, it seemed there would be a backer.
The firm of Charles W. Morgan—dean of the New Bedford
whaling magnates—agreed on April 5, 1861, to finance a voyage using Roys's rocket-harpoons. But through a twist of fate,
Roys's hopes were again dashed, for when he returned two

days later, on a Monday morning, for an "appointment to draw writings, he was dead."[14]

From New Bedford, Roys journeyed to New York City, where he experimented further with the rocket gun and found he could fire a longer harpoon line.[15] There he began to produce the gun commercially, first from the city, then from across the East River in Greenpoint, Brooklyn, during midsummer 1861. To promote business, he placed this advertisement in about a dozen issues of the New Bedford *Whalemen's Shipping List:*

Rocket Harpoons and Guns.

These weapons will fasten to and kill whales of all kinds at a distance of one hundred feet or less, and there is no recoil or inconvenience to those firing them. I can furnish three guns and harpoon bombs sufficient to kill thirty whales and fasten to them at the same time for three hundred and sixty dollars, and will give a lawful warranty if these weapons fail to give satisfaction to return the money at the termination of a voyage. Gun patented January 22d, 1861.

Whale Raiser

This instrument will attach any number of lines to whales that are dead on the bottom, and can be furnished for forty dollars; it can be done in any thing less than one hundred fathoms of water. If it fails to give satisfaction if tried, the money will be refunded at termination of the voyage. Patent ordered to issue at my convenience; any person wishing to see the weapons fired, can do so and fire themselves by giving me a weeks notice. No orders for these weapons can be accepted unless thirty days time is given to supply them.

Address

Thomas W. Roys

263 East Ninth Street, New York[16]

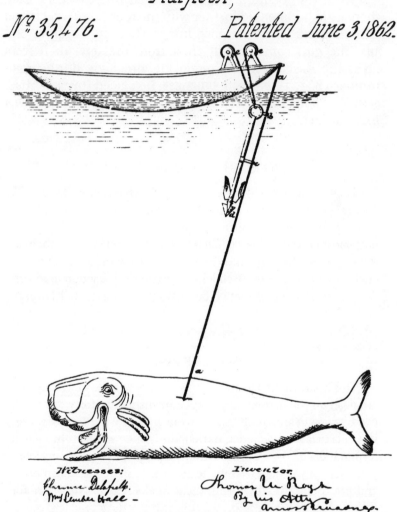

T. W. Roys,

Harpoon,

N.º 35,476.   *Patented June 3, 1862.*

Witnesses: *Inventor:*

FIG. 17. ROYS'S WHALE-RAISER

Another of Roys's early inventions, this device was conceived as a means of raising sunken whales, especially rorquals, from the ocean floor. The barbed, 10-foot-long "whale-raiser" was sent down the harpoon line, its 200-pound weight driving it into the dead animal. The hawser secured to it then was drawn in by the ship's windlass, bringing the whale to the surface. This drawing is from the specification for Roys's patent 35,476 of June 3, 1862.

(Courtesy of U.S. Patent Office, Washington, D.C.)

Intermezzo

Whether Roys sold any of these inventions during this period is unknown, but perhaps he did, for whaling masters should have been impressed by his bold claims and strong guarantees. It must have seemed to Roys that success at last was at hand and that soon the work of years might be rewarded. Now his gun only had to be proven in actual use, then it might take hold as standard to the industry. Finally, his dreams of a great rorqual fishery and the revival of the whaling industry itself—which at that time appeared to be dying of the effects of the Civil War and the discovery of petroleum in 1859—seemed about to be realized!

8

Enter
Mr. G. A. Lilliendahl

Iт was principally through his enlightening friendship with Lt. Matthew Fontaine Maury that Roys began to embark upon, not one, but two new facets of his already brilliant career. He emerged not only as a self-taught and acutely aware naturalist of the sea but as an equally bold and innovative inventor. In these dual roles he became a strange paradox. While his fellow whalemen were concerned with little more than the economics, or even the thrill, of the chase and kill, Roys sought a more complex, intellectual understanding of the relationship of man and nature. He would observe and tend his flock, so to speak, and would harvest only selected creatures, the untapped stocks of rorquals, for their then vitally essential products, while permitting others—particularly the overworked traditional catches such as right, sperm, and bowhead whales—to thrive and multiply and thus to always maintain the stocks. Roys, moreover, had been influenced by his mentor, Maury, to attain a closer biological awareness of cetacea than he had ever had before, and he began cataloging various species; observing and registering their anatomical features, habits, migratory patterns, and ecology; and applying all this information toward furthering his own professional development and improving the industry to which he was to devote his entire adult life.

As an inventor he also transcended the stereotyped *Moby-Dick* character of the old-time whaler, for even Herman Melville would have been forced to admit that of all professions, whaling was one of the most rigidly bound by custom and antiquated methods, some even traceable back to prehistoric times—with the most stubborn inclination to avoid change and not to attempt anything novel. Yet an inventive and probing spirit always lived within Roys. Had he been cast in an academic or industrial role, rather than as a forever-roaming and rootless mariner, his agile and fertile mind would have worked just as intensely and would unquestionably have produced some scholarly gift or wonderful machine. Instead, Roys was destined to direct his inventive powers toward the sea, to whaling.

Roys's first attempt at bettering his craft was an effort toward an improved whaling gun. The common, hand-held irons thrown by Queequeg (the Polynesian harpooner of *Moby-Dick*), and his kind were simple, cheap, and—if the eye was steady and sure—deadly. But if the harpoon failed to partially or entirely penetrate the immense blubbery mark, the wounded leviathan would either continue on his way or perhaps be driven to such a rage as to smash the fragile whaleboat and its puny crew to smithereens. Yes, everything depended upon the skill and pluck of the boatsteerer on whaling vessels—the agility of his muscle, the position and alertness of the prey, and the vagaries of wind and weather. But a gun was more certain. While not a new invention in Roys's era, it had never been fully perfected. To the first of the "modern" whalers, like Roys, it represented a far more efficient—and in many ways more humane—approach to the age old hunt. Its longer range considerably reduced exposure of the whaleboat and crew to the animal, thereby insuring additional safety. The gun, firing a shell or bomb harpoon into the whale's vitals, was instantaneous in effect, eliminating the long, tortuous effect of the wound made by the honed steel lance. True, some more progressive whalers already were using the so-called bomb lance—which had been invented in 1852 and consisted of nothing more than a shoulder gun that fired explosive missiles to kill whales within close range—but the combination harpoon-bomb gun Roys envisioned was potentially far more efficient than anything Queequeg would dare have dreamed.

As we have seen in chapter 6, Roys actively investigated the possibilities of a whaling gun from at least the mid-1850s, while he was master of the brig *William F. Safford,* and he eventually developed and tried his own modifications of the basic concept. Remember, in this first work he used traditional guns with rifled shells, but later switched to the more novel rocket mode of propulsion. Unfortunately, what is missing in Roys's memoirs is word of his actual "discovery" of the rocket principle. We do know that he had applied for his first patent for a harpoon using the rocket-propelled method by September 1857[1], although he continued to use the traditional rifled-type guns for at least one additional voyage in *William F. Safford.* After that, he was committed to perfecting the rocket.

Just how and when the idea may have occurred to him we can only surmise. No doubt during Roys's visits to Capt. (later Maj. Gen.) Edward M. Boxer at Woolwich, England, during the late 1850s, the subject of rockets was discussed. Boxer, who had been appointed superintendent of the Royal Arsenal there during the Crimean War (1854-55), had assumed responsibility for the manufacture of Congreve war rockets as well as of conventional arms. In addition, he instituted improvements in both combat and lifesaving rockets, the latter having been officially introduced into British shore rescue stations the same year that Roys applied for his rocket patent, 1857. Then, Roys may possibly have been exposed to the concept of rockets during his recuperation at Oporto, Portugal, after the loss of his hand in *William F. Safford.* Not so many years before, during 1832-33, that city had been bombarded with British-made Congreve rockets while it was under siege during the Portuguese civil war.[2]

Enter Mr. G. A. Lilliendahl

The Congreve rocket itself, developed during the dark days of the Napoleonic wars by the Englishman William (later Sir William) Congreve, was a very simple affair by today's standards, but at that time it was considered a powerful auxiliary to artillery and could itself inflict devastating damage when fitted with explosive shells, incendiaries, or shrapnel. Its morality, particularly when fired against raw troops or cavalry horses, was questionable. The rocket per se was an iron tube, fitted at one end with the warhead and having the exhaust gas holes at the other end. A wooden guide stick was screwed into a flange in the center of the base plate and was surrounded by the four or five exhaust holes. Gunpowder served as the propellant, just as it had in the very first, more crude Chinese and Indian war rockets.[3]

Roys was not the first to conceive of the rocket as the propulsive means for a whaling harpoon. Congreve himself had also fashioned some small rocket-harpoons, and they had been very successfully tested in the Arctic during the 1821 whaling season.[4] We can trace the germ of this concept even further back. In 1638 the Dutch pyrotechnist Abraham Speeck of Amsterdam built a rocket for a well-known Dutch whaling master; he fired some of these rockets off Spitsbergen, but they proved too heavy.[5] In Congreve's day, the rocket had simply failed to catch the imagination of the conservative whalers, and consequently his rockets proved to be a commercial fiasco. One contemporary traveler reported seeing thousands of unopened boxes of the rockets in the warehouse of Congreve's private factory. It is likely, however, that Roys was totally unaware of Speeck's, and possibly even of Congreve's, efforts. He proceeded to develop his own rockets vigorously, as an entirely new and potentially revolutionary tool for the whaleman.

Always the innovator, Roys was most impressed by the advantage of the rocket's lack of recoil, a feature which facilitated its use from the bobbing bow of a small whaleboat. It also possessed extensive range in relation to its light weight and was less costly than the gun type of propulsion, yet it could be fired with just minimal instruction. Once perfected, the rocket could expel gas from its warhead, which, in the manner of gun-fired bomb harpoons, would likewise contribute toward keeping most species of whale afloat (although, of course, some species had a tendency to sink after being killed). Lastly, he hoped the rocket would prove far safer than the traditional gun, which had deprived Roys of his hand.

Roys's invention—which he continued to refine and to protect with British, American, and French patents that followed—fundamentally consisted of a narrow explosive-shell-rocket having a conical, or other suitably shaped, metal head with an ordinary harpoon flue, or barb, at the tip of it, to insure its hold once it had penetrated the whale. From the rear, projected a standard guide stick, though Roys's was made of metal rather than wood and was designed to be bent onto a detachable whale line or chain. The rocket was fired, bazooka fashion, through a pistol-operated open tube. The igniter was a length of quick-match. The "aiming tube," or launcher, provided with a pistol lock, was thus placed upon the shoulder of the harpooner, aimed, and fired. Later models were improved by adding a hinged protective flap, or curtain, that shielded the operator's eyes from the gaseous discharge. Roys's overall concept was sound, but his rocket needed both further technical development and field trial. It also required manufacturing facilities and—for those tight-fisted days—plenty of financial backing.[6]

In Gustavus Adolphus Lilliendahl, a wealthy New York City pyrotechnic manufacturer, Roys apparently found the perfect collaborator. After joining forces, they formed a partnership that was to last almost three-quarters of a decade. How they actually met is not too difficult to surmise. The date must have been about 1861, and the introduction might have come through a curious sideline of Lilliendahl's, a whalebone-cutting house, that he owned, or Roys might have approached him directly to manufacture rockets. In any event, we know that Roys was actively seeking backers during this period, for a printed form letter survives in which he describes his methods and inventions, boasting that:

I estimate that One Million, Two Hundred Thousand Dollars, is annually lost in the whaling fleet, through the sinking of Whales that are captured by harpoon and line; and to prevent sinking saves all of that, besides leaving nothing in the way to prevent the taking of every kind of Whales that inhabit the sea. I have the means to prevent the loss of any Whales, by sinking on shoal water of one hundred fathoms or less. Since the weapon and gun is perfected... Whales of every description are killed as easily and as quickly as the smallest bird could be by the hunter, without the slightest inconvenience, and the impossibility of the recoiling of the gun. . . .

I wish all persons who may receive this, to keep it and compare my prediction with the proofs of coming years, and the very day you have the proof that Whales can be prevented from sinking, will also prove the Whaling business is in its infancy, although existing 250 years.[7]

Strong statements; and perhaps just the spark that may have brought Roys and Lilliendahl together.

Lilliendahl was born in 1829 in New York City. He attended King's College (now Columbia University), but as a youth of nineteen he decided to try his hand at the gold placers of California. He embarked for his El Dorado on Christmas Day 1848, filled with hope, but after arriving on the West Coast, he experienced spotty luck at mining. Ironically, it was the mercantile skills learned from his father, Christian Lilliendahl, the well-to-do owner of a fancy goods and toy store on the fringes of the Wall Street area in New York, that enabled him to return home with a substantial profit from the sale of supplies to forty-niners and investments in prime San Francisco land. After joining his brother in a grand tour of Egypt, the Holy Land, parts of Africa, and the Continent, he settled down and married Lucinda Detwiller of Easton, Pennsylvania, in 1854.[8]

The elder Lilliendahl's store sold fireworks on a seasonal

basis, and as a young man, Gustavus had become interested in their manufacture. In time he converted his father's business into the Excelsior Fireworks Company, with offices on Dey Street in lower Manhattan, and built it into one of the largest and most reputable pyrotechnic firms in the area. In fact, a successor firm, Unexcelled, Inc., while no longer manufacturing fireworks, is in business to this day. Lilliendahl had the distinction of being invited to set up the fireworks spectacular in celebration of the successful completion of his friend Cyrus Field's Atlantic telegraph cable, but the festivities were marred by a stray spark, which ignited and partially destroyed New York City Hall. In 1859, the following year—his business apparently burgeoning despite that unfortunate accident—Lilliendahl removed his manufacturing facilities to Jersey City, New Jersey.[9]

At the outbreak of the Civil War, Lilliendahl espoused the cause of the Union and succeeded, practically out of his own pocket, in raising a full company of over a hundred men— Company D, second New Jersey Militia. He himself was elected its captain. After serving only four months, he was called by the Secretary of War to a classified position with the Secret Service in Washington, D.C. Apparently his knowledge of explosives was considered too important to be neglected, for he was soon back at the Excelsior plant, manufacturing Coston and other signal rockets for the Union forces.[10]

Thus, by the time Roys approached him, Lilliendahl had earned a well-deserved reputation in business and pyrotechnics, beside having substantial capital and rocket-manufacturing facilities at his command. He also was willing to experiment and even to gamble a large portion of his considerable fortune on the new venture proposed by Roys. Moreover, Lilliendahl was by no means ignorant of whales and whaling himself, for his father had been interested in the uses of whalebone commercially, and Gustavus had established his own whalebone-cutting factory in Jersey City.[11]

Roys's own credentials in the field of rocketry and technology were becoming more impressive during this period too. He was awarded a British patent for his improved rocket guns and harpoons in February 1861,[12] and on June 3, 1862, he received three American patents for an "Improved Rocket-Harpoon," an "Improvement in [Ship's] Propellers," and an "Improved Apparatus for Raising Sunken Whales to the Surface of the Water."[13] That same year he had commenced working with Lilliendahl, and they received a joint patent for an improved war rocket on July 22.[14] Lilliendahl, of course, was most intrigued with the rocket-harpoon. They worked well together, agreeing "to make a voyage to control the sinking [of whales,] which was now the only obstacle to get large cargoes of oil." A partnership was formed, and by early June, Roys had sold one-fourth of his patent rights for $500 to Lilliendahl.[15]

Meanwhile, in mid-May, Lilliendahl had purchased the 158-ton bark *Reindeer,* registered her out of New York, fitted her out for whaling, and appointed Roys her master.[16] In effect, Lilliendahl was financing an experimental voyage. To equip *Reindeer,* Roys had had built, in New Bedford, "two large boats, 36 feet long, 7 feet beam, and about 4 feet deep for the purpose of holding whales when sinking."[17] But there were difficulties, one of them totally unforeseen and almost disastrous. Roys recalled in his memoirs:

> When the *Reindeer* was ready for sea, the United States Marshall, Murray, jumped on board and seized the vessel on suspicion of being a slaver, turned everyone ashore and locked up the ship. It seems letters had been sent from New Bedford that these boats were not [ordinary] whale boats. Thus the very means I used to make the whales float were the cause of the seizure. I took my patents and my contract with Mr. Lilliendahl, which clearly showed how I was engaged, to the marshall and he turned his back on me; would not even look at my papers.

Some legal and political machinations ensued, with Lilliendahl eventually having to sign a bond for the release of the ship, which—it later was found—had indeed once served in the odious capacity of a slaver. Nonetheless, she was now a whaler, but reached Iceland too late to serve in her new role that year. It

FIG. 18.   GUSTAVUS ADOLPHUS LILLIENDAHL (1829–1907)

A New York City based pyrotechnist, Lilliendahl teamed up with Roys to produce a working whaling rocket. They became partners in the venture and spent several years in Iceland attempting to perfect their method, which never really succeeded. Sketch by Peter Copeland, based on a photograph.

(Courtesy of Smithsonian Institution, Washington, D.C.)

was the end of the season, and Roys was compelled to return home and wait for the next opportunity.[18]

Yet, despite this temporary setback, there began an interesting relationship between a rough-hewn seaman, self-educated and outspoken, and a respected New York gentleman. Even the Norwegians—those developers of the art of mechanized whaling—are ready to admit that Roys and Lilliendahl were to become the link between the old-style methods of whaling and the new, highly efficient mode.

9

Beginning

The Inventive Years

In 1863 Thomas Roys began a new chapter in his varied career—and far more significantly, in the history of the whaling industry. That year Roys and his partner Lilliendahl commenced their full-scale whaling operations off Iceland, which reached a pinnacle in 1865 with the establishment of the first modern-type shore whaling station. From here they ranged out after rorquals in small steamers, killing leviathans with their rocket-style harpoons. The use of mechanized methods to process the enormous carcasses was in itself a radical change, and proved infinitely more efficient than the old-type whalers' shipboard cutting in—an extremely dangerous operation—or their boiling out oil in the huge try-pots on deck. Naturally, such innovations attracted widespread attention, and soon Roys and Lilliendahl were being imitated by Danish and Dutch rivals. Even the so-called Father of Modern Whaling, Svend Foyn, a Norwegian, made a brief appearance in Icelandic waters to observe the Americans' strange goings-on, thus reinforcing his own ideas; then he went his own way, which led him to brilliant success. Foyn rejected the rocket-harpoon, and by the late 1860s he had developed a large, rifled harpoon gun, thereby perfecting the means by which hapless whales are killed to this very day. In the interim, the enterprises of Roys and Lilliendahl and their imitators waned one by one and had finally petered out by the early 1870s.

Every summer from 1863 to 1872 the awed Icelanders—who were themselves completely unacquainted with whaling—peered down from their high coastal mountains to watch the several steam whalers which cruised along their coast whenever the variable weather permitted. At times they were even lucky enough to see the catcher boats drop from their davits or if towed from astern, being rowed off in pursuit of high-blowing whales. Sailors were usually stationed in the bows, popping rockets at fleeing animals, or crews were to be seen tugging at whales which had slipped beneath the surface. The waste of human effort, material, and lost whales must have been immense during these early years, though probably not much worse than in the first seasons of modern pelagic whaling in the Antarctic. Fortunately for the frugal Icelanders, some of the dead whales drifted ashore, and they could claim a portion of them by virtue of some very old laws and could purchase blubber and meat at reasonable prices.

Unquestionably, these times were the zenith of Roys's life. It was during this decade that he reached his full potential and that success seemed within his grasp. Not quite though, for again he failed, and he was eventually forced to withdraw from Iceland in 1866. Thereafter, his career became a series of sad reverses, ending in his inevitable ruin. Although Roys's rocket-harpoon concept continued to be tried and retried after this period, eventually it had to be abandoned, for it could not compete economically with Foyn's cannon.

In one special respect, however Roys's experiments at Iceland were to have a significant impact on the future of the whaling industry, because the Americans employed many foreigners and shared their vast whaling experience with them. Most of these Europeans had no knowledge of the trade, but several were fine seamen and observed these Yankees with critical eyes. Eventually a few even established their own competing enterprises, aimed at catching the rorquals, which they had previously neglected, using Roys's and Lilliendahl's radical new methods. The imitators included two Danes, Captain-Lieutenant Otto C. Hammer (a former naval officer) and a Captain Tvede, as well as a Dutchman, C. J. Bottemanne. As we shall see, the Norwegian, Svend Foyn, also borrowed some of their ideas.

If they could speak to us today, perhaps these imitators could give us some hint of why Roys and Lilliendahl failed. These Europeans were self-made mariners, and their back-grounds—coupled in some cases, with formal maritime edu-cations—had imbued them with habits of exactness and precision. The Danes were especially critical of the Americans, who were always excusing away their own failures in a casual way; Foyn, on the other hand, hardly bothered to comment, for he preferred to work independently. Captain Bottemanne re-mained silent altogether, because he adhered to the American method exactly and did not want to upset his Dutch partners by pointing to their failures. Although they never received much credit from historians, Roys and Lilliendahl did play an important role in carrying the whaling trade into the industrial age. Even more significantly, Roys proved that the once undis-turbed mighty rorquals—finbacks, blues, and seis—could be harvested, providing a vast, untapped supply of whale oil and eventually of meat and by-products.

The vast American venture began modestly enough in 1863, when Roys refitted *Reindeer* with a crew of twenty-three professionals and cut a course northward. As luck would have it, once on the coast of Iceland the ship's rudder was torn from its pintles. With considerable effort, Roys managed to work her into the Reydarfjördur on the eastern shore, arriving on July 20. There he determined that the rudder pintles were gone, and after considerable searching, was able to come up with replacements. His luck was good this time, however, for even while lying in port with the rudder on deck, a crew from *Reindeer* killed an enormous blue whale. At first they thought it was lost, for it had sunk in seventy fathoms of water, but

PATENT ROCKET HARPOONS AND GUNS.

FASTEN TO AND KILL INSTANTLY WHALES OF EVERY SPECIES.
WITH PROPER LINES AND BOATS,
SUCH AS WERE USED BY THE OFFICERS OF BARK REINDEER IN 1864,
ALL WHALES ARE SAVED.
N. B.—Two Months' notice required to fill an Order for the Season of 1865.
——FOR SALE BY——
G. A. LILLIENDAHL,- - - - - - - - - - NEW YORK

FIG. 19.   ADVERTISEMENT FOR THE WHALING ROCKET

This advertisement, over the names of Thomas W. Roys or G. A. Lilliendahl, appeared many times throughout the mid-1860s in the New Bedford, Mass., *Whalemen's Shipping List and Merchant's Transcript,* the trade paper of the American whaling industry. The woodcut, although somewhat inaccurate, gives a good idea of the whaling-rocket principle.

(Courtesy of Smithsonian Institution, Washington, D.C.)

somehow, through brawn or ingenuity, the leviathan was saved. Back at the ship it turned out a spectacular yield of oil. This catch was truly a milestone, for this animal was the first that Roys had been able to pluck from the depths and to salvage out of the hundreds killed and wasted in seven years of experiments.[1]

This massive creature must also have been one of the first of its size—if not *the* original—ever taken anywhere by whalers. An enormous animal, it measured almost ninety-five feet in length, with a girth of thirty-nine feet, and it yielded approximately 800 pounds of baleen in lengths up to four feet from its twenty-one foot jawbones. The oil rendered was about 110 barrels. The entire animal was estimated to have weighed

[*101*]

between 137 and 147 tons. Roys, in his memoirs, reckons its size thus:

Blubber	20 tons
Kinka (edible underside "bacon")	12 tons
Bones	20 tons
Flesh	75 tons
Blood and innards	10 tons
Total	137 tons[2]

Coincidentally, Lilliendahl later donated a massive twenty-foot set of jawbones to Lafayette College in Easton, Pennsylvania, where they still repose in that school's vertebrate collection.[3] We wonder if they were not cut from this very same animal.

Having repaired the rudder, Roys put to sea, killing many more whales, but saving none of them because his harpoons could not hold them. While it is not too clear whether Lilliendahl had accompanied Roys during this 1863 voyage, we do know that he had retooled his Greenville, New Jersey, factory about this same time to produce rocket-harpoons. It is also thought that Roys assembled and serviced some defective units at Dundee, Scotland, as a matter of convenience.[4]

In August 1863 an Icelandic newspaper published a letter from a local farmer who had joined Roys's crew for the summer. First, he stressed that the captain was no stranger to the coasts, having sailed off Iceland from 1855 to 1858. Likewise, he pointed out, Roys's brother Sam cruised there in the Sag Harbor whaler *Parana* about that same time. The article continues—although somewhat inaccurately and obscurely— that: "Captain Roys owns the vessel. He is now in company with another man whose name is Liljendahl [*sic*] and lives in New York, very rich and runs many vessels. If Roys will be successful in his enterprise this year, he intends to send up here 5–6 other ships next year, all for whale-fishing."[5]

It is obvious that despite the setback of the 1863 season, hopes were running high. Writing of the venture almost a century later, Norway's distinguished chronicler of modern whaling history, Dr. Arne Odd Johnsen—although freely admitting that Roys and Lilliendahl ultimately failed—emphasized that "this American entry into modern whaling was so intelligent and on so large a scale and it showed such important results that one can ascertain that Roys and Lilliendahl were establishing a new industry of substantial size."[6] After 1863, the curious Icelanders were to see a great deal more of the American strangers over the next few years. While Roys, with his red beard and hair, his alert blue eyes, and his missing hand, engendered the appearance perhaps of some crusty, Yankee Civil-War naval hero, Lilliendahl looked for all the world like the indigenous people of Iceland. He was, so to speak, a Viking son returned to his homeland. Almost six feet tall, his Scandinavian blond hair and beard, fair complexion, and blue eyes bespoke his unmistakable ancestry, and his Nordic surname only seemed to confirm that fact.[7]

The following season of 1864 proved far more encouraging, for out of twenty whales killed, eleven were saved—in open sea, no less—and one was even retrieved in the waters of a shallow fjord.[8] Roys had financed and refitted *Reindeer* this season by selling another quarter of his patent rights to Lilliendahl,[9] and the ship sailed with stronger harpoons and better lines than ever before. This time, however, Roys was plagued by the uncertainties of the Icelandic weather. Recounting the season's results in his memoirs, he mentions taking some 500 barrels of oil and 5,000 pounds of baleen. "Some of these whales," he wrote, "were held from sinking by the large boats, but when there was [a] 4 foot sea on, it was no use as the boat being only two feet above water, [it] must go under or the line must part as the great surface of the whale cannot be moved suddenly."[10] Furthermore, writing from Iceland on June 25—the season halfway over—he reported that although a respectable 350 barrels of rorqual oil were stored aboard already and another 390 barrels or so were boiling out, working *Reindeer* was difficult, because of "eddying winds and calms under the highlands of the coast." Still, he was confident of success.[11]

Meanwhile, the officials and citizens of East Iceland, off

which Roys was operating, looked upon his enterprise and ambitious plans with interest. Rorquals previously had not been hunted there, partly because they are considerably faster swimmers than the usual prey, the slow-moving, docile Greenland whale, and partially because some said they were very vicious. In fact, many Icelanders feared them. While the populace habitually complained of intrusions of British and French codfishermen into Icelandic waters, they welcomed the Americans, for they believed that whaling would aid the traditional fisheries. The local fishermen disliked the rorquals because they frequently pursued great schools of herring and sardines into the fjords, consuming the fish in tremendous quantities. On a single day during the spring of 1864, for example, some thirty rorquals had been seen gorging themselves in the Seydisfjördur. Fishermen nearby would usually wait in safety until the whales moved on; only through sheer necessity would they dare to venture out among them. Then too, the Icelanders were pleased when dead whales floated ashore and they could share in them, adding to their previously meagre incomes.[12]

The Americans' presence had other substantial economic advantages also. During the summer of 1864, for instance, Roys had employed three Icelanders in *Reindeer,* paying them a fixed monthly wage of forty rix-dollars each, plus a bonus of ten rix-dollars for each whale they saved. On a much broader scale—should the government grant a permit to him—Roys planned to establish a shore whaling station at the former trading post of Örum and Wulff in Vestdalseyri on the Seydisfjördur. If he could buy the station, he intended to bring a large sailing ship there on which to store coal and whale oil, as well as two smaller steamers, which would be able to hunt spouters regardless of the vagaries of wind and weather. Ole Smith, the prefect in that district of Iceland, embraced Roys's ambitious plans enthusiastically, pointing out to his superiors in Copenhagen that the populace of East Iceland could benefit from the project in terms of employment and the sale of whale products—and perhaps, he injected with some optimism, his own people might be able to learn the trade and to take it up for themselves. Lastly, Smith was aware that the whalers traditionally abandoned all save the blubber and baleen, so the killed whales could be a source of virtually free red meat for the people of his district.[13] Obviously he knew that such a vast enterprise would be a boon to this previously sleepy, destitute coastal area.

To secure permission for their shore-based venture, however, Roys and his associates were expected to meet certain conditions imposed by the Danish government: he and his men would have to establish legal residence in Iceland, and he must agree to register his ships in Denmark. Apparently he had no objection to either requirement. On November 24, 1864—through the Danish Ministry of Justice, which had overall jurisdiction over Iceland—he obtained residency and fishing rights so that he could legally establish a land station. From Copenhagen, where he wisely took the precaution of applying for a patent for the rocket-harpoon in the names of Lilliendahl and himself,[14] he sailed for Scotland. At Inverkeithing, opposite Edinburgh, he ordered a small twelve-ton, sixty-two-foot iron steamer. "I called her the *Visionary*," he wrote later, "in remembrance of those who said that a man who would undertake to kill the rorqual must be visionary, as good whalemen have tried it repeatedly and always failed."[15]

Roys returned to Iceland in the spring of 1865. Arriving at the Seydisfjördur on May 14, he found that his three-masted bark *Reindeer* had arrived in April, with his half brother Samuel in command of some forty men. Remembering back to the dark days when he had taken *Superior* through the Bering Strait, Thomas Roys liked to work in later years with men he could rely upon: old friends, relatives, and in-laws. Of his own family, five of his six half brothers were sailors. Four of them, all purportedly experienced whalemen, joined him in Iceland, one even bringing along his wife—to the dismay of the other sailors, who thought she would bring them bad luck. Of the seafaring Royses, only James, who was in his mid-twenties, was not there. He was away on his own four-year adventure in the famous old *Charles W. Morgan.* Sam was the most experienced and capable of the lot, for he had skippered the Sag Harbor whalers *Parana* and *S.S. Learned,* spending most of his adult life in the trade. Andrew Roys was the youngest of the brothers, being in his mid-twenties when he arrived at Iceland, but he quickly became a good whaler. He had previously been a sailor in Great Lakes ships. At Iceland he supposedly killed his first whale on his twenty-fifth birthday and fared well thereafter, for even the cynical foreign observers noted that he seldom missed any whale he tracked. John was said to have been a poor sailor, but later, it is claimed, he had owned an otherwise unidentified cargo schooner named *Union.*

William Henry Roys did not share any of his brothers' skills. As third mate and boatsteerer of the bark *Black Eagle* of Sag Harbor during the 1855 season, he had earned himself the reputation of a "do-nothing," and while second officer of the New Bedford whaler *Lancaster,* he was accused of being "an extensive KNOW-NOTHING! Too ignorant to catch a bowhead, and afraid as death of a right whale. Would make a good deck walloper." So strong was resentment against him, the entire crew of *Lancaster* chipped in to print broadsides cautioning all "Masters of Vessels" against shipping him and a fellow officer, "as it was through their ignorance, inefficiency and utter incompetency that the '*Lancaster*' was 'SKUNKED!' "[16] In fairness to his memory, perhaps there was more to the story than is told here. It should be said, however, that of the entire clan, only Thomas commanded the respect of all who worked with or observed him.

Soon after arriving, Thomas Roys purchased five warehouses in Vestdalseyri (an east-coast hamlet on the Seydisfjördur) from the firm of Örum and Wulff for £1,000.[17] This place was to become the nucleus of the first modern whaling station. Meanwhile, Roys was disappointed to learn that his brother had had poor luck at whaling so far that season. Lilliendahl (who, he felt, should have known better) had supplied

MASTERS
OF
VESSELS!

And all others interested, are hereby publicly cau-
tioned against shipping the following officers of the
"LANCASTER," of New Bedford, as it was through
their ignorance, inefficiency and utter incompetency
that the "Lancaster" was "SKUNKED!"

WILLIAM HENRY ROYCE,
SECOND OFFICER,

Was 3d mate and boatsteerer of the Bark "Black
Eagle" for the season of '55, during which time he distinguished himself as an excellent DO-NOTHING,
whilst as 2d officer of the "Lancaster" he won for himself the reputation of an extensive KNOW-NOTHING!
Too ignorant to catch a bow-head, and afraid as death
of a right whale. Would make a good deck walloper.

CHAS. BUSHNELL,
THIRD OFFICER,

Is equally incompetent and worthless. Was boatsteerer in the "Washington" when lost--no oil! Then
4th mate of the "Wm. Badger--no oil! Again 4th mate
of the "Huntsville," brought no oil to the ship! And
finally 3d dickey of the "Lancaster"--SKUNKED!
Was fast six hours to a ripsack which drove him out of
the head of the boat and from which he finally cut.
Would make a good blubber room hand.

Of the mate we will say nothing, preferring to consign
him to the tender mercies of Captain Carver.

Before shipping any of the above wor-
thies, Masters of Vessels are requested to
ascertain their true characters.

(Signed by the entire Crew.)

FIG. 20. A CURIOUS BROADSIDE

Not all of Roys's five half brothers who were also whalemen shared
his skill and competence. A broadside, apparently circulated in
New Bedford ca. 1860, gives some indication of the reputation of
William Henry Roys (Royce) among his fellow whalers.

(Courtesy of New Bedford Whaling Museum, New Bedford, Mass.)

Sam Roys's crews with defective rockets, and they had shot only two small whales for their efforts. The rockets, it should be remembered, required particularly delicate and uniform charges, and Roys was simply furious that Lilliendahl had not followed his explicit instructions. "After great difficulty," Roys groused, he was able to concoct the proper mixture by mealing the defective powder (i.e., dampening it with spirits, then drying and grinding it), but it was mid-July before he could resume whaling.[18]

On the voyage out from New York, *Reindeer* had been loaded with a cargo of special whaling equipment, boilers, steam engines, timber, bricks, and the like for the construction and outfitting of a shore base. In addition, there was a unique mill for grinding bones, as well as huge tanks for steaming blubber.[19] Yankee ingenuity had invaded Iceland, but the gears of industry were not yet grinding, for until the new shoreside equipment could be set up, the crews had to haul the dead whales alongside *Reindeer* and cut them in in the traditional manner—flensing and cooking the blubber aboard the ship, which served as a temporary station until permanent processing facilities were ready ashore.[20]

Meanwhile, the whaling station began to take shape. Roys was anxious to get it operating, for the base afforded a safe place for cutting in whales and cooking blubber, reducing the risk of doing this messy work in stormy seas or while drifting along threatening ice packs. Roys preferred to establish his station in eastern Iceland rather than in Scandinavia, where off Finnmark County, northern Norway, his rival Svend Foyn had been centering his own whaling hunts since 1864. Roys was of the opinion that Finnmark had too few good anchoring places and that the waters in that locality were too deep to recover sunken whales with ease.[21] He chose Iceland also because fin whales abounded off its rugged coasts, and there were plenty of enormous blues—called sulphur-bottoms by the Yankees and *Steypireidir* in Iceland—as well. The largest being alive on earth today, these amazingly graceful and beautiful animals rival even the largest prehistoric dinosaurs in sheer bulk and size. Quite a match indeed for Roys and his daring crews!

The captain selected his sphere of operations carefully. The south coast of the island was ruled out, for it has few very good harbors, and the adjacent seas, while shallow, are extraordinarily dangerous. Likewise, the northern coast is barred by floating ice for several more weeks in the spring than the others, and the western shore—while studded with deep, navigable fjords and safe harbors—is battered by frequent gales from the northwest and southwest which make entering and leaving a risky business, especially for ships under sail. By process of elimination, the east coast remained. Here, several deep fjords with safe moorings—protected from floating ice— offered ideal locations.

Nineteenth-century Iceland was a cold, harsh, barren country, with a very indigent and sparse population. The Seydisfjördur, where Roys finally settled his base, was an especially fine choice, for it has a small village at its head. At least here minimal supplies and a labor market were accessible. Fortunately, the whales were as abundant here as at any other place on the coast. Naturally there were drawbacks as well. As elsewhere in this strange land, these coasts too were often hammered by sudden and heavy storms and were smothered in unpredictable fog. Ice floes and bergs blocked its entrance every season save summer, while hidden underwater ledges and shoals lurked in unsuspected places.

Approached from the sea, Eastern Iceland is awe-inspiring— its high and naked mountains crowned by icecaps, snowclad in winter, and furrowed by silver streams in spring. When co-author Dr. Cornelis de Jong visited this area some years ago, he was deeply moved. While he did not expect that the pragmatic whalers had paid much attention to the stark beauty of this amazing land, he did find at least one fleeting, yet admiring reference in an old diary. Cruising off the southeast coast, Roys's rival Capt. O. C. Hammer wrote, "Öster and Vesterhorn and the glaciers in between showed one of the grandest sights I have seen anywhere. The boldest mountain shapes combined with a rich play of colors are in the light we saw, truly a view of which we had hardly ever before seen a match; it could not possibly be reproduced by the greatest artist."[22]

In his memoirs Roys sketches a fine word picture of Iceland in the 1860s. The population, he said, numbered about 60,000 in those days, and most of the inhabitants lived along the coasts to a distance of about thirty miles inland. The center of the island was uninhabitable, being blanketed by perpetual snow and glaciers. Although there was a parliamentary form of government, there were no schools save for a college in Reykjavik, the capital. Each family had to educate its children at home. The church was an integral part of their stern, demanding lives, and the effects of rigorous religious training were reflected, perhaps, in the curious fact that there were no jails or prisons. Roys regarded the people in general as very honest, and he provided possibly another key to their good behavior by remarking casually that ". . . sometimes whipping is resorted to."[23]

Some of the Icelandic customs perplexed and even provided great amusement for the Americans. The people, for instance, greeted each other with a kiss instead of shaking hands, and chuckled Roys, no doubt with a glint in his eye for the flaxen-haired ladies, "before the custom was known to us, some of my seamen were quite delighted at this extraordinary condescension of some of the Icelanders."[24]

He continues this rather entertaining vignette:

There is also another custom in which I was initiated. . . . Having gone from Seidisfiord to Nordfiord about 20 miles in my boat I was overtaken by a storm and obliged to remain overnight. I obtained lodgings for myself and boat's crew in the house of an Icelander. The house was built of stone and covered with turf, quite airtight . . . underneath the main part they kept their cows. Here was a trap door where they went up to where the whole family lived, having no fire but keeping warmth by the exclusion of fresh air and the number of people in the room.

In the sides of the room were tiers of berths. They gave one end of this to me and my 5 men. Being tired I soon fell asleep. In the night I awoke, breathing with great difficulty with scarcely life enough to get out doors while my men were sleeping apparently without difficulty. I then got the Icelander to dig a small hole through the top of his house that let in sufficient air to keep me alive until morning.[25]

The sequence that followed was equally comical, even for a man of Roys's almost fifty years of age. The storm continued, forcing Roys to remain another night in Nordurfjördur. Having had enough of odoriferous lodgings, he rambled about two miles down the road to the house of the minister. Here the accommodations were more civilized, with a comfortable room and his own bed for the night. Well, thank heavens Roys was a prudent man—a direct contrast to his notoriously lusty fellow whalemen—but let us tell the episode that followed in his own cautious words:

A few moments after [retiring], a young woman of 17 years, or thereabouts, came into my room and shut the door and stood with her back against it. She could speak no English and I no Iceland, and I was entirely at [a] loss to understand what she wanted. We gazed at each other until the position was painful. I then took off my coat and hung it up to intimate that I was going to bed, expecting she would go, but she did not move. I then took off my vest, still there she stood. I then sat down in the chair and she came at once and pulled off my boots and stockings and carried them away with her in order to dry them overnight for the morning. This is Iceland hospitality and fashion.[26]

The only mode of transportation that Roys observed there was small ponies, which either were saddled or carried packs. The Icelandic people raised cattle—for milk and beef—and sheep. They made their own clothing and exported wool, skins, salt beef and mutton, cured fish, the oil of seals, sharks and fish, salted fish, eiderdown, and peat moss to Denmark, receiving in exchange what necessities they might require for themselves. Roys found little illness in this robust country, save for some isolated cases of leprosy. But he did find that "they are universally liquor drinkers and snuff takers. Their mode of taking snuff, which they carry in a horn similar to a powder horn, is to pour upon the back of the hand a train of snuff 3 or 4 inches long and drawing it across the nostril, imbibe a considerable [amount] at once, which seems to give them great satisfaction." A curious practice, considering their strict, churchgoing ways. But Roys is digressing, for getting back to his life's work, he recalled:

> When I began to kill the rorqual whale there, they looked upon us as wonders. Although the right whales have been killed there until only a few is left, no one supposed it possible to kill and save a rorqual. They flocked around us in great numbers to try a part of the whale called Kinka [underside "bacon"]. . . . It is held by them in the highest estimation. They would have come for it 100 miles of distance, paying us in silver amounting to some thousands of dollars.
>
> They boil this article until all the oil is extracted, then slightly pickle it. In this state it keeps a long time. It is quite palatable. I have eaten it many times with satisfaction.[27]

After the rockets had been rebuilt at the shore station—with some assistance from Lilliendahl, who had arrived by steamer in August—Roys and his crews were seen cruising off the neighboring coasts in the steamer *Visionary*, towing a string of whaleboats astern, for the mother vessel was too small to hoist them all on deck. As soon as a spout was sighted, the crews scrambled into their respective boats and began the chase, hoping to kill the fleeing animal with pops of their curious guns. It must have taken a steady hand and a mighty good aim to strike a fast-moving target from a small, bobbing boat's bow. But if they were lucky and the whale was killed, the crew of *Visionary* would take over the harpoon line, then heave the enormous animal to the surface with the steam winch, fasten it alongside, and return to the base in the Seydisfjördur. Once at the shore station, the carcasses were moored to *Reindeer* and the processing work began. The whale was stripped, and the blubber was cooked on board in try-pots in the traditional manner.[28]

Roys's brothers filled all of the key billets in his expedition, making it essentially a family affair and giving a rather clannish impression to outsiders. There even is some evidence that he hoped in this way to keep his novel processing methods secret. Thomas Roys, quite naturally, was the general manager and supervisor of the overall operation. His brother Sam commanded *Reindeer* for part of the season, but his health deteriorated over the summer. Eventually he was forced to recuperate ashore for several weeks, and once he was well enough, he returned to Scotland in the coal-supply schooner *Jan en Albert*. About this time another half brother, William Henry, arrived and skippered *Visionary*, chasing whales until the ship was lost in a storm. Thereafter he served as a mate in *Reindeer* under Thomas's watchful eye. John Roys was second mate and a gunner, while half brother Andrew sailed as a gunner. The crews had a definite cosmopolitan makeup, for Roys hired Americans, Scots, Danes, and Icelanders to man his vessels and the shore station.

Beside defective rockets, other problems plagued the expedition. Some of the whales which had been harpooned, for instance, did not die quickly and towed the boats so fast or far away that the harpoon lines had to be severed and the monsters permitted to escape. Others sank and could not be retrieved, since either the line snapped or the harpoon drew out. Despite these setbacks, for the 1865 season Roys and his crew took twenty whales or more (there are several conflicting reports of higher numbers), of which six were humpbacks killed in the Seydisfjördur late in the season, during October and early November. Unfortunately, Roys lost about twenty whales, so his process was still far from perfected. Incidentally, the humpbacks taken yielded much less oil than blues or fins, and the numerous barnacles and parasites on their skins hampered cutting the blubber.[29]

But the most serious problem came in September. Heavy gales of almost hurricane proportions tore three expedition ships from their moorings in the fjord. The whaling steamer *Visionary* was wrecked on some rocks, the supply schooner *Jan en Albert* was driven ashore, and the Dutch ketch *Concordia,* which had just arrived with a load of coal from Britain, went ashore, then slipped off and sank in thirty fathoms. Only the station ship *Reindeer* remained unscathed. *Visionary* was found to be a total wreck. Since she was uninsured, Roys immediately hoisted out her boiler and masts, then rolled her over, cut off the rivet heads, and took all of the iron plates that could be salvaged back to Scotland in *Reindeer*. There, Roys says, she was reassembled, and she was still in service at the end of the decade. About the same time, *Jan en Albert,* skippered by Capt. C. J. Bottemanne (of whom we shall hear more in a later chapter), was declared formally lost after having run ashore. Her somewhat-hasty Dutch owners quickly sold her for the insurer's account. She was picked up, very conveniently, for a song by Roys and Lilliendahl, who hauled her off the strand the following day. A bargain she was, for the ship was so sound she was able to sail under Sam Roys for Dundee, Scotland, without repairs, taking along whatever still remained of *Visionary*.

By November 20, 1865, the Americans had left the Seydisfjördur with the season's takings (variously estimated at between 900 and 1,300 barrels) for Scotland,[26] then a major market for whale oil, where it was utilized in great quantities by local jute spinneries. In all, the season had been a substantial loss financially, but the vision of a successful rorqual fishery was still clear, for Roys and Lilliendahl soon afterward were investing more money and purchasing additional ships for an even more massive assault in 1866.

FIG. 21. CAPT. THOMAS WELCOME ROYS (CA. 1816–1877)

Portrait taken in Edinburgh, Scotland, in the mid-1860s. Note Roys's missing left hand, lost in an unfortunate accident while experimenting with a rocket harpoon in 1856.

(Courtesy of Mrs. David Byington, Aurora, Col.)

[*115*

10

Defeated Again

During the winter of 1865-66 Roys and Lilliendahl toiled continuously toward an all-out assault on the hapless rorqual whales that abounded in the waters off Iceland. At Dundee, Scotland, they converted the salvaged wooden schooner *Jan en Albert* into a screw steamer, utilizing the engine removed from the wrecked *Visionary*. On completion, she was renamed *Sileno* and was fitted out with two whaleboats, flensing equipment, and other whaling gear from *Reindeer*, which apparently had been sold. In addition, the Americans ordered two iron steamers built at Renfrew, on the opposite coast near Glasgow. These ships were designed from the keels up especially for the whaling trade, and they included a number of novel features. Although they had not been fully perfected at this earlier time, these ideas were later successfully adapted on a much broader scale by Capt. Carl Anton Larsen, a Norwegian, who pioneered modern pelagic whaling by outfitting one of the first whaling factory ships at the beginning of the twentieth century. Although Larsen probably was not aware of Roys or his work, he surely was influenced by his fellow countryman Svend Foyn. And—as we shall discuss later—Foyn had borrowed liberally from the Americans' innovations. To begin with, Roys's new ships had steam tryworks right on board. These were combination steam cookers and hydraulic presses, which were capable of exerting a pressure of 1100 pounds per square inch. Also, there were power winches to heave aboard large strips of blubber as well as to tend the anchors. The steamers were identical: bark-rigged, clinker-built of iron, 116 feet long, 22 feet wide, and with a depth of hold of 14 feet. Each carried two whaleboats. The steamers were named *Staperaider*—blue whale in Icelandic—and *Vigilant*. The former was owned by Roys and Lilliendahl, while the latter was under charter from Henderson, Anderson and Co. of Liverpool, England. Possibly this firm also had a financial interest in the enterprise. In keeping with Roys's agreement, both ships were registered in Denmark.[1]

While Roys hastily was tending to final preparations for the 1866 season, the following article, quoted from the New Bedford *Standard,* appeared back home in the Sag Harbor *Corrector* of March 10, 1866:

IMPROVEMENTS IN THE WHALE FISHERY.

The sulphur-bottom [blue]whales are very plenty in the Iceland and Spitzbergen seas, and, though of large size, and yielding an excellent quality of oil, have always been neglected by whalemen because their specific gravity is greater than that of sea water, and they sink as soon as they are dead. The elder Captain Roys, of New York, after a long series of experiments in which with Mr. G. A. Lilliendahl, he perfected the Lilliendahl rocket-harpoon, made an experimental voyage, which proved successful, in bark *Reindeer,* from Glasgow in steamer *Visionary,* built for the purpose, though she was too small for the business, took a thousand barrels of oil, and three large iron steamers are now being built at Glasgow, to be commanded by three of the Roys brothers, while a fourth will sail in a steamer prepared for him at Copenhagen by another company. The *Reindeer* is to sail from New York during the season to supply the Glasgow vessels with coal &c.[2] Mr. Lilliendahl is concerned with them in the enterprise, and his agent, with two of the Messrs. Roys, have been in this city a few days, buying machines and other whaling gear, and endeavoring to engage some of our old whalemen as officers, but they seem to be rather shy of the project, as old whalemen are invariably crochetical in regard to the manner of taking the monsters of the deep.

The harpoons contain each a pound of gunpowder, with a ten second fuse, and one of them is sure and instant death to a whale. They are fired with a three-inch line attached, the other end of which passes through the bottom of the boat, so as to buoy up a dead whale. For this reason larger boats are used than in ordinary whaling being thirty to thirty-five feet long. When the vessel arrives at the scene the whale is brought to the surface, and the blubber hoisted on board by steam power.

A tract of land has been purchased in Iceland, and experiments will be made in the manufacture of guano and bone dust from whales' carcases [sic], and also in securing more oil from them.

An independent concern is fitting a steamer from Liverpool for the same business and as the British Isles is a few days' steaming of the whaling-ground, we should not wonder if the business increased to considerable magnitude.

The parties interested in this new fishery and the means of prosecuting it, seem to have undoubted faith in its success, considering that steam is to supersede the old style of whaling, and that a sailing vessel is as far behind the age as a hand printing press, or any other thing of the past. A steam whaler from St. John's visited Hudson's Bay last season, and was very successful and the Scotch have for several years employed steamers in the Greenland fishery.

Well appointed propellers [steam whalers] can visit either Hudson's Bay, Davis Strait, Spitzbergen, or Iceland, take the whales if they are to be found, and make their way out of the ice and return home the same season, without having to undergo the hardships of a winter's incarceration in the ice. Will not some of our merchants take hold of this matter? They can as well fit steamers from this port, as can be done at St. John's, and we have no doubt but that the voyage will prove entirely successful.[3]

Sileno sailed from Dundee on April 3, 1866, for Seydis-fjördur—her port of registry—under a Captain Bistrup of

Copenhagen. *Staperaider* cleared the Clyde River on April 14 skippered by Capt. C. Fotel, also of Copenhagen. G. A. Lilliendahl, as well as Capt. C. J. Bottemanne, who had been master of *Jan en Albert* when she was wrecked during the previous season, came along as passengers. Bottemanne, incidentally, had joined the cruise to acquaint himself with the Americans' whaling methods, since he was hoping to establish a whaling firm of his own back in the Netherlands, utilizing RoysLilliendahl equipment. *Staperaider* arrived in Iceland after a week's passage, only to encounter stormy and heavy weather and winter ice, making it difficult to enter the fjord, and keeping the whales away from the nearby hunting grounds for the months of May and June. *Vigilant* was not ready for sea until May. She departed the Clyde on the sixteenth under Captain Tvede, another Dane, making the run up to the whaling station in just six days. Once there, however, she too encountered heavy ice. Finally, forging her way into the station, Tvede's ship met with *Sileno,* which had had no luck at all. *Staperaider,* however, had at least taken a runt (undersized or sick) whale that yielded a token thirty barrels. With the weather so bitter and damp, the season certainly was not yet conducive to hunting.[4]

At Iceland Andrew and Sam Roys both received their citizenship papers on April 23, and on May 24, William Henry took an oath of loyalty to the Danish crown.[5] Actually it was all for appearances' sake, but now at least the Roys brothers could command the ships legally and could engage in whaling. Sam became captain of *Staperaider* upon becoming an Icelandic citizen, William Henry assumed command of *Vigilant* from Captain Tvede as soon as they dropped anchor in the fjord, and Andrew took over as master of *Sileno* when she arrived at the station. Most of the ships' officers were Americans, some of whom were experienced whalemen. Foreigners held few key billets. The deck crews, the engineers, and the land-station laborers were a mixed bag of Americans, Danes, Swedes, Scotsmen, and Icelanders, with even a Russian, a Hawaiian, and a Portuguese from either the Azores or Madeira, where

Yankee whalers frequently recruited. Among the engineers, Scotsmen were most numerous since the British were then most advanced in the principles of steam engineering.[6] At least half of the crews were Danes shipped on at Copenhagen: former artisans, ex-soldiers, fishermen, and plain adventurers. Only a handful could really be considered sailors.

Whaling, of course, was very crude and dirty work, and few self-respecting, able-bodied sailors would lower themselves to ship on blubber hunters. Therefore it was not at all unusual to find some rough characters among the Royses' crews. In fact, the magistrate at Seydisfjördur was moved to remark that "among these people there were not a few bad characters, especially from Copenhagen."[7] Ironically, for all of the care they had taken in selecting the officers, the Americans had been careless when hiring greenhands in Denmark and Britain. It is no wonder though, for whaling was not very popular in either country, and the dangerous, dank surroundings of Iceland held little appeal for any but the desperate or broke wharf rats that could be rounded up.

There were also communication problems. The Americans did not speak the Danish language, but the officers expected strict discipline and quick execution of orders. Moreover, the Yankees regarded the Europeans with slight contempt as greenhorns at whaling, forgetting that there were some fine sailors among them. Captain Tvede complained that the foreigners, especially the Danes, were often bullied and beaten by the American officers—the Roys brothers included—without reason and that the American and British sailors always were among the preferred.[8] Perhaps it was simply that the English-speaking people communicated better. Then too, the Britons, most of whom were engineers, knew more than their superiors in most cases, which engendered more respect for them. In general, the English-speaking crew members earned higher wages because they were either skilled whalers or experienced machine operators.

Naturally, therefore, there was a lot of bickering and conflict between the Americans and the foreigners, and for the

Europeans' part, trifles developed into major problems. The dispute probably had its roots when they shipped aboard at the British Isles. Before *Staperaider* sailed from the Seydisfjördur on a cruise, six or seven of her crew, Danes and Swedes, had enjoyed a brief liberty ashore. At midnight they returned tipsy and began scuffling among themselves in the fo'c'sle. Next morning they complained—in rather insubordinate tones—to Sam Roys, the captain, about their treatment, refusing to report for duty. Roys became enraged, at first tying them to the stays, then clapping them in irons in the squalor of the foul blubber hold. There they wallowed for several days, subsisting on nothing but bread and water until finally they acquiesced and returned to duty. When the ship returned to Seydisfjördur—with four whales—the embittered men headed straight for the local magistrate and filed a formal complaint against the officers and captain, claiming maltreatment. Two days later the judge handed down a verdict: Sam Roys was fined fifty rix-dollars, payable to the village welfare fund. He was criticized for having taken matters into his own hands, for he should have brought any grievances before the proper legal authorities. As for the recalcitrant seamen, the magistrate declined their request to be paid off and returned home, ordering them instead to return to their ship and serve until the end of the season.[9]

The second confrontation beyween Americans and a foreign crew occurred aboard *Sileno*. When she arrived at Iceland, the Danes aboard refused to serve under a Yankee skipper. Again the local magistrate, Ole Smith, mediated, and after the crewmen had received a promise of a considerable increase in wages, they became willing to work for an American. But beneath the surface they remained moody and nearly mutinied when the captain—Andrew Roys—did not provide them with warm water for bathing. Again the magistrate conciliated. He commanded the men to resume work, but their spokesman, a certain Beckmann from Copenhagen, rebelled, so Smith had him placed in handcuffs and shipped back to Denmark to stand trial for what amounted to contempt of court. Roys seemed just as satisfied to be rid of him and to have the troublemaker tried back in Copenhagen.[10]

The ten Icelanders who were employed by the Americans received relatively high wages considering their humble circumstances, so they stayed satisfied and quiet.[11] A competing whaling ship operator said that the Americans paid local common hands from twenty-five to thirty rix-dollars (presumably monthly) and five rix-dollars per 100 barrels of whale oil. They also received free room and board. Probably the foreign-whaling-company manager was jealous that he could not afford such high wages and fringe benefits.[12]

This season it was Thomas Roys's intention to move at least part of the processing operation to the land station at Seydis-fjördur so that the ships would have greater flexibility in hunting whales. To this end he had bought and set up an array of expensive equipment on shore. The oil-rendering concept was revolutionary in comparison to the time-honored—yet primitive—method whalers had used for decades: boiling out blubber aboard ship in try-pots. Roys brought the tryworks operations ashore; they now consisted of metal tanks with steam powered worm drives that turned the blubber as it was rendered. Then, to squeeze out the very last drop of precious oil, Roys devised steam presses that compressed the remaining scrap. In addition, the immense bones, which had previously been discarded by whalers, although they contained large measures of fat—were utilized. They were sawn into smaller pieces, crushed in a special machine, then the residue was tried out. The crushing machine was a failure, though, for lack of a powerful enough engine.

The oil from both blubber and crushed bone was rendered under considerable steam pressure in great fifty-barrel-capacity vats. It was dangerous work because there was the very real possibility of a boiler explosion and frightening quantities of boiling oil were being handled. Nonetheless, it was probably safer and infinitely more efficient than working on the deck of a rolling ship. The new process, it is said, yielded much more oil of a purer quality than the old, depending on the

FIG. 22. WHALING STATION AT ICELAND

This wood engraving of a whaling station was published in the *Illustreret Familie-Journal* in Copenhagen in 1889. It supposedly was based on a photograph taken under the midnight sun around 1870. While the exact identity of the station is unclear, the picture is typical of Roys's operations at Seydisfjördur. The whale is a blue, largest of the cetaceans.

(Courtesy of The Royal Library, Copenhagen, Denmark)

freshness of the blubber. The plant itself was housed in a barnlike building, and once the crushing machine—or bonemill, as it was also called—had been abandoned, very little oil was extracted from the bones, which were scattered everywhere, giving the place the weird appearance of some herculean slaughterhouse. In fact, a visitor was prompted to write, "The skeletons of whales are now lying scattered on the beach, bleached by the sun and rain and without use."[13]

As mentioned before, the two largest steamers, *Staperaider* and *Vigilant,* were equipped with costly pressure cookeries and appurtenant hydraulic presses capable of squeezing oil out under pressure of 1100 pounds per square inch. But like the bonemill ashore, this innovation was not very efficient either,

[*123*]

for the oil tended to leak while the press was operating. In addition, the shipboard boilers seemed incapable of driving such complex equipment. Consequently, little blubber was tried out on the steamers, and most was brought ashore, where the processing was carried out under the watchful supervision of two skilled engineers. If the catch was really good, the blubber overflow was boiled in the four traditional try-pots that were installed at the land station in July.[14] We find that even Roys himself was surprised by some of the substantial yields his shoreside equipment produced. When the bonemill functioned, he claimed, it could extract "as much as one pound of oil from 3 pounds of bones." And after the machine was no longer used, he found a ready market for the bones as a by-product, for they were shipped to England, where they netted about eight pounds per ton. He later concluded that:

> It was found by actual trials, of which we made several, that the skull bone of a Rorqual made about 3 bbls. of oil, that the jaw bones made 5 bbls., that the tongue made 10 bbls. and the flesh, when the whale was fat, made 1 barrel to the ton, and this only could be extracted by steam. Thus, one of these whales, towed to shore and all the oil extracted by steam, would crowd hard 300 bbls. of oil.[15]

Toward the end of May that season the weather remained testy, and choking ice prevented the ships from clearing the fjord. Then June blossomed, and with it came favorable weather—clear, warm, and quiet—yet still the ice remained. *Staperaider* attempted several times to sail out, but was forced to turn back. Finally, on June 7 she and *Vigilant* were able to leave. That same afternoon *Sileno* arrived at the base, having taken no whales, and reported numerous growlers and small bergs combined with stormy conditions on the high seas. In all, she had taken quite a beating since sailing on a cruise on May 22, steaming slowly and under sail and spending part of the time waiting out the weather laid up in one of the northern fjords.[16]

Meanwhile, workmen ashore were busily constructing a quay next to the tryworks, while coopers were assembling numerous barrels in optimistic anticipation of a good harvest. Dikes had to be built along the Vestdals River, which threatened to flood the developing whaling station as the winter snows began to melt far inland. The work progressed slowly, for there were only three Icelanders to do the labor, and of necessity, it stopped when there was blubber to process. But when *Staperaider* came in on June 12 she was empty, having been forced into port by stormy weather at sea. She recoaled and sailed again the following day. Fortunately, the ice was beginning to melt by this time, and when she returned again on the seventeenth, she had a whale in tow. *Sileno* was in and out, but the unpredictable weather checked her progress. *Vigilant,* however, brought in a whale on the twenty-fourth, buoying somewhat low spirits. Ironically, on June 26 a small fin whale swam right into the fjord and circled *Vigilant.* Apparently it was a runt not worth the trouble, for Capt. William Henry Roys did not bother to waste a rocket on it. *Sileno* brought in a small humpback on the twenty-sixth, but obviously such slim pickings could not sustain an extensive expedition such as Roys and Lilliendahl had envisioned.[17]

Again this year, the rockets did not perform well. They were—as in the past—often temperamental. In fact, one of the Danish observers at one point said that eighty out of a hundred were inoperative. Roys had personally supervised the manufacture of the rockets in Dundee, and he insisted that they were good. Still, at least one careful observer noted that these were not even as good as those Lilliendahl had made only the year before. In the new rockets, for instance, the powder charge often was wet and not flammable. Then, many of the harpoons did not penetrate far enough into the whales for the explosive charges to perform their deadly task. Further, when the rockets misfired and were reloaded again, it was discovered that the iron casings had warped and did not fit together properly. Added to all of these troubles, the sights were not always properly aligned, and the fuses sometimes did not work right, causing the shells to explode at incorrect intervals or not at all. There seemed no end to the problems. Wherever possible, the rockets were reworked at Seydisfjördur. Meanwhile, only the Roys brothers had had any real experience in firing the unique weapons, so they had to spend considerable time teaching the difficult art of shooting moving whales in heavy seas to shivering boat crews. It was beginning to seem that the disappointments of the previous season were being repeated all over again.[18]

True, some of the troubles could be attributed to the in-experience of the harpooners alone, but most were due to shortcomings in the rockets themselves. Several times, for instance, a bomb actually penetrated the blubber but was stopped short by the tough white layer of sinews that separates the fatty tissue from flesh. On other occasions, the harpoons tore clear through the bodies of the whales and exploded harmlessly in the air. Some just glanced off the animals. Since the harpooners fired the rockets from a position in the bows just a few feet above the surface of the choppy seas, more than once the deadly devices struck a rising wave crest before their mark and ricocheted harmlessly away from the fleeing targets.[19] It seemed that Roys was experiencing the same frustrations he had had aboard his earlier experimental voyages in *W. F. Safford*. The following is excerpted from his memoirs:

> The steamer *Stapraider*'s [sic] boat at Iceland shot a rorqual whale and the shot passed through the top of his back simply harpooning him and this whale ran with great speed. They held on to the whale in the boat one hour, then cut the line. A patent log was thrown from the steamer and she followed and took up the boat that had lain still after cutting from the whale and the distance was 22 miles that this whale had run. . . . This is the way the speed of the whales has been obtained, of the Rorqual and some other kinds & from these data all the others are easily calculated.[20]

So, at least one misadventure proved of some benefit.

But the seeming incompetence of the harpooners must be excused. After all, the rockets were still experimental devices. While we read of the many and often bitter complaints of Roys and the other whalers about the quality and performance of the rockets they manufactured in different places, we must realize that in many countries in those times the Industrial Revolution was still in an early stage of development; that the skilled personnel needed to fabricate the strange new equipment Roys had developed were scarce—even in Great Britain, the cradle of modern technology; and that even the most careful supervision could not always prevent carelessness or ignorance on the part of the factory workers who manufactured and assembled the various components.

Strangely enough, the rockets used this season probably represented Roys's and Lilliendahl's latest technology, for on April 24, 1866, they received an American patent for an "improved" rocket-harpoon. It incorporated significant revisions over previous American, British, and French patents they held. The device consisted of five main parts: (1) the rocket itself; (2) a pointed harpoon bomb, screwed or otherwise secured into the end of it; (3) the stock of the harpoon; (4) the barbs; and (5) the shank of the harpoon, to which everything was fastened. The shank end was formed like a bow or loop, to which was secured a large iron ring which slipped back and forth freely. The harpoon line was bent onto this link.

When the gun was loaded, the barbs closed on the shank and slipped into the gun barrel, with the link hanging loosely in a special cutout slot in the launcher. It was fired by a pistol barrel fixed to the launcher, which ignited the rocket propellant contained in the stock portion of the harpoon. As the rocket-harpoon left the launcher tube, the barbs sprung open and the securing link slipped to the end of the harpoon shank. Shortly after impact, the bomb portion of the harpoon exploded, killing the prey, and the barbs held the whale fast until it could be reeled in by the whaleboat.[21]

Judging from an existing specimen in the Smithsonian Institution of the so-called California whaling rocket—a direct descendant of the Roys/Lilliendahl harpoon—the device of their Iceland days must have been close to seven feet long and have weighed maybe thirty pounds, including the unloaded rocket shell. The bomb head itself was about ten pounds and measured about three inches at its maximum diameter. If the performance claimed for the older version of the Roys harpoon matched that of the later California version, it must have been capable, when it did work, of fastening to a whale at 130 feet, "which was a considerably greater distance than could be reached even by gun lances." Unfortunately, a full-sized launcher has not been discovered to date, so its dimensions are only subject to conjecture. Though the Suffolk County Whaling Museum at Sag Harbor, Long Island—the home port of Roys's first voyages—possesses only a very handsome miniature patent model of his 1861 launcher (U.S. Patent 31,190), handcrafted of brass, we can deduce that its life-sized counterpart was quite hefty and that fully loaded, it must have exerted considerable weight on an operator's shoulder.[22]

Roys finally arrived at Iceland for the 1866 season on July 9 as a passenger in a sailing ship from Dundee. He brought along two spare whaleboats, together with a munitions press to refill defective rockets. After hearing the crews' complaints, he determined by further tests that the rockets were indeed not as powerful as they should be. In addition, he discovered that the explosive charges in many shells were wet because the holes through which they had been filled with powder had absorbed water while the harpoon tips were being honed. In addition, the fuses were no good; sometimes the pistol ignitor for the rockets misfired, or the fuses in the rockets did not catch and fire the charges. Realizing that he should begin again from scratch, Roys had all of the charges burned out then refilled the shells. During this dangerous operation, several of the rockets exploded, throwing shrapnel about, but fortunately, no one was injured. Earlier in the season it had been found that the rockets' power could be increased to some extent by boring out the interiors with a steel tool especially fabricated for the purpose. Tests were conducted on land at the whaling station. A target was set up approximately seventy feet away from the firing position. After the sights were corrected some of the rockets hit right on the bull's-eye, but others overshot the target—some by almost double the distance. Surely, for the sake of safety, and perhaps of economy, the explosive shells must have been fired with sand instead of gunpowder during these exercises.[23]

On July 10 *Sileno* came in empty, but on the thirteenth *Vigilant* arrived with two whales, and she brought in another pair on the twentieth. Ambrose W. Landre, second officer of *Vigilant*, wrote home to New Bedford that, "the [catcher] boats are large; if they were not, a whale could not be held, for they go with lightning speed after they are first struck,—but the rockets finally sicken them [i.e., the whales] and no mistake. We are very busy now, coaling and watering, discharging oil, repairing boats, &c., and go to sea again to-morrow. Mr. Andrews, our cooper, and the other men from New Bedford, are well."[24] Unquestionably, their luck was turning, for on the twenty-first *Staperaider* arrived with three more whales and *Sileno* with one, and two days later *Vigilant* brought in two more—big ones. Within the next month the modern whale hunters had taken another sixteen.[25] It appeared that at last Roys's efforts were finally paying off.

That summer Roys introduced another innovation which was not very successful. He took an ordinary whaleboat of the traditional kind and fitted her with a steam engine. Unfortunately, the boiler was too small. With a full head of steam she could cruise at a respectable twelve knots, but in a few minutes the steam load dropped and she could not back down—an important maneuver when taking a whale. According to the captain, the boat was used for only one hunt; the load dropped before the boat could be reversed and she ran right onto the writhing, dying animal's back. Roys concluded that she "was not very safe, but had she been with more boiler, [we] would have shot more whales than 6 ordinary whale boats and only required 2 men to man her [vs. the typical six-man crews of rowed boats]."[26]

The catching methods during the 1866 season usually proceeded according to the following pattern. The three steamers would go out, each with some whaleboats in tow. As soon as one of the steamer crews sighted a spouter, seven men jumped into each of the boats and chased the whale. It was important to get within a specific range, so that the harpooner could take exact aim. After the shot was fired, the harpoon burst out of the firing tube and took the whipping line with it, so that the whale was held fast after being struck. Ideally, the bomb portion of the harpoon then exploded, and if the whale died instantly, the whole affair was very simple. As the oarsmen pulled toward the whale, a hand harpoon was planted in it for good measure, and the steamship would move in and pick up the dead carcass on signal. If the whale sank immediately (as many did) and became so heavy that the boat could not hold it, the harpoon line had to be paid out until the animal lay on the sea bottom, and the crew had to give the end of the line to the steamer, which started to winch the whale in. If the leviathan was wounded only superficially, with the harpoon still fast in, it often took the boat in tow for a terrifying but thrilling "Nantucket sleighride." Usually this was the result of poor marksmanship, the whale having been either shot when it was too far away or not hit in a vital spot, where the explosive charge could effect an immediate kill. Quite often an animal in these circumstances would run away with the velocity of a locomotive, and there was the added risk that it might draw the boat under if it sounded. In these cases, there was no choice but to cut the line. According to one report, Roys had mounted a capstan in the rowing boats, which made it almost impossible to haul the line in near enough to harpoon the whale again should the first attempt have failed its mark. A second boat, therefore, had to move in and dispense the final death blow with another explosive harpoon.[27]

All of the whales that they took that season were rorquals, including some blues. As we noted in the previous chapter, blues are, of course, the kings of the leviathans and can grow to enormous sizes. On the sulphur-colored bellies of these animals lie numerous rows of large folds of blubber—known as *rengi* to the Icelanders, and which they served as a delicious native dish prepared like bacon. Unfortunately for the whales, it is still served as a delicacy in Japan. Most of the American and European whalers avoided whale flesh, but the Icelanders relished it and reported that it was a very palatable substitute for beefsteak. Finbacks were the second most common species caught. These too yielded good-tasting *rengi*. The Americans had seldom hunted fins in the past, for they gave proportionately less oil per foot of length than other species such as the bowhead, right, or sperm, and they were considered to be quite dangerous to approach in small cedar whaleboats. Humpbacks, as mentioned before, were also harvested, but they were not among the whalers' favorite catch because they only rendered forty barrels of oil at the most, and their bodies were covered with numerous parasitic crustaceans, such as "whale lice" and barnacles, making it difficult to cut the blubber.[28]

Now we already know that rorquals have a tendency to sink when dead, so they had to be either heaved up from the ocean bottom, or if this was not feasible, they had to be left to putrify until natural gases brought them to the surface.[29] In his memoirs Roys complained, "The difficulty of getting all [of these sunken rorquals] up still remained in the want of a chain compensator at the mast head [of the steamer,] which was not yet known, and the soft bottom in some places making it impossible to lift them from the mud, which is now remedied by holding them from going down."[30] On April 3, 1866, Roys patented an "Improved Tackle for Raising Sunken Whales and Other Bodies," which he saw as a partial solution to the problem. In his patent specification Roys noted that, in the past, part of the difficulty in recovering sunken bodies was that there was not sufficient elasticity in the harpoon lines to counteract the rolling and pitching of the ships at the surface. Consequently, the harpoon would draw out of the animal, which then had to be abandoned. Very simply described, Roys's contraption consisted of an ordinary block and tackle, to which was fitted a counterweight and a dual set of pulleys connected with huge rubber bands. The device would thus take up the slack in the whale line in heavy seas, in much the same way as a snubber is used aboard yachts today to keep mooring lines taut.[31] Roys subsequently patented the whale compensator in England and the Netherlands that same year.

Apparently the oil-processing equipment at the shore station presented some problems. Captain Tvede, the Dane who superintended the sophisticated works during the 1866 season, regarded the American's system as "time-consuming and

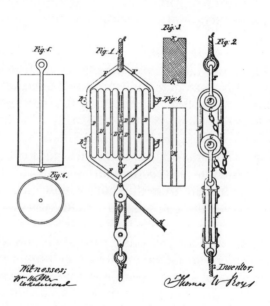

FIG. 23. ROYS'S WHALE COMPENSATOR

While in Iceland, Roys continually lost rorqual whales that had sunk after being harpooned. His "Whale Compensator," patented in the United States, Norway, France, and the Netherlands in 1866, seemed the solution. Lines secured to harpoons set in sunken whales tended to draw out if the catcher vessel rolled violently. Through an ingenious combination of weights, pulleys, and springs or huge rubber bands, Roys's contraption steadied the whaleline. A Norwegian, Svend Foyn, later took credit for the concept, called an accumulator on modern catcher ships. This drawing is from the specification for Roys's patent 53,684 of April 3, 1866.

(Courtesy of U.S. Patent Office, Washington, D.C.)

fuel-wasting, because for the extraction of 80 barrels of oil 3 days and about 8 tons of coal were required. . . ." At the same time, however, Tvede did admit, "the oil extracted in this way was much finer than that boiled at the same time in the traditional way in cauldrons." He felt that the old, weak boiler they were using was the real cause of that problem, and believed that increased steam pressure would have improved efficiency. In addition to operating at far less than its rated specifications, its heating coils tended to clog and had to be cleaned every twelve hours. Moreover, the grates under them did not fit properly, and a lot of coal dropped through into the ash pits below and was wasted.³²

The 1866 season wound up in late fall. The rockets continued to fail, nearly all exploding prematurely before hitting their marks, which made them very dangerous to use. In a last-ditch effort before the ice formed, Roys had the entire stock burnt out and reloaded. Of some hundred rockets on hand, only twenty were any good. During the reloading process, some of them broke to pieces under the pressure, and a certain Captain Dennis narrowly escaped injury when he was hit by a piece of flying iron while burning out one of the rockets.³³ In terms of having proved the potential of the rorqual whaling industry, the season might be termed a mild success, for of some ninety whales killed, about half (forty-three or forty-four) were saved. These yielded approximately 3,000 barrels of oil. The rest of the whales were lost while heaving them up from the sea bottom, so Roys's whale compensator must not have functioned as well as he had envisioned.³⁴ An official report from magistrate Ole Smith of Seydisfjördur states that the expedition took 2,350 barrels (possibly the *official* figure reported to the authorities), divided between the steamers as follows:

Staperaider	Capt. Samuel Roys	1,050 barrels
Vigilant	Capt. William Henry Roys	920 barrels
Sileno	Capt. Andrew Roys	380 barrels

The takings of oil, baleen, and *rengi* were worth, by the magistrate's estimate, almost 100,000 rix-dollars. Smith had no doubts "that the rocket will become an effective weapon and yield good results when more accuracy is applied in its manufacture and when pyrotechnists with the necessary theoretical insight will be employed." Pleased with the Americans' presence, he concluded, "the inhabitants have profited in various ways from the whaling business here, among others because they could sell many bulls and fowls at good prices. The share of a harpooner in a whale driven ashore in the Vopnafjördur was given to the poor fund here and on the whole the Americans have not insisted on the harpooners' shares in the whales stranded this year."[35]

It is difficult to fully assess the financial aspects of the American experiment. From his own standpoint, however, Roys did prove the success of the rorqual fishery, having taken more than 100 of those whales during the few years he worked out of Seydisfjördur. For some reason—probably money-related—he and Lilliendahl parted company at the end of the season. Roys returned to England, where he sold out to his partner and Henderson, Anderson and Company—which bought half interests in the ships and all of the capital equipment. Then he sailed for New York.[36] There were rumors that the venture had run up deficits so great that the brothers Roys were forced to withdraw.[37] Lilliendahl, on the other hand, decided on one last try alone and readied himself for another season in Iceland. In early May 1867, his party arrived on the east coast with the steamers *Staperaider* and *Vigilant,* but initially they had to lie offshore because of the thick ice. There was nothing to do but wait, for the rockets were to be loaded on land this year to insure fresh charges. While standing offshore, *Staperaider* damaged her screw and had to return to England for repairs. Finally, at month's end, the ice began to clear, and the ships came to rest near shore. In a few days a sufficient number of rockets were filled, and hunting began during the first or second week of June, just as the floating ice began to disappear from the fjords.[38]

This season, *Staperaider* was commanded by an Englishman, a Captain Ridge, and *Vigilant* by a Dane, Capt.

Christen J. Klitgaard—neither of whom had previously sailed in whalers. Except for the mates, who were Americans and had served in these ships before, and the chief engineers, who were Britishers, most of the crews were Danes and Swedes, and there were a few Icelanders. Because the ships had been reregistered under the British flag, the captains were strictly forbidden to hunt within the existing territorial limit of three miles. But the ships carried sea passes, so they legally could unload blubber ashore and could sell *rengi* to the inhabitants, for it had been taken on the high seas.[39]

Some years later, the good natured Captain Klitgaard wrote fondly of his adventures as master of *Vigilant*. He reminisced about a contest between himself and Captain Ridge, in which the sister ships *Vigilant* and *Staperaider* challenged each other to a race up the Seydisfjördur—a distance of sixteen miles. Klitgaard was peeved with his British adversary, who might have won the contest, he thought, had he not tried to ram *Vigilant*. Klitgaard was not intimidated by him and responded in kind, but one of his men fell overboard in the process and was towed the rest of the way. "So," remarked the captain in a light vein, "poor fellow, he received a good bath for *once* in his life." The Stars and Stripes were hoisted ashore in *Vigilant*'s honor as she passed the finish post.

The next day spouts were reported at the mouth of a nearby fjord. Although the ice was thinning, Ridge, who was the senior man, procrastinated. Klitgaard jumped at the opportunity and was rewarded with a whale for his trouble, to the great annoyance of his rival. He lost several other whales in deep water though, and even accused Ridge of stealing a few. Then one particularly testy animal towed Klitgaard and his men in an eight-mile-wide circle, at speeds that seemed to be sixty miles per hour. The water surrounding them during the rambunctious ride was bloodred, and everyone aboard the catcher boat looked like a butcher by the time the frenzied beast took one last breach and succumbed in seventy fathoms of water.

Another whale—a gigantic, thrashing, leaping blue—upset the whaleboat, spilling all hands into the frigid waters. Then off he went, snapping the harpoon line—which wrapped itself around Captain Klitgaard's legs in the process, towing him along at a breakneck rate. After what seemed like hours, the wild animal finally tired, and the captain, half drowned and half clothed, was fished out. None the worse for the experience, he remarked cheerfully, "if *that* is the way one must go to see the North Pole, I am not interested in seeing it at all." A large party was held to celebrate his narrow escape, and Ridge and he patched up their differences. Klitgaard, incidentally, took the biggest whale of the season and carried its massive twenty-foot jaws home with him to Denmark, using this enormous souvenir to frame the entrance to his home—a memento of his "happiest time as a sailor!"[40]

In the final tally, Klitgaard had taken about 1,000 barrels of oil in *Vigilant*, while his rival had taken 800 in *Staperaider*. Lilliendahl personally looked after the rocket loading that season, and on at least one occasion he took charge of one of the catcher boats, taking two small whales close inshore in the Seydisfjördur with an Icelandic crew. These yielded a total of more than fifty barrels. The total baleen for the season was ten tons. Lilliendahl's idea of freshly loading the rockets himself at the land station proved very satisfactory. Ole Smith reported to his superiors that "in my opinion the experimental period may be considered to have ended and I do not doubt that in the future in general good leadership and the Danish flag will permit [them] to hunt whales in the fjords from 1 April to 1 September. The ships will be able to each produce 1,200 to 1,500 barrels of oil, a yield which will leave a very considerable profit."[41]. Smith, it seems, was overly optimistic or somewhat naive, for Lilliendahl had taken only thirty-six whales in all. Again the business ran a sizable deficit, and Lilliendahl's company went bankrupt, thus ending the first American attempt at modern whaling.[42]

Some months later the newspaper *Nordanfari* (July 4, 1868) published the firm's "obituary," having noted in an earlier issue a loss of £1,000: ". . . the whale-fishing of Lilliendahl, Henderson and Anderson in Icelandic waters was left off, and this is a great loss for the country, though not least the inhabitants of [counties] Múlasýslur. This summer their houses and all the property here in Seydisfjördur concerning whaling will be sold at an auction."[43]

Lilliendahl went home to Jersey City, where he developed a lifesaving rocket which was used widely for years afterward. In 1870 he turned his fireworks business over to his brother-in-law, Jacob J. Detwiller, who conducted it for many years, later merging it with several other companies. The successor company survives to this day. An active Republican, Lilliendahl ran for the New Jersey legislature in 1878 and served one term. In 1903 he joined his sons, Alfred, Frank, and William, in their flourishing railroad, mining and smelting, and electric-power-plant interests at Saltillo, Coahuila, Mexico. The mining and smelting operation, Mazadil Copper Company, alone employed 7,000 men. The senior Lilliendahl, it is said, devoted his energies to the promotion and building of the Coahuila & Pacific and Coahuila & Zacatecas railroads. He enjoyed the climate immensely and made his retirement home there. Liliendahl died at Saltillo on December 4, 1907.[44]

Considering their influence on the modern whaling industry, it is ironic that until now there has been little to be found in the standard whaling histories concerning the pioneering efforts of Lilliendahl or Roys. Gunnar Sveinsson—a leading historian in Iceland, who was himself born in Seydisfjördur—admits that his home village, which now numbers about 850 inhabitants, is more interested today in fishing than in history. Coincidentally, he grew up just two miles from the former whaling station at Vestdalseyri, yet he never knew there had been a processing plant there. It seems that the old warehouses in which Roys had installed his equipment burned to ashes in 1894.[45]

The best—and probably the only—overview and evaluation of the American effort is found in Arne Odd Johnsen's *Finnmarksfangstens historie, 1864–1905*. As mentioned above, Johnsen's admiration for Roys and Lilliendahl is entirely unabashed, and he grants them full credit for the transition from the old to the new whaling methods. He felt, however, that the Americans failed, not through lack of intelligence or inventive spirit, but in the practical application of their ideas. Johnsen believed that they did not succeed because they implemented their concepts on a grand scale from the outset, wasting capital before they really had had an opportunity to prove the feasibility of their ideas. Such mistakes were necessarily costly in time, energy, and money.

Unquestionably Johnsen is correct. If a more substantial boiler had been employed at the shore works, the yield of oil would have been far greater. The rockets were expensive and were manufactured without good quality control. If from the start they had been filled and maintained with the care that Lilliendahl exercised during the final season of 1867, many of the initial failures would have been overcome. More experienced crews would have been an asset too. Many of the men in the combined endeavors of 1863–66 and the solo effort of 1867 were strictly greenhands. Roys' age—he was over fifty years old at the time—may have lessened his vitality, industry, and initiative.

Lack of capital was one of the Americans' greatest handicaps. They might have succeeded, however, if only they had not embarked on such an ambitious program from the very outset. Johnsen points out also that whaling was increasingly becoming less attractive as an investment. Prices of oil and baleen were tumbling, and other, more profitable, ventures— such as textiles and the opening of the West—plus the discovery of petroleum, which promised cheaper substitutes for whale-oil products, threatened the industry's capital and market bases. True, the Civil War had brought a temporary boom in prices which likely motivated Roys and Lilliendahl to begin their Iceland venture in the first place. But after the war was over, prices plummeted, declining in 1867 to half the levels of a few years before and cutting deeply into the profitability of the whaling business.

In closing, Johnsen observes that, ". . . Roys and Lilliendahl share the merit to have opened fairly successful modern whaling in the northern seas. They were pioneers in an industry which later on would take on international dimensions and their enterprise evidently inspired Danish, Dutch, and Norwegian whalers, i.e., Captain-Lieutenant O. C. Hammer, Captain C. J. Bottemanne, and Svend Foyn."[46] We shall deal further with all of these individuals in the next chapter.

11

Competition Arrives

Steam and rocket whaling so excited the attention of mariners operating in and around Icelandic waters that several captains who either had served directly with the Americans or had studied their methods firsthand decided to imitate them, thus truly giving expanding dimensions to Roys's and Lilliendahl's rough original ideas. These foreigners, all of whom were careful and critical observers, benefited in many ways from knowledge of the Yankees' shortcomings. The general conclusion is that the American equipment was never perfected technically, although there is no question that, in principle, the basic ideas underlying their innovations were excellent. In fact, they were so important that their influence still can be seen in the modern whaling industry.

Their new devices—the rocket-harpoon, whale compensator, whale-raiser, bone crusher, and steam pressure cookers for extracting oil from blubber and crushed bone—all offered promise, but they needed further refinement. The rockets had often failed before Lilliendahl took personal charge. Roys was never fully able to cope with the problem of whales which sunk. True, his compensator helped ease the tension exerted by the yawing and pitching ship on the harpoon line and the iron itself, and his whale-raiser—a contraption designed to plant a second heavy harpoon into sunken whales and to double the tether to the animal—was a useful invention, but his lines and harpoons were not themselves strong enough for the difficult job of heaving dead whales to the surface. As a result, at least half of the whales killed were probably lost.

One of the imitators, Capt. O. C. Hammer, wrote of the American whalers, "They lack any sense of theory and have only a superficial practical ability,"[1] and he later commented sarcastically, ". . . The men whom we considered masters of the trade are not yet past children." Only Roys was the driving force and mastermind behind the basic ideas and their implementation. The Danes got the impression, however, that he was lacking in the ability to direct and orchestrate the expedition. Perhaps his rapport with his half brothers made him too lax and informal. Hammer, again criticizing the Americans' operations in Iceland, wrote, "The only one who is able or has been able in whaling is the [fifty-year] old Thomas Roys, but he is almost too old."[2] We shall return to O. C. Hammer later in this chapter and shall describe his Danish whaling enterprise. While Hammer was first to imitate Roys's operation, we should realize that his bitter criticism of the Americans was engendered in part by his own failures and frustrations.

Another firsthand witness of Roys's methods—and a whaleman of the highest caliber himself—was Svend Foyn, the father of modern whaling. His meeting with the Roys brothers was brief but decisive. It is difficult to compare Roys and Foyn—the two great pioneers of mechanized whaling. It is a pity that the American should have come so close to complete success then have met failure in the end, while his Norwegian counterpart—who borrowed some of his concepts and ideas—should himself have succeeded after a similar long and trying spell of almost heartbreaking disappointment and should therefore have reaped the credit and reward. Perhaps, as indicated above, the difference was not so much in their persistence as in their own carefulness in applying basic principles. An apt analogy might be that between the alchemist and the true chemist: empirical methods vs. logical scientific experimentation.

No mistake though, Svend Foyn should receive credit for

the real breakthrough between the old and the new whaling methods. Seen in perspective, Thomas Roys was an intriguing forerunner of the modern whalers who emerged later in the nineteenth century. It is remarkable that the capital-intensive and highly technical and sophisticated industry that we know today originated—more so than any other business—in the initiative and resourcefulness of only one man. Ironically, Foyn's homeland, Norway, was a country which had taken only a peripheral interest in the whaling trade before his appearance, for it was too backward and too poor to engage in such large-scale endeavors. It is true that during the early Middle Ages Norway was the original homeland of the proud Vikings who discovered and colonized Iceland and Greenland, who touched at the Maritimes and New England, and who were regular hunters of whales, and petroglyphs in northern Norway reveal whale-hunting enterprises there as far back as 2,200 B.C. During the late Middle Ages, however, Norway came under the economic domination of the German Hansa League, and it was subsequently subject to the political and cultural influence of Denmark, falling into economic and cultural poverty. Finally in 1814 Norway broke this yoke and gained her independence when Denmark—which had sided with Napoleon—shared in the Little Corporal's defeat. From this time Norway began to emerge gradually as a seafaring and fishing nation.

Svend Foyn surely was one of the early exponents of this economic restoration—a link between early and modern capitalism.[3] He was born in 1809 in the small but lively port of Tønsberg near Oslo. Foyn's biographer, Arne Odd Johnsen, describes his life and career as an epic—which it was. His father was a skipper and had perished at sea when Svend was only four years old, but the younger Foyn also turned to the sea. Serving as a sailor, he had to educate himself, which he did quite successfully (just as Roys had done). Foyn rose rapidly through the ranks to captain and shipmaster in the merchant navy and was already well-to-do when in 1846 he began a new Norwegian industry: seal hunting near Jan Mayen Island,

FIG. 24.   SVEND FOYN (1809–94)

Foyn observed, then rejected, Roys's rocket-harpoon methods in favor of his own whaling gun, which revolutionized the whaling industry. He did, however, borrow heavily from Roys's mechanized whaling concepts, refining and adapting them and earning himself the title "Father of Modern Whaling."

(Courtesy of Vestfold Fylkesmuseum, Tønsberg, Norway.)

north of Iceland. The industry continues to this day, somewhat
to the consternation and disapproval of conservationists. For
his sealing enterprise he constructed a specially designed ship,
which he commanded personally. Sealing brought him considerable wealth and many imitators throughout southern
Norway.

Other much more populous and prosperous nations, such
as Great Britain and Germany, also conducted extensive seal
hunting operations in the vicinity of Greenland, however, and
after fifteen years of hunting, Foyn concluded that the heyday
of sealing—and the times of substantial profit—had passed. He
again laid his wealth on the line to establish a second new
industry in his homeland. Naturally, it was whaling. At this
time Foyn was fifty-five years old, and being the richest citizen
of Tønsberg, he could well have retired and lived comfortably
and quietly on his means. It might logically be questioned why
he did not retire and why he once again choose to be a pioneer,
especially in a venture much more difficult than sealing had
been.

Arne Odd Johnsen provides the answers, explaining that
this unusual attitude was engrained in Foyn's work ethic. He
was a deeply religious man, which influenced him to lead a
sober, frugal, and very active life, establishing and expanding
business enterprises to generate profits for the benefit of his
budding nation and for the expansion of "God's kingdom on
earth." Unlike the so-called robber barons of America who
were amassing immense personal fortunes about this same
time, Foyn appears to have been motivated more by the spirit of
expansionism than by profit, much the same as the Japanese
are today. Remember too that he was a puritanical capitalist
and entrepreneur in a strict Lutheran country. There were
other early industrial/religious enterprisers in Norway during
this period, and two centuries earlier this type of person had
contributed much to the development of early capitalism in
Western Europe. Old-style whaling, for instance—as it was
practiced by the Dutch, Germans, and Britons in the seventeenth and eighteenth centuries—had operated more or less

under these influences, and a century later whaling flourished under stern Quaker shipowners on Nantucket in America. Herman Melville takes note of this in *Moby-Dick*. The puritanical entrepreneur appeared at a somewhat later time in Norway because of her backwardness in relation to her stronger neighbors. But more than any of his contemporaries, Foyn successfully applied the techniques of the Industrial Revolution to whaling, transforming it into a modern, capital-intensive industry.[4]

Just as he originally had done in his sealing venture, Foyn had a whaleship built to his own specifications. She was the first whale catcher with mechanical propulsion. He christened her *Spes et Fides* ("Hope and Faith"), and as Thomas Roys had done, he set out after the big fin whales that his European forefathers had considered too large to catch. During 1864 Foyn collected as much knowledge as he could about these cetaceans off the coast of Norway. At first he worked the coast of northern Norway—the province of Finnmark—where in the summer, fin whales were often numerous. Foyn acted as both skipper and gunner in *Spes et Fides*. Like Roys, he encountered personal dangers in the course of his experiments and was also almost killed. Several of his guns exploded, and on one occasion, while in the process of shooting a whale, the trailing harpoon line twisted itself around his leg and he was hurtled overboard. Fortunately the plucky Foyn was able to free himself and to swim back to his ship.

At first Foyn utilized the standard guns of the Greenland whale fishery, save that his shells were somewhat heavier than those previously used. His first innovation, however, was his use of *Spes et Fides* itself in pursuing the whales, for he knew that the fragile standard whaleboats were no match for leviathans in a flurry. This first season was for the most part a time of learning. Foyn soon realized though that the traditional tools which he had aboard were too weak and had to be reworked and strengthened and redesigned to match the awesome power of the rorqual whales, previously untouched by the blubber hunters. Like his competitor Roys, he too was plagued by the fact that these whales tended to settle to the bottom after death. And Foyn was none too pleased that he had only three whales—and a portion of a fourth—to show for the season's efforts.[5]

In 1865 Foyn did not whale. In order to cover his financial losses of the previous season he returned to his old trade of sealing with his three ships near Jan Mayen Island east of Iceland. Again this effort was very profitable. For the remainder of the year Foyn worked continuously at improving his inadequate whaling equipment. In February 1866, he again cleared on a seal-catching expedition, but this campaign was a failure. He returned home and stayed only a month, steaming off on June 10 from Tønsberg—bound with a fourteen-man crew for Iceland in *Spes et Fides,* with a brig, *Haabet* (Hope), trailing behind, crammed to the gunwales with coal and other supplies that would be scarce in Iceland. The purpose of this voyage was to study firsthand the methods of Roys and Lilliendahl. He had contacted the two Americans previously—in the winter of 1865—when they had offered to sell him some of their patented devices. Unquestionably their novel ideas had piqued the old Norwegian's curiosity.

Svend Foyn recorded his impressions during his visit to Iceland in a daily journal of his whaling voyages and experiments, detailing his difficulties and repeating his fervent prayers to the Lord to grant him help in this new and risky enterprise. Despondency and jubilation alternate in this human chronicle, in which Foyn wrestled with his God like Jacob did with the Angel at Pniel. It ranks as one of the most interesting documents to reflect the thinking of a Puritan capitalist.

According to his journal entries, Foyn arrived at Nordurfjördur on the east coast of Iceland on July 1, 1866. Seven days passed before he found one of the American whaling steamers, either *Staperaider* or *Vigilant,* with a leviathan in tow. He goes on to describe the American activities in meticulous detail:

Competition Arrives

Monday, 8 July [1866]. The wind SWW and NNW, strong. Sailed and steamed northward to Langnaess Bay. Did not see whale. May God be merciful to us. In the afternoon [we] found in Langnaess Bay an American steamer which had caught a fin whale. The steamer went into Funnafjord, anchored, and flensed the whale. We accompanied him in order to observe. He had started to cut in at sea but stopped because there was too much swell. The Americans are whaling with three boats; these are 33 feet long, presumably 7 feet wide, have 7 men each, an iron capstan at one third of the length from the bow, whence a line descends through the bottom of the boat. Likewise at one third of the length from the stern there is a leeboard [keel] 18 inches deep and 2 feet broad, which is drawn up with an iron rod of one half inch from the after end and has a line in its front part. A watertight box for containing the line is fore in the boat. The harpoon to which the line is spliced is fired from an iron tube, placed on the shoulder, and is driven by a rocket ignited by a pistol. In the forepart of the rocket there is an explosive shell fired by the rocket when this is burnt out. The line is 3¾ or 3½ inch manila rope, 300 fathoms long. The leading part [of the harpoon line] lies likewise coiled up in the box in the hold of the bow, [and] in a box somewhat behind the center of the boat lest the line would be fouled. When the harpoon is fast and the whale is dead or has sunk, the line is reeved through a pulley in the top of the mast which hangs from a frame filled with rubber ropes, 16 rubber strings of 5/4 inch in circumference, each string 3½ [long]. By these means the line resisted the rolling [of the ship]. On the main mast he [Roys] had 3 tackles of 4½ inch manila rope, one double pulley below and 3 single pulleys at the top. From there a warp ran to the foremast. . . .

The railing was taken away 1½ foot from the deck. He drew the blubber from the whale in strips 6 inches broad. He also took the lips by cutting along the jaw bone; this he discarded; he hoisted the upper part of the head on the deck and there he removed the baleen. He said it was best to boil the blubber immediately. He took the fat of the intestines. On the middle pulley there was a loop on which to splice ropes or to haul away at a great angle.

Because we believed we had seen all there was to be seen we left [after one day and night], with good weather and smooth sea. We saw several whales but could not come near enough. So we cruised in vain from one o'clock in the morning on 10 July during the whole day. The whales had been frightened by the people in the American ships owing to extensive hunting and there was no harbor within 16 miles distance. I thought our prospects for a catch were bad, so we loaded coal from the *Haabet* and decided to steam to the Lofotes [north Norway] for God's sake. We fixed the venue at Stokmarknaess. I truly believe that it would be better to have a whaleboat with the *Spes et Fides,* so that there would be two chances to fasten to a whale. Having no rocket harpoon I believe that in such a big boat one can place a harpoon gun forward with 3¼ inch line 400 or 300 fathom [long] and a dart gun on each side upon high pivots. Perhaps this arrangement would be as good.

The harpoon and the dart must be fired at the same time. The transport [ship] always remains necessary for the provision of coal, barrels, and tryworks and for flensing the whale. The steamships and whaleboats must have a light color under water. The whale caught by the Americans was a fin whale as meagre as that off Vardø [north Norway] but nevertheless he said that this kind was the best one there.[6]

And so we see how Roys and Lilliendahl came to influence Foyn to some degree. Even before this encounter, however, Foyn had independently been seeking the solutions to much the same problems that Roys, Lilliendahl, and their imitators had sought to solve by perfecting a reliable, cheap, and trouble-free whaling projectile. By the time that he arrived in Iceland, Foyn had already established the basics of his whaling gun and was more in favor of a rifled gun bore and shell than of any other form of harpoon launcher. While Captain Foyn found these rockets to be a most interesting departure from other means of capturing and killing whales, he believed them to be impractical. In 1868 he wrote that, "These . . . [rockets], however, appear to me to be not efficient and too expensive for my enterprise."[7] After observing the rockets firsthand, he judged them to be primitive in comparison with his own weapons, and he left Iceland for Norway that very day to experiment with Swedish and German gun-fired shells. In the final analysis, Foyn's appraisal proved entirely correct. The American rockets remained imperfect as well as costly and needed considerable refinement before they could be of any practical use.

Upon reaching Finnmark in northern Norway, Foyn did not meet with success either. He had left Iceland because the whales there were too fast for his equipment. At Norway, however, he found very few whales. Then, two of his guns exploded, and a man was injured. After steaming all the way to Russia and finding nothing, he returned to Tønsberg, where he arrived in early August. Nevertheless, the season of 1866 probably taught him a great deal—especially his encounter with the Americans at Iceland. Although Foyn discarded the concept of the rocket-harpoon, other devices which the Americans had developed sparked his interest and were incorporated eventually into his own methods. He decided, for instance, to use the same 3¾-inch manila harpoon lines that Roys and Lilliendahl utilized. Then he fitted *Spes et Fides* with a steam winch—similar to those on board the Americans' steamers—to raise dead whales. He patented his version in Norway in 1875.[8] Foyn was also very impressed with Roys's whale compensator, or "rubber rope" as he called it, which he described and even sketched in his journal. Roys wisely had patented this invention in Norway on November 17, 1866, for five years, but when the patent expired, Foyn incorporated it into his own equipment. He received a patent himself for a similar device in 1873 for a period of ten years. True to character, however, in the description that accompanied his request Foyn honestly admitted that it was not his invention. Foyn also adopted rowed-type whaleboats during his experiments off Finnmark, but later abandoned them for a gun mounted right on the bow of the steamer. He had paid close attention to the Yankees' flensing methods and learned that oil had to be tried from the blubber immediately after the animal was caught to insure the best quality oil.[9] This imitation and subsequent adaptation of the American whaling methods into modern technology by Foyn and his successors was the real legacy of Roys's work.

Unquestionably then the meeting between Foyn and the Americans was decisive for the future of the whaling industry. The Norwegian was most impressed with the Americans' taking of fin and blue whales, an untapped resource. Before this Foyn had been uncertain which direction he should take, but after the day when he and the Americans parted ways, Foyn followed his own course to success. His resources apparently strained, Foyn sailed again in the spring of 1867 as skipper of a sealer, *Eliezer*, and filled his ship. His other two sealers were similarly lucky, so he now had sufficient funds to continue with his whaling experiments. Later that year he caught three whales but lost another three, and with them a lot of money. He solved most of the urgent technical problems, however, in 1867 and 1868, improving his equipment, which had repeatedly been shown to be too weak when matched against powerful rorquals. Previously Foyn had fitted *Spes et Fides* with a battery of guns which fired harpoons and bombs separately, but in 1868 he developed a gun-fired harpoon that contained a grenade charge. In that year he killed thirty whales—salvaging twenty-three of them and receiving part of the other seven, which had stranded. This was the success he had worked for, and that year is hailed as the birth date of modern whaling. It was also the first in a series of very successful seasons for Foyn. Eventually his harpoon was to become the standard of the industry, and—with slight modifications—it continues to be used from the bows of whale catchers to this day, to the sorrow of the leviathans.

Toward the twilight of his long and admirable career, Svend Foyn paid indirect homage to his unsuccessful, yet influential, predecessors. In 1892, two years before he died, Foyn wrote: "For the achievement of my purpose I needed three years, winter and summer. The work of the first two years was almost hopeless but finally I beat four comrades, an American, a Scot, a Belgian and a Dane who did not succeed in

catching whales in a profitable way and had to stop."[10] These
comrades must have been Thomas Roys, Captain Ridge (the
Englishman who commanded *Staperaider* for Lilliendahl in
1867 and who in 1868 skippered *Columbia* for the Tay Whale
Fishing Company off Iceland and Greenland),[11] the Dutchman C. J. Bottemanne, and the Dane O. C. Hammer.

Naturally the question arises of why Foyn triumphed
where Roys had failed. The answer has much to do with good
fortune perhaps, but is related to character as well. The
similarities between the two men are interesting. Both devoted
their thoughts, energies, and wealth entirely toward the improvement of whaling and risked their lives, pleasure, and
capital in the pursuit of this business. Both of their wives felt
neglected and left them. Roys's second wife, Marie, eventually
eloped with his former first mate, and Foyn's first spouse, a
local Tønsberg teacher, separated from him on friendly terms
in 1842, after three lonely years of marriage. Six months later
Foyn wed a more self-sacrificing woman.[12]

Yet there were important differences between them too.
Foyn weathered his numerous difficulties because he did everything himself and delegated nothing. With an iron exac-
titude, he checked all of his equipment time and time again,
thus preventing many unpleasant surprises and adversities.
There is the impression that Roys sometimes failed in this
regard and relied too much on other people, specifically his half
brothers, some of whom were given to waste and neglect.
Though Roys was about half a dozen years younger than Foyn,
he seems to have retained less energy, for the Norwegian's
enormous vitality could hardly be matched by any person his
age. Remember, Capt. O. C. Hammer called Thomas an able
and amiable man, but added that he was "almost too old."[13]
Also, Foyn had the advantage of commanding homogenous
crews from Tønsberg and environs whom he knew personally
and had carefully selected. These men were all inexperienced
in whaling, but he drilled them well. As we have seen, Roys's
crews were polyglot bunches. They did not understand each
other well and did not always cooperate with each other. Then

too, the Americans among them generally were the experienced whalers and conveyed a feeling of superiority. Possibly these factors—and a little luck—were the components of Foyn's success.

The second pioneer in the transitional phase between old and modern whaling was Roys's imitator Captain-Lieutenant Otto C. Hammer of the Danish Navy. Born in 1822, he had fought bravely in the first and second wars against Prussia in 1848-50 and 1864, when he was taken prisoner. After the second war, Denmark lost the duchies of Schleswig-Holstein to the Prussians, but a group of patriotic Danes—civil servants and businessmen— resolved to find something to compensate to an extent for this painful loss of territory and national pride. They decided to expand the fisheries industry because a small nation like Denmark could recoup its losses only at sea. After the war, Hammer resigned his naval commission, and—with a patriotic desire to create a Danish fishing industry based in Iceland—he founded Det danske Fiskeriselskab (The Danish Fishery Company) in December 1865 with a capital of 180,000 Danish rix-dollars. Hammer became the general manager and the driving force of the new enterprise, which was essentially a nonprofit patriotic endeavor. In fact, the prospectus carefully informed potential shareholders that they should not expect to receive a dividend during the first year. The company proposed to catch cod off Iceland, seals off Greenland, and whales near Iceland using the Roys's methods. Investor interest ran high, for the following year another 70,000 rix-dollars was poured into the enterprise.

From the beginning, whaling became the main thrust of The Danish Fishery Company, for that enterprise seemed to offer the greatest promise of profit. Hammer entered into a contract with Thomas Roys, who agreed to help the Danes and to instruct them in his methods. Hammer, it should be pointed out, was no stranger to rocketry, for he had surely seen modified versions of Congreve war rockets himself during the Schleswig Wars. He was particularly intrigued by Roys's and Lilliendahl's curious adaptation of these devices to whaling.

Iceland was an ideal base for the Danes because only the Americans were whaling there. The Danes had chosen this barren, stormy island far to the north because there were many rorquals and because there are several good harbors there for processing the whales, in contrast to other northern coasts adjoining seas abounding with whales. Iceland was also nearer to ports with repair facilities, supplies, and markets for whale products than other whaling grounds, such as Portugal, the Azores, the coast of Brazil, or elsewhere off South America. The waters surrounding the island had been frequented in the past by codfishermen—poor Icelanders in rowboats, French and British companies in fine sailing ships—but by very few Danes, who had preferred to work their nets nearer home, off their own coasts and the Faeroe Islands.[14] Hammer's company bought six ships: a 297-ton steamer, which was renamed *Thomas Roys,* for Hammer expected technical and practical advice from that gentleman, whom he intended to imitate; the small steamer *Vikingen* (displacement unknown); the schooners *Garder* (137 tons), *Emmanuel* (displacement unknown), and *Skallagrimur* (147 tons); and the yacht *Gudrun* (48 tons).

Most probably the Americans realized that it would be useless to oppose Hammer's competition, for the Danish government in Iceland—on whose good will they were dependent—would back Hammer if a controversy arose. Perhaps also they welcomed the new Danish firm as a potential customer for their mass-produced, expensive rockets. It was agreed that Captain Tvede, who commanded one of the Danish company's ships, would first spend a season with the Americans to learn their catching and processing techniques. They, in turn, were to give the Danes all the information and help they needed to get started. John Roys and three other American whalers—gunners and boatsteerers—would sail in Hammer's own ship and would teach his men all about whaling. In return, Hammer was committed to giving them a fifth share in the voyage and to purchasing a large quantity of Roys's rockets.

Tvede has been mentioned before as one of Roys's foremen

at the Seydisfjördur station during the season of 1866, and we have quoted from his critical report of the Yankee enterprise.[15] He pointed out correctly that the rockets left much to be desired, owing to a lack of careful inspection; that the pressure

FIG. 25.   CAPT. OTTO C. HAMMER (1822–92)

A former Danish naval officer, Hammer founded The Danish Fishery Company in 1865. He contracted with Thomas Roys and his half brothers to provide equipment and technical advice for a Danish whaling operation at Iceland, but later became disenchanted with his American advisors, accusing them of incompetence and suspecting sabotage. Hammer attempted to operate on his own, utilizing rocket-harpoons, but was finally forced to liquidate his firm in 1871, after suffering continual losses.

(Courtesy of The Royal Library, Copenhagen, Denmark.)

cookers and hydraulic presses in the steamers did not operate properly; that the bone crusher was faulty; that the main boiler at the shore station was too old and leaky; and, finally, that the whale compensator was not practical, at least as Roys had designed it.[16] All of his devastating criticism was valid and these defects were the reason for the undoing of the American effort.

Hammer may have christened his steamer *Thomas Roys,* but he soon began to wonder about the faulty rockets the old gent had supplied to him and about the lack of whales in the areas he was directed to—once even questioning in his diary why he had ever given the ship that name. Toward the end of April 1866, Hammer arrived in *Thomas Roys* at Hafnarfjördur, near the capital of Reykjavik on the southwest coast of Iceland. Meanwhile, John Roys and three of his men had come aboard Hammer's ship, but soon afterward the Dane became disillusioned by their queer behavior. In the first place, John was often seasick—a bad omen. Then, we get the impression that John (to the great embarrassment of his half brother Thomas) was the least talented of the family, which was probably the reason that the Americans so readily permitted him to work with the Danes. Hammer said that he was a braggart and made the Danes feel they were only neophytes at whaling—which enraged them, since John was a poor sailor himself and had always worked under the close supervision of his older brother. According to Hammer, he also lacked initiative, shirked responsibility, and neglected his duty. The other Americans with him were said to have had no experience at firing the rockets, yet John left the first shots to them.

And when Hammer wanted to chase fin whales and humpbacks on the west coast of Iceland, John Roys told him that only blue whales were worth pursuing, to Hammer's great annoyance and disbelief. Roys should at least have told him sooner, he thought. The cruise was a loss, so Hammer returned to his base at Hafnarfjördur, then set out for the east coast to meet with Thomas Roys. Owing to the carelessness of his American "instructors," he lost two whaleboats in a gale and was forced to return to the shore station for replacements. Realizing the difficulty of the situation, John Roys and his companions took this opportunity to cancel their contracts with the Danes and (to their mutual relief) left the ship, having accomplished nothing.

It is just as well that events turned out as they did, for toward the end Hammer began to suspect Roys and his men of deliberate sabotage. Shamed, these men were banished from the Icelandic whaling enterprises, both at the new Danish station at Hafnarfjördur, which Thomas Roys had helped build, and at the original American site at Seydisfjördur. Throughout the 1866 season—even after the Americans had left his employ—Hammer complained almost daily in his diary about their indifference in setting up and checking the complicated whaling gear and in preparing the rockets, on which all the sights had been set incorrectly, despite John Roys's assurances. Hammer remarked bitterly that "this carelessness and unreliability in all seems to be a basic feature of these Americans. They lack all sense for theory and have only a superficial practical ability."[17]

There is the possibility that Hammer's criticism was exaggerated. After all, he most probably had the typical European attitude of that day toward the pragmatic Americans, or they could simply have served as handy scapegoats for his own failures during the 1866 season. The truth, as always, probably lies somewhere in between. So great was the division though, that Hammer and his crew even suspected the Americans of purposely supplying him with bad rockets. As we have seen previously, however, Hammer's own man, Captain Tvede, observed similar difficulties with the weapons at Thomas Roys's land station. Even Roys's whale compensator, for which he had paid £100, gave Hammer trouble—five of its straps snapping while his men were attempting to raise a whale.[18]

Eventually, as he gained experience himself, Hammer attempted to improve upon Thomas Roys's equipment. He eliminated, for instance, the complicated system Roys had devised for handling the whale line aboard the catching boats, returning to the simpler method that had been used by old-time whalers. It was most difficult, as we have seen, to take a second shot at a whale using the Roys's method. To improve the effectiveness of the rocket-harpoon, Hammer had it mounted on a swivel or pivot at the bow. This made it much easier to take aim at a fleeing whale from a bouncing boat than with Roys's way of firing the weapons from the shoulder.[19]

Since Roys had not complied with a condition in his Danish patent requiring him to establish a factory for the manufacture of his rocket-harpoons, the patent expired in 1866. Therefore by mid-season Hammer was able to order weapons based on Roys's model—combined with others—from the navy yard in Copenhagen, through his old connections. Next, he turned to Tivoli Garden's noted pyrotechnist Gaetano Amici, an Italian by birth who had migrated from Rome to Copenhagen many years before to conduct the fireworks displays at that famous amusement park. Amici continued to work at the problem while Hammer was in Iceland, and over the winter of 1866-67, he became completely disillusioned with Roys's rocket idea. He developed his own shell-type harpoon gun, which injected poisonous gas into the animal upon impact, and he patented this device on September 3, 1867. It is possible that Svend Foyn borrowed some of its principles for his own successful gun.[20] Oddly enough, Thomas Roys had indirectly fostered yet another imitator in Amici.

While at his shore station at Hafnarfjördur during the 1866 season, Hammer received word that conditions for whaling were particularly favorable on the southeast coast of Iceland. There, he laid out a second station at Djupivogur in the Beru-fjördur, not far from Roys's own base in the Seydisfjördur. Without delay Hammer visited his neighbor, for he wanted to vent his anger about his alleged mistreatment by John Roys and his assistants and possibly to exchange experiences with "the old, practical gentleman," as he called Roys. Hammer arrived in Seydisfjördur on September 26 and renewed his acquaintance with Roys, whom he had met previously in Dundee in the spring of 1866.[21] Roys was most friendly and ready to settle differences. He immediately proposed that they test the rockets he had supplied the Danes against those made by Amici and lastly against those which had been reworked at the Seydisfjördur land station. In his diary Hammer recorded that the Danish rockets were the strongest—in Roys's opinion too strong—while the reworked American units were much better than those Roys originally had sold him for six pounds each.

Roys admitted that the rockets he had supplied to Hammer were weaker, then courteously escorted his visitor around his

FIG. 26. WHALING STEAMER *THOMAS ROYS*

The *Thomas Roys* (297 tons) was the principal ship in the Danish-backed whaling venture of Capt. O. C. Hammer. In the foreground is a whaleboat crew utilizing the rocket-harpoon. Woodcut after a drawing by Carl Neumann (1833–1891) in *Illustreret Tidende,* February 25, 1866.

(Courtesy of Kendall Whaling Museum, Sharon, Mass.)

spacious station. Hammer, the exacting ex–naval officer, was not too pleased with the housekeeping. He did take note of the newly invented and more efficient way of extracting oil from whale bones. "These parts," he observed, "are collected in a big cooking vessel and the oil is pressed out by steam, which enters by a tube in the bottom of the tank."[22]

Roys then asked Hammer what he thought of his whale-boats and their outfits. The Dane responded that they were too big and too heavy, that he intended to replace them. The hand winch and the arrangement of the harpoon line were ineffi-cient, in his opinion, so he had had them taken out of his own boats. Roys was quick to admit that he too realized that this innovation was a failure, but he was taken aback to hear that Hammer had adapted his guns to swivel mountings at the bows of his whaleboats rather than shooting them from the shoulder. Lilliendahl had done the same thing, but the Roys brothers refused to install them in their boats.[23] After this meeting the paths of Hammer and Roys did not cross again.

Shortly thereafter, Hammer brought his first whale into his station at Djupivogur, without the Americans' help but using their methods entirely. With his steamer *Thomas Roys* he took only six whales and part of one or two that were driven ashore—a paltry 250 barrels in all—compared to some thirty or forty animals he had killed and lost through inexperience. For all of his energy and good qualities, Hammer lacked the practi-cal knowledge of seasoned whalers like Roys—which would have been a deciding factor in this instance between success and failure. The rockets also contributed significantly to this poor showing.[24] Ens. L. Loizillon, a young Frenchman who was an observer aboard *Thomas Roys*, confirms this: "The [rocket] apparatus . . . employed on board the *Thomas Roys* did not give good results. In some cases the harpoon penetrated and the rocket did not burst; in others, the rockets burst and the harpoon did not penetrate. Fourteen whales were struck during my stay on board, and none were taken; it was generally attributed to the bad quality of the rockets."[25]

The 1867 season was a disappointment too; only fourteen

whales were captured. For the 1868 effort, Hammer was delighted to engage Capt. Christian Klitgaard, who had skippered the whaling steamer *Vigilant* for G. A. Lilliendahl. But Klitgaard backed out at the last minute, complaining that, ". . . when I found we were not allowed to use American rockets, I refused the job, as the Danish rockets were in my opinion not much good." Perhaps he is referring to a new type of rocket that Hammer had made up in Copenhagen, which utilized gunpowder and dynamite, "just invented by a Swede named Nobel." The new explosive, it was boasted, was fourteen times more powerful than gunpowder. Only half a dozen spouters were saved in the 1868 season. The following year *Thomas Roys* was partially wrecked, so only one whale was caught. By 1870 she was repaired, and Hammer decided to turn his hand to seal hunting, but during the voyage out the old, weather-beaten ship began to leak terribly, and she was eventually lost when she arrived at Iceland.[26] For all of his criticism of the Americans and his intellectual superiority to them, Hammer had little to show for his own efforts.

Toward the end of February 1871, after the loss of thousands of rix-dollars, it was decided at a general meeting to liquidate The Danish Fishery Company. Hammer's reputation appears not to have suffered by his failures, however. His nephew and biographer, R. Hammer, mentions that in 1871 he was invited to lecture in Moscow on whaling with the rocket-harpoon. He accepted, and the talk was well received. Hammer was likewise flattered by a visit at Copenhagen from none other than Svend Foyn in 1868.

Since the Danes had made few basic improvements in the American methods, they, in essence, merely replaced Roys and Lilliendahl, and it was through them that Foyn came to adopt many American ideas. Foyn already had established an international reputation after his own highly successful 1868 season, and no doubt the conscientious Norwegian pioneer hoped to learn even more from the Danes. He listened carefully to Hammer describe his lack of success, then Foyn suggested that the Danes mount his own harpoon guns on the bows of their steamers, as he had done aboard *Spes et Fides*. Hammer said, however, that to do that he would have to rearrange his equipment completely, which he could ill afford to do. During the visit, Foyn also spoke with the fireworks maker Amici. There was little the Italian could tell him, though, and it is more likely that the Danes could have learned more from the successful Norwegian whaler than he from them. In this respect, the hope expressed by the Danish newspaper *Faedrelandet* that Foyn's visit would be fruitful to both parties was not fulfilled.[27]

Actually, it is no wonder that The Danish Fishery Company failed. After all, Roys and Lilliendahl—who had had far more experience and technical knowledge than the Danes—had both given up, so it stands to reason that the Danes had had little chance at such a radical venture as modern whaling. Again it was proven that rockets were not the solution, for the future of modern whaling hinged on the heavy harpoon gun and not on the American or Danish methods.

The Dutch had been the leading whaling nation during the seventeenth and eighteenth centuries, but they had abandoned the industry almost completely thereafter because of foreign competition from the Basques and the English, coupled with the overexploitation of Greenland whales, the main object of their quest. Among their successors Britain then became the leader, which provoked strong patriotic feelings among the proud Dutch. There had been an abortive attempt at the beginning of the nineteenth century to revive the halcyon days of Dutch Arctic whaling, but it was for naught. It fell therefore to Capt. Caspar Josephus Bottemanne—who was literally blown upon the American whaling operations at Iceland—to make still another attempt at reviving their past glory.

Bottemanne was born in Dordrecht, an old Dutch seaport, in 1829. In time, he became a sailor in the Dutch merchant navy, and during his service he came to observe and admire the whalers who operated in the East Indies—probably Yankees chasing down volatile, oil-rich sperms. These cruises engendered an interest in whales and whaling. Bottemanne's big chance to see whalers work firsthand came soon after he received his mate's certificate. He signed on as skipper of the schooner *Jan en Albert,* taking her up to Iceland in 1865 with a load of coal consigned for the Roys-Lilliendahl station in Seydisfjördur. As we have already noted, a wild tempest blew *Jan en Albert* ashore. She was sold at auction to Roys and his company on the following day, and Bottemanne and his crew were taken in at the American station. Here he became fired with ambition to learn all he could about Roys's new method of whaling. He offered his services in a high or low position, and was rewarded with a mate's berth in one of the steamers. He regularly went whaling. You will recall that *Jan en Albert* had been salvaged by Roys and his men without difficulty, and was then taken to Scotland, where she was fitted with the engine of the wrecked *Visionary* and renamed *Sileno.* Bottemanne returned with Roys to Dundee, Scotland, in *Reindeer* late that fall. So a pure accident produced yet another rival for Roys, for Bottemanne soon was dreaming of revitalizing a Dutch whaling trade based on the Americans' new methods.[28]

In the spring of 1866 Bottemanne returned to Iceland in company with G. A. Lilliendahl, as a passenger in the steamer *Staperaider.* He worked at the whaling station in Seydisfjördur for the season. The Danish observer Captain Tvede, it will be remembered, was also there at that time, and he mentions in his report that even then Bottemanne was enthusiastic about the idea of a Dutch whaling company. Another opportunity came when the brothers Roys withdrew from the venture toward the close of the 1866 season. Bottemanne approached Lilliendahl—who was continuing the venture alone after Roys's withdrawal—anticipating a good chance for promotion, and he decided to postpone the establishment of his own company until he had had another year's experience at whaling to his credit. During the 1867 effort he became the manager of the land station and had permission to whale in *Sileno.*

With three years' practical experience to his credit, it could be said that Bottemanne had received an education in whaling in all its aspects. To promote the idea of a great Dutch whaling revival, he began to publish a few articles in newspapers. He even wrote an informative piece for the new Dutch journal *De Economist*, touching on the history of early Dutch and foreign whaling, various kinds of cetacea, and Roys's new methods,

FIG. 27.   CAPT. C. J. BOTTEMANNE (1829–1906)

Bottemanne, who was Dutch, worked at the whaling station in Seydisfjördur, Iceland. When the Roys brothers withdrew from there in 1866, Bottemanne became manager of the land station under Roys's former partner, G. A. Lilliendahl. Finally, having gained enough experience, he founded his own firm in 1869 and attempted to imitate Roys and Lilliendahl exactly. He too failed and had closed his own company by 1872.

(From the private collection of Cornelis de Jong.)

with a commentary on his own experiences in the Americans' service. Finally, in 1869 he founded his dream, *De Nederlandsche Walvischvaart, N.V.* (The Netherlands Whaling Company, Ltd.), supported by a handful of investors from Rotterdam. Bottemanne's company purchased an auxiliary steamer then under construction in the yard of W. B. Hornby Willington at Newcastle, England, and christened her *Noordkaper*—the old Dutch name for the right whale, which had been the first species to be caught off the North Cape of

Norway. Bottemanne, of course, became general manager of
the firm, with additional duties as captain of its steamer.

When he finally reached the whaling grounds off Iceland,
Bottemanne, unlike Captain Hammer, followed Roys and Lilliendahl's methods closely. He used their rockets as patented
and manufactured in Britain, with the gunners firing them
from their right shoulders while standing in the bows or
rowing-type whaleboats. He did not use swivel-mounted guns,
as did the Danes. Bottemanne worked off the east coast of
Iceland during the 1870, 1871, and 1872 whaling seasons. He
wrote extensive reports on the first two cruises, based on his
ship's journals, and he laid these before a general meeting of
the stockholders. The catch of 1870 was embarrassingly
meagre: one small fin whale. This poor showing was due to a
general lack of experience, since only Captain Bottemanne
had had any practical knowledge of whaling and the rockets.
Two whales were killed but lost. In 1871 the catch was better—
thirteen whales in all—but another thirteen were lost. Bottemanne was satisfied now with the rocket-harpoon and was
crowing that his efforts looked more promising. No report of
the 1872 season can be found, however. Perhaps it was never
written, for after three unfavorable seasons, the fate of Bottemanne's enterprise was sealed. Toward the conclusion of
1872 *Noordkaper* was sold and the company was dissolved.
This ended any viable tries to revive Dutch whaling until
1946.[29]

Noordkaper was about 200 tons and was fitted with a
seventy-horsepower steam engine and a screw-type propeller.
Schooner-rigged, she was outfitted with three traditional
whaleboats, each manned by seven hands. She had a steam
winch for working the whale alongside and for taking in pieces
of blubber. There was a furnace on deck for trying out, but
Bottemanne felt that a land station would be more desirable,
for it would enable the steamer to function more efficiently in
the variable Icelandic weather. Processing the animals ashore
seems to have been an important step in the transition toward
modern whaling.

For the 1871 season Bottemanne hired experienced Shetland Islanders, who had sailed annually in British sealing and whaling expeditions to the Arctic. Naturally, he had a much higher regard for these whalemen than for the greenhorn Dutchmen who had shipped on the year before. Financial considerations precluded the establishment of his own base, but Bottemanne was fortunate enough to acquire Lilliendahl's abandoned station in Seydisfjördur. Among the equipment scattered about there, he found a machine he described as a *klauwduiker* ("clawdiver"), which had never been used. Perhaps this was Roys's whale-raiser. Lilliendahl had probably left it behind. Anyway, Bottemanne appropriated the contraption, and in 1871 he raised three whales with it. He was so satisfied with the device that he bought it for his company. It consisted mainly of a fairly heavy oblong iron box with claws at the bottom. If a whale sank after being harpooned, the clawdiver was sent down the harpoon line by gravity, and upon reaching the bottom, the claws seized the harpoon shaft protruding from the dead whale. At that point, the steam capstan in *Noordkaper* was engaged and slowly drew the whale to the surface.[30] From the 1867 season on, O. C. Hammer was also using a special apparatus for raising whales which he called a *plumpeharpun,* or "plumping harpoon."[31] It employed a heavily weighted harpoon, which was released above the sunken whale and was intended to fasten a line to it.

The failure of the Dutch venture in 1872 capped the transitional phase of modern whaling as far as Thomas Roys's methods were concerned, for in 1883, when the industry resumed operations off Iceland, Foyn's methods were in vogue, and Roys's work and that of his imitators were only memories. Curiously, one of Bottemanne's rockets survives in the Zuiderzee Museum at Enkhuizen, Netherlands. Other than references to it in a few dusty journals, Bottemanne's work had been forgotten, and it was rediscovered only in 1965.

The Norwegian whaling historian Arne Odd Johnsen has researched a comparison between the rocket method of whaling—as practiced by Roys, Lilliendahl, Hammer, and Bottemanne off Iceland—and Svend Foyn's harpoon gun, employed off northern Norway. Johnsen constructed a table to prove that Roys's method gave results and could have led to a profitable whale fishery, and these data are reproduced

RESULTS OF HUNT FOR WHALES USING MODERN METHODS
(1865 - 1872)

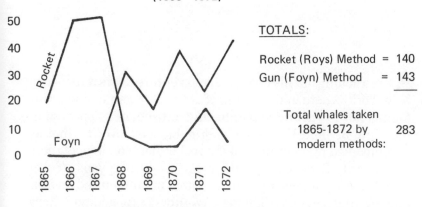

TOTALS:

Rocket (Roys) Method = 140
Gun (Foyn) Method   = 143

Total whales taken
1865-1872 by   283
modern methods:

FIG. 28. RESULTS OF HUNT FOR WHALES
USING MODERN METHODS

graphically below. Note that in 1868 the tide turned; Foyn, with the invention of his harpoon gun, had opened the way to successful whaling, and the rocket method was abandoned a few years later by Roys's struggling followers.[32]

12

One Last Try

AFTER selling out his failed Iceland venture, Roys returned to New York, where in the spring of 1867 he began manufacturing his novel whaling apparatus. Advertisements appeared in the New Bedford *Whalemen's Shipping List* over his name, accompanied by a woodcut of the rocket-harpoon in operation. He offered "Rocket harpoons, rocket shell harpoons, rocket shells, and whale raising compensators manufactured and for sale by the patentee, Thomas W. Roys." In addition Roys boasted that "forty-three Sulphurs, seven Humpbacks and two Finbacks were taken last season, at Iceland; yielding 3,000 barrels; one of the Finbacks making sixty, and the other eighty barrels. No order can be accepted without sixty days time to execute it. Address 211 East Thirty-Sixth Street, New York. There are no agents."[1]

Meanwhile, Roys's half brothers scattered far and wide. William Henry spent several years whaling off the coast of Alaska, returning home to Pultneyville from California in 1869, about the time that their father, Philander, died. Sam Roys purchased a farm in Nebraska and settled there.[2] John, who had left Iceland in disgrace, supposedly bought the cargo schooner *Union,* selling out in 1869 to a Captain Burgess. No further word of him can be found.[3] Andrew, on the other hand, drifted out to the West Coast, made a voyage to the Orient, then became one of the first settlers of David City, Nebraska, purchasing a homestead near there in 1870 or thereabouts. He is credited with having helped to establish the town, building a general store, and then being instrumental in securing a post office for the community. Later he moved from his farm into David City proper, where he became an undertaker. Andrew became a prominent resident, and a few senior citizens can still recall to this day his vivid sea stories. The last of the legendary Roys brothers, he passed away on June 18, 1932, at age ninety-one.[4]

After his brief attempt at manufacturing, Thomas Roys became restless. In December 1867 he raised $1,000 by selling another share (one sixth) of his three major patents to Albert M. Wickes and Edward B. Arnold of Troy, New York.[5] Seed money in hand, Roys boarded a ship at New York in December and sailed for San Francisco. On reaching California he planned "to go down the coast to kill whales and make further experiments to prevent the sinking of whales. For this purpose," he later recalled, "I had placed the harpoon on the point, making it much stronger, and when we began to fire at whales, it glanced [off] and flew up in the air, thus making it useless for that small voyage."[6]

Roys returned to San Francisco, improved the weapon, then headed north to British Columbia to continue his experiments. Just after his arrival in the early summer of 1868, he was joined there by a competing whaling company headed by James Dawson and a group of San Francisco men. The entire vicinity was filled with enthusiasm over the arrival of the whalers; and the Victoria *British Colonist* editorialized that: "Whale fishing in our waters has been too long neglected; and now that it will be shown what can be done, it is to be hoped that the business will be followed up thoroughly. There is plenty of room for more companies to operate."[7] Roys had hoped to utilize the rocket-harpoons extensively, but again he was plagued by minor problems. Working quickly, because the humpbacks would soon be migrating south, the defects were corrected, and it was soon predicted that "certain annihilation awaits any of those deep sea monsters. . . ."[8]

There is some conjecture that Roys began the 1868 season in the steamer *Holmes,* working in the Strait of Georgia between Vancouver Island and the mainland.[9] Later in July, however, he engaged the steamer *Emma,* which was owned by Joseph Sprott, an engineer and iron founder of Victoria. She was barely a year old.[10] Perhaps it was Sprott who helped Roys revise his rocket-harpoons at British Columbia. It also appears that Edward B. Arnold, who had purchased a share in the key Roys patents a year earlier, had joined him in British Columbia, along with a man named Meeker.[11] The initial trials during late July and into August were a failure. Once again the rocket-harpoons ricocheted off the surface of the water and did not penetrate the animals. It was all very exasperating, for they were encountering whales measuring sixty to eighty feet. But hopes ran high, and the editor of the *British Colonist* crowed that "when the rocket is remedied, fear need hardly be entertained of failure." Within the month, the rockets had indeed been improved. Roys sailed in *Emma* with eighteen men on September 5, and within a week they had taken two whales, yielding sixty-five and forty-five barrels respectively. Several more were wounded and lost but were later recovered. Perseverance had again paid off, for the rocket gun now worked perfectly.[12]

Emma returned to Victoria on October 6. She had lost three out of every four whales through lines and harpoons breaking. The weather was terrible too, characterized by dense fog; of the thirty-one days she had been out, only two and a half had been clear enough for whaling. Despite these troubles, community interest in the new industry ran high. On October 22 a meeting of Victoria merchants and businessmen was held at the store of Edgar Marvin. They agreed to actively support a whale fishery in local waters upon the opening of the following spring season. A company was formed with a capital of $10,000, and before the meeting adjourned, 82 out of the original 100 shares had been subscribed. Meanwhile, Roys was dispatched to Honolulu to engage competent hands for the new venture, the Victoria Whaling Adventurers' Company,

Fig. 29. Steamer *EMMA*

In 1868 Roys attempted one last try at rocket whaling. He chartered the small steamer *Emma* out of Victoria, British Columbia, on the west coast of Canada, finding backing from local businessmen. This venture also failed following the wreck of his second ship, the brig *Byzantium*, in 1871. *Emma* is pictured here as a towboat, ca. 1870, docked at Victoria.

(Photo courtesy of Maritime Museum of British Columbia, Victoria, B.C., Canada.)

Ltd. At Hawaii Roys gammed with every captain, mate, or whaleman he could buttonhole, extolling the advantages and conveniences of whaling out of Victoria. In three weeks he had signed on a party of experienced whalemen.[13]

Over the winter, rockets were being loaded in a warehouse at Clover Point, and the steamer *Emma* was fitted for an all-out assault on leviathans. After testing and loading his rocket-harpoons, Roys sailed on February 23, 1869, for Barkley Sound, on the western shore of Vancouver Island, to commence operations for the 1869 season. No doubt he had been encouraged by the success of his competitors, the Dawson Whaling Company, which had gathered over 10,000 gallons of "oil . . . beautifully clear and as good quality as any ever brought from the Arctic Ocean." Dawson and his people, incidentally, used traditional—and certain—methods, including bomb lances, which consisted of an explosive shell fired from a shoulder gun.[14]

This year Roys had outfitted *Emma* with two whaleboats, six rocket launchers, and a plentiful supply of rocket-harpoons of the most recent design. He intended to tow the dead whales ashore on Barkley Sound and to boil them out there. Recent arrivals at Victoria were reporting that several pods of whales had been seen sporting in the vicinity, so it was soon predicted that Captain Roys would succeed "in striking oil worth 60 cents per gallon." Hopes in Victoria were running high, with optimistic suggestions that this port would supplant Honolulu—then the center of the whaling industry. People reasoned that food and chandlery were cheaper in British Columbia, markets were closer for whale products, and, most important, there was a steady quantity of oil-rich sperm whales and sea elephants nearby. Whaling ships out of Honolulu often cruised six months in quest of a full cargo. Freight costs, communications by telegraph, and a steady supply of reasonably skilled labor accented the advantages of Victoria over Honolulu.[15] Responsibility fell heavily on Roys's shoulders to make these predictions come true.

Arriving at Dodger Cove, Barkley Sound, Roys began constructing a shore station. A house was erected and tryworks apparatus was set up ashore. The first whale shot was killed instantly, but the harpoon broke and the whale was lost. Bad iron was the cause. The animal was picked up later by coastal Indians, and they appropriated it for their own uses. The weather was terrible. The second whale shot also was killed immediately. After it had been towed about twelve miles, however, the animal was abandoned because of a heavy gale. By the end of March *Emma* had been out five times and had seen many whales, but she could not get near them, because of poor weather conditions. In April it was reported that she had two large whales in tow and that a third had been lost by the parting of a line. Still, bad weather kept *Emma* from whaling a good portion of the time.[16]

Roys turned his interests to the shore station next, and here he built a wharf 150 feet long at Dodger Cove, erecting more buildings and installing furnaces, try-pots, and the like. Disgusted with the weather, he set out for Deep Bay, above Nanaimo—his old whaling ground—until conditions became more settled. It was at Deep Bay, incidentally, that he had killed several whales the previous summer. But this year he saw only two spouters, both of which evaded him. At Nanaimo Roys learned that a large pod of leviathans had been sighted several hundred miles to the north, spouting in Knight Inlet off the mainland and quite close inshore. The waters in that vicinity had never been surveyed fully, but he was lucky enough to get piloting directions from the sailing master of H.M.S. *Sparrowhawk,* which was in port at the time. Roys set out immediately.[17]

The whales in Knight Inlet proved difficult to approach. Then misfortune struck. *Emma*'s propeller blades broke. Roys beached the steamer and repaired the screw, but on going out again it broke a second time, and the steamer *Fly* was sent up to tow him back to Victoria. He returned on June 3. The condition of the steamer ended the voyage, and within two weeks the stockholders of the Victoria Whaling Adventurer's Company decided to liquidate. It is absolutely ironic that on the day following Roys's departure from British Columbia, "a dozen great whales, spouting, sporting and fighting like mad all day long;" appeared off Victoria, "and, to make the case all the more provoking, if possible, one of the big fish [sic] impudently runs aground at low water and actually lies upon the beach over one tide—as much to say, come and catch me, if you can!—before he floats off. Too bad," the author laments, "Too bad!"[18]

Meanwhile, Roys had set his course for the Hawaiian Islands, arriving on July 12 in *Byzantium* from Burrard Inlet, British Columbia. How ridiculous it is that throughout that summer, whales spouted and sported right off Victoria. "The oily rascals," a local newspaper claimed, "seem to be aware that Roys has abandoned his whaling enterprise and gone away." The most outrageous event of all, however, occurred in August, when a whale steamed right up the harbor, intending, according to some wags, to tie up at one of the wharves "for a few days and 'drop a line' to Captain Roys at the Sandwich Islands to come and take him—if he could." All this drew the attention of another company from San Francisco, which decided to try their luck. And speaking of that, the rival Dawson company was doing especially well that summer, having taken seven whales totaling 9,450 gallons of oil, utilizing their old-fashioned methods. By the end of the season the Dawson firm had taken over seventeen whales, their ships' holds bursting with success.[19]

At Honolulu Roys chartered the locally registered coasting schooner *Anne* in early February 1870 and sailed for Kalepolepo Bay to engage in whaling. Feeling fully confident, Roys was claiming that "no whale that allows him [the harpooner] to get within one hundred feet of it with his gun, can escape alive, as the weapon is carried with extraordinary accuracy, and its striking or entering the whale causes instant death by explosion." Tryworks were set up at Olowalu, some five or ten miles south of the old whaling port of Lahaina on Maui, where the whales were to be cut up and the blubber tried out. The first two weeks of the cruise were quite stormy, but during the third, Roys shot two whales off Maui, heaving both up off the bottom. Roys had had some rockets manufactured by a local Honolulu brass founder, J. A. Hooper, just for this voyage, and apparently they worked quite well, for the two leviathans taken were killed instantaneously. *Anne* returned to Honolulu on March 29 with seventy barrels of oil.[20]

Perhaps the real reason for Roys's cruise in *Anne* was to engender the interest of new investors, for a notice appeared in the April 9 issue of the Honolulu *Pacific Commercial Advertiser:* "There will be a trial of Capt. Roys' whaling gun today at 4½ p.m. at the market wharf. Those who have seen it in use say that nothing can surpass it." The report of the actual trial in the April 16 number of the *Advertiser* was most promising:

> The experiment made with Capt. Roys' whaling gun last Saturday afternoon in the harbor, was very satisfactory to all who witnessed it. A target consisting of a sail cloth, was sunk a little under the surface, and the weapon fired twice from a boat. The first shot was fired about 25 fathoms from the target and hit it, passing through the cloth. The second about 35 fathoms distant, passed a few feet from it. A whale, in both instances, would have probably been struck. Although this instrument is somewhat expensive, it is considered by old seamen as one of the best ever brought into notice. It is proposed to fit out a brig and send her to the Arctic this summer. Two weeks of good whaling would suffice to fill her up with the aid of such a deadly weapon as this.[21]

How, one might ask, could any investor resist?

On May 31, 1870, a party of three otherwise unidentified gentlemen, "possessing experience, energy and capital," arrived at Victoria in the brig *Byzantium* from Honolulu for the purpose of embarking on a new whaling venture on Barkley Sound. It is not known whether Roys was among them, but surely they were under his influence, for it was reported that they had been "armed with the Roys rocket." During the 1870 season there also were two other companies operating out of Victoria, but using traditional methods: the Howe Sound Whaling Company and, again, Dawson Whaling Company.

The Dawson firm was the most successful, however, and took twenty-one whales in all during an otherwise lean season. Of the Honolulu venture we hear no more for this year.[22]

Capt. Rufus Calhoun—a wealthy shipowner from Washington Territory who regularly carried lumber from the Pacific Northwest to Honolulu and had brought Roys out to Hawaii in his old, British-built packet brig *Byzantium* in the summer of 1869—was very impressed with Roys's whaling methods, so much so, that he agreed to advance $8,000 for a new whaling expedition during the 1871 season, utilizing Roys's rocket-harpoons. Together they returned to Victoria on May 10, where *Byzantium* was fitted out to cruise Queen Charlotte Sound—to the north of Vancouver Island—in the summer and the Strait of Georgia in the fall. No expense was spared; tryworks and tanks were installed on deck, and every contemporary whaling appliance—including, naturally, a good stock of Roys's rocket launchers and harpoons—was provided to insure a substantial catch. The Calhoun-Roys party sailed in mid-May for Cape Flattery, which juts into the Juan de Fuca Strait from Washington Territory, amid reports of "numerous schools [of whales] disporting themselves in the vicinity."[23]

The 1871 season seemed to offer real promise, and the Douglas-Strachan Whaling Company had reported eight whales and about 10,000 gallons of oil by the end of July. In August word reached Victoria that Captains Calhoun and Roys had established a shore station on Queen Charlotte Island at Cumshewa where they had erected buildings and were setting up casks to receive oil. The whales were numerous, and a great catch was anticipated. In addition, the weather was promising at last, and the "Indians as docile as lambs." Roys killed several whales off the northern end of Queen Charlotte, saving six.[24] It looked like a good season.

But *Byzantium* encountered some peculiar weather during October, experiencing seventeen days of alternate calms and head winds in the strait between Vancouver Island and the mainland—a foreboding of disaster. Let Roys tell the rest of the story in his own words:

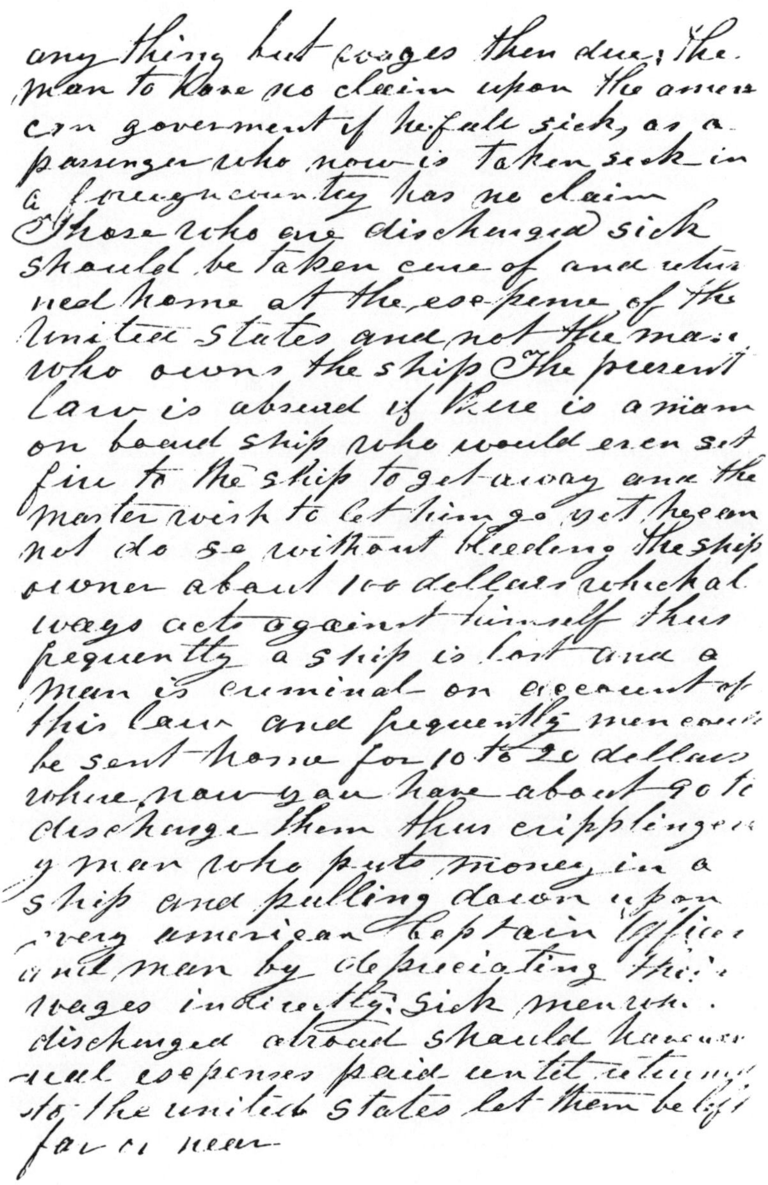

any thing but wages then due; the man to have no claim upon the American government if he fall sick, as a passenger who now is taken sick in a foreign country has no claim. Those who are discharged sick should be taken care of and returned home at the expense of the United States and not the man who owns the ship. The present law is absurd if there is a man on board ship who would even set fire to the ship to get away and the master wish to let him go, yet he can not do so without bleeding the ship owner about 100 dollars which always acts against himself thus frequently a ship is lost and a man is criminal on account of this law and frequently men can be sent home for 10 to 20 dollars where now you have about 90 to discharge them thus crippling every man who puts money in a ship and pulling down upon every american captain officer and man by depreciating their wages indirectly. Sick men when discharged abroad should have their real expenses paid until returning to the United States let them be left far or near.

FIG. 30. THOMAS ROYS'S AUTOBIOGRAPHY

Toward the end of his long career, perhaps about 1871, Roys wrote "The Voyages of Thomas Welcome Roys," a manuscript account of his knowledge of the natural history of whales, descriptions of his methods and ideas on the fishery, and most important, a chronicle of his life's adventures. Nothing was found on his person when he died at Mazatlàn, Mexico, in 1877—a pauper, save for a sheath of papers. Perhaps this autobiography was among them.

(Courtesy of Suffolk County Whaling Museum, Sag Harbor, N.Y.)

Then came a gale at southeast, very quick and stormy, and right at a little before midnight she [*Byzantium*] struck upon the rocks, stoving two holes in her, and we escaped in the boats, knowing well when the tide turned she would swing off and go down as there were 150 tons [of] ballast on board. This she did, for a few hours afterward she had disappeared altogether with everything on board.[25]

Later it was learned that the ship had struck a sunken reef in Weynton Passage, Johnstone Strait, off the northeastern shore of Vancouver Island. The impact was sharp, and the brig began to take on water rapidly. A fresh breeze was blowing and the weather was what is known in sailors' parlance as dirty. Both anchors were dropped with forty fathoms of chain. Within an hour the ship had to be abandoned, and the thirteen officers and crewmen threw a few articles, including the ship's chronometer and their personal belongings, into the boats and escaped to shore, where they camped until morning. After daylight they tried to return to the wreck, but a fierce gale kept them off until nearly dark, when they found water within three feet of her deck beams. Unable to salvage anything, Roys and his men rowed off ashore and made their way to Fort Rupert, where they remained until picked up by the steamer *Otter*, which was on her way down from the north. Next day they went to survey the scene of the wreck, but found no traces of the ship. It was presumed she had drifted off the reef and had sunk nearby in sixty fathoms. Later it was learned that the brig had floated off with the next tide and had been lying at anchor with four feet of water in her hold when some Indians discovered her. The natives had cut the anchor cables and had taken the ship behind an island while *Otter* was searching the area. When she had left, the natives plundered the ship of cabin furniture, sails, and anything else of use to them, and *Byzantium* was last reported floating out to sea by the northern passage of Queen Charlotte Strait.[26]

When she was wrecked, *Byzantium* had on board several hundred barrels of oil and a quantity of stores, and it was estimated that the total loss would reach $15,000—of which only $5,000 was covered by insurance. Most of the financial loss was incurred by Captain Calhoun. The emotional strain on Roys—who had failed once more, although again not through his own fault—must have been devastating. After four years in British Columbia, his only accomplishment had been to prove that he could prevent whales from sinking by utilizing his methods. Meanwhile, the crew of *Byzantium* was stranded without money. "One at least of their number," the editor of the local *British Colonist* reported, "an Englishman—is friendless, homeless, and starving. Cannot," he implored, "something be done for their relief to-day?" Unfortunately, this man, William Cooper, who had been the ship's cooper, died soon afterward of exposure. Broke himself, Roys was able to bum a passage to Port Madison, Washington Territory, where he boarded the lumber coaster *Wildwood* for the journey back to San Francisco. He arrived there on November 24, after a passage of nine days.[27]

Despite his hardships, Roys enjoyed the rugged beauty of British Columbia, and a few years later he had this to say in his memoirs:

> At Queen Charlotte's Island, British Columbia, there is a fine race of Indians . . . who live by fishing, hunting, raising potatoes and going down to Victoria to barter their furs. Many of them work on board sailing vessels and steamers, in coal mines, and other places, and are fast being civilized.
>
> The Inland waters of British Columbia and Alaska south of Cross Sound, has the finest stream navigation in the world, a great amount of navigable channels with fine land and fine harbors with timber, coal, and iron in profusion accessible to navigable water. The climate is mild, warm in summer, and not very cold in winter, being dry in summer, and rainy and wet in winter with very little snow or frosty weather.[28]

It is truly a pity that a man of such depth should have fallen short of his life's ambitions. As we shall see in the final chapter, however, Roys remained true to his dreams to the last.

13

"So Ends."

Roys arrived in San Francisco at an opportune time. The port was just beginning to develop as a major whaling center. After all, following the purchase and opening of Alaska in 1867, and because California was far closer to the fabled Arctic whaling grounds than east-coast ports, San Francisco offered the ideal rendezvous for the Yankee fleets. In 1870, for instance, six ships entered San Francisco, bringing in over 4,000 barrels of oil and 66,000 pounds of bone. By the end of the decade the all-out transition began, and by 1883 San Francisco had thirty-six ships in the trade—in comparison with the dowager queen of whaling capitals, New Bedford, which had only twenty-three.[1] Here, Roys might find a receptive market, at last, for his inventions.

While laying over at San Francisco in November 1871, Roys took his harpoons and rocket guns—full of difficulties and errors—to Hawkins & Cantrell's Machine Works on Beale Street. As this firm was equipped to fabricate anything from steam engines to mill and mining rigs, it could easily fill Roys's orders for a new rocket press, a mold, and rammers, as well as for the steel and brass rocket hardware.[2] At the shop Roys became acquainted with a Scottish-born machinist named Hugh Hamilton Lamont, to whom he sold an eighth part of his chain compensator, boat-detaching floats, cartridge-shot and rocket guns, and harpoons inventions on June 17, 1872, in return for a rocket press worth $75 and a mold and rammers for charging rockets worth $300. The work was completed within a year by a Mr. O'Brien of Hawkins & Cantrell.[3] Lamont became, in effect, the middleman in the development of what was to become known as the California Whaling Rocket. While he did not improve upon or even use Roys's inventions for himself—acting more as a custodian for the basic ideas— Lamont was instrumental in their later implementation in the west-coast whale fishery.[4]

Roys's activities for the next few years are hazy. His wife Marie, it will be remembered, had run off from their home on Blubber Row at Peconic, Long Island, sometime after 1870 with their three children, Thomas, Jr., Willis, and Matilda, presumably to New York City. Roys himself is listed as residing at 868 Lexington Avenue, New York, circa 1873-74. And Charles M. Scammon mentions in his 1874 book *Marine Mammals of the North-western Coast of North America* a "recent" interview with Roys regarding his discovery of the Arctic whaling ground in 1848.[5]

Besides this, we can learn nothing of Roys's activities until the winter of 1876-77, when he turned up in San Diego, California. He joined a ship a few months later and contracted yellow fever. He was then put ashore at the grubby little Mexican fishing port of Mazatlán. Here Roys was found, "in the street sick, destitute, and wandering in mind," by an American doctor, D. M. Brown, who took the old captain to his own home out of charity. Roys lingered about a week, then passed away at 5 A.M. on January 29, 1877, of a stroke. On his person Roys had "a roll of papers," no doubt the manuscript of his memoirs and his patents, and a portfolio which contained some letters from his half brother Andrew and his son Philander, his only identification. These were his sole effects. The local United States consul, E. G. Kelton, called on resident Americans immediately after Roys's death and collected $60 for a fitting funeral, contributing $10 himself. Kelton made all of the arrangements and read the service at the grave. Upon learning of Roys's sad demise, a contemporary editor back home placed his life in perspective. Noting his accomplishments as well as the fact that the old captain had died of "want and exposure," the newspaperman moralized that it "goes to show that energy, pluck and ambition are not the sole elements of success."[6]

Roys died intestate, so his eldest son, Philander, was appointed administrator of his estate, which was valued at a scant $200 or less. The son filed posthumously the last of his father's patents—probably found among the papers on Roys's person when he died—in March 1879. The specification is the culmination of Roys's seventeen years of experimentation, representing improvements in his former patents, remedies for defects, and devices to render the weapons more practical. Oddly enough, Philander Roys filed a similar patent application in the then-independent Hawaiian Islands in February 1879, perhaps as a precaution against imitators.[7] Roys's work was done, but—as we shall see—his rocket-harpoon idea endured a while longer.

Roys's experiments with rocket-harpoons were continued with the arrival in San Francisco of an intriguing pair of characters. John Nelson Fletcher, an itinerant pyrotechnist of dubious background and the senior of the two, was originally from Ohio. He had used the alias "John Baird," for reasons unexplained, while serving in the Union Army toward the end of the Civil War.[8] Conversely, Robert L. Suits, Fletcher's partner in the whaling-rocket venture, was a former Confederate soldier, having been raised in North Carolina. At the age of fifteen, he began his career as a machinist in a local gunsmith's shop, helping to fit locks and assemble guns for the war effort. When he came of age, late in 1863, he enlisted and was stationed at the arsenal at Fayetteville, North Carolina, where undoubtedly he assembled Fayetteville rifles, pistols, and carbines. The experience was invaluable when he began building California Whaling Rockets.[9]

Fletcher and Suits met after the war in Baltimore, where they were probably working as a pyrotechnist and a machinist respectively. In 1873 Fletcher married Suits's younger sister Salena (Lena), and two years later the brothers-in-law and their families again pulled up their tenuous roots and headed for San Francisco.[10] Robert, now skilled in his craft, was hired by the old (by Western standards) Hinckley & Company Fulton Foundry, then located at Fremont and Tehama Streets. Established in 1855, the hallmark of the Fulton works was versatility, their output running the gamut from locomotives to quartz mills and crushers. Among the machinists at Fulton was Hugh Hamilton Lamont.[11] It is difficult to determine precisely when Lamont broached the subject of the whaling rocket to the new employee, but it certainly must not have been more than a few months after Suits's arrival, for by 1877 the year of Captain Roys's demise a thousand miles to the south, the California Whaling Rocket was born.

"California" probably was added to distinguish it from its predecessor, the Roys-Lilliendahl whaling rocket. So far as we know, with Roys's death and with Lilliendahl's having made a concession shortly afterward to Fletcher, the California-brand whaling rocket was without competition. Fletcher, Suits & Co., 407 Front Street, San Francisco, became the sole manufacturer of whaling rockets in the country—indeed, perhaps in the world. At a nearby factory it was Suits's job to machine the harpoon's metallic parts and to install the intricate firing mechanism.

In 1878, John Fletcher began negotiating with Gustavus Lilliendahl, then of Jersey City, New Jersey, for further manufacturing and patent rights. Interestingly enough, he reverted to the use of his alias, "John Baird," for these negotiations and was to continue to do so everytime he had any connection with New Jersey. By the end of the year the harpoon was still known as the Roys and Lilliendahl whaling rocket, though Fletcher and Suits had sold several sets already to prominent Pacific Coast whalers and had some glowing testimonials in hand.[12]

As Fletcher promoted the rocket, he and Suits were striving at the same time to eliminate its drawbacks. They were determined to go into mass production on a cheaper and more profitable basis. Lilliendahl and Roys had made the harpoons too lightweight, they found, and the weapons consequently were not charged with enough powder. Fletcher and Suits's modifications produced a rocket bomb lance six and one-half feet long, and weighing thirty-two pounds; even a cabin boy

Fig. 31.   The California Whaling Rocket, ca. 1877

This is the modified harpoon device developed in San Francisco by John N. Fletcher and Robert L. Suits. Its popularity reached its zenith from 1878 to 1880, when at least fifteen whaling ships out of San Francisco were equipped with these rocket-harpoons. From *The Wasp*, July 28, 1877, p. 566.

(Courtesy of California Historical Society, San Francisco, Calif.)

could operate it. The Church & Co. pyrotechnic laboratories, which shared the same address as Fletcher, Suits & Co., also came up with an exclusive, more powerful black-powder formula for the improved rocket. Fletcher and Suits began to boast that their harpoon could fasten to a whale at thirty fathoms (180 feet), which was a considerably greater distance than could be reached even by a gun-fired bomb lance.[13]

The resourceful Fletcher also acquired the use of a small steam launch to ply California coastal waters to test the rockets. This vessel was probably the *Rocket,* a small five-and-one-half ton steamer of San Francisco registry. The boat apparently was built and owned by Robert Suits's foundry. Throughout 1878, the brothers-in-law killed thirty-five whales outside the harbor with the rocket. These were humpbacks, blues, and finbacks.[14]

Around Christmastime of that year they also gave a public trial of the rocket in the Oakland Creek (now the Oakland Estuary), with a tub serving as the target. Observers were reported to have been highly pleased with the demonstration, and one newsman declared that any of the rockets would easily have killed a whale. "Already some six vessels," he added, "have [been] outfitted with this apparatus for the Arctic, each carrying from five to fifty shots." By 1879, Fletcher and Suits seemed firmly established. In May of that year they began regularly advertising in the *Whalemen's Shipping List* of New Bedford, just as Roys had done. The publisher and proprietor of this unofficial organ of the American whale fishery, Eben P. Raymond, was even induced to serve as an east-coast agent for the whaling rocket after witnessing a special trial.[15]

Between 1878 and 1880 at least fifteen whaling schooners, brigs, barks, and steamers out of San Francisco were equipped with the new California Whaling Rockets. Most of the vessels were New Bedford owned and registered, though San Francisco was almost a permanent home port for them. Just about all of them hunted in the North Pacific and Arctic, principally for bowheads that calved in the Sea of Okhotsk, by Russia.

Capt. Thomas W. Williams of the famous Williams dynasty of whalers and shipowners out of New Bedford, and later San Francisco, was one of the first to be shown the harpoon and became its largest buyer. He purchased a great number for his ships, the barks *Francis Palmer, Coral,* and *Dawn,* and the brig *Hidalgo,* and "would not go on a whaling voyage without . . . the apparatus." Another New England man, Capt. James Caughill of the schooner *Newton Booth,* was reported to have "been using these rockets down the [California] coast so successfully that he has telegraphed for a new supply of shots."

Perhaps an even more unequivocal testimonial came from Capt. Bernard Cogan of the bark *Rainbow*. Though the co-inventor himself of another improved method of catching whales—the Cunningham and Cogan breech-loading bomb gun—he was "so favorably impressed" upon seeing a few fired that he ordered "a number of them." Whaling master Ebenezer F. Nye of the bark *Mount Wollaston* took out fifteen shots and two launchers. And the forty-four ton San Francisco whaling steamer *Daisy Whitelaw* "very successfully" hunted finbacks with them through the Farallon Islands off San Francisco and up to Drake's Bay. She caught an unusually large female during a short Independence Day excursion in 1880 and moored it at the Second Street Wharf for public exhibit before processing it for oil. The ship's skipper (Stutzman) and owner (Thomas P. H. Whitelaw) went so far as to advertise their seventy-three foot, ninety ton catch in the local papers and to charge admission. Similarly, the tiny steamboat *Rocket* took Fletcher, Suits & Co. "bomb rockets" regularly up as far as Point Reyes. In one close shot at a blue whale, the harpoon went completely through the whale and burst on the other side.[16]

Some were purchased also by the Northwest Whaling Company, or Northwest Trading Company, of Killisnoo Island, near Sitka, Alaska. They successfully harvested finbacks and humpbacks, apparently firing the rockets from the deck of the company's small steamer *Favorite*. Even a ship flying the Russian ensign was "plentifully supplied." Though commanded by a Yankee captain, the steam brig *Siberia* was legally bound to fly the flag of imperial Russia in order to fish off Vladivostok.[17]

For all Fletcher's glowing claims and wide-ranging salesmanship, the California Whaling Rocket venture was doomed to fail within a decade after it was launched. By 1890 the whale fishery everywhere was on the decline. Primarily the industry's death knell was sounded by the sinking of petroleum wells and by the increasing substitution of cheap natural gas and kerosene for whale oil. California had experienced its "black gold" strike in 1860; thereafter, the state's whale-products market slumped. Sperm oil that once fetched $2.55 per gallon on the San Francisco market had dropped to twenty-five cents by Fletcher's day. By 1878, while Fletcher, Suits & Co. still exhibited their wares to Barbary Coast whaling masters, the San Francisco *Chronicle* began advertising wholesale dealers of "water white in barrels" (kerosene) and Downer's mineral sperm oil (a petroleum derivative).[18]

There were also difficulties with the rocket itself. It was far too bulky and expensive. Hand irons cost only seventy-five cents each, bomb lances (exclusive of guns) were several dollars, but Fletcher demanded as much as fifty dollars for his rockets. The charge also remained uncertain, particularly its ignition. Despite built-in precautions, rocket blasts might also sear whale lines, causing them to part. A more subtle drawback was that veteran mariners were apt to regard the newfangled whaling rocket or anything else so radically innovative with the gravest skepticism and preformed prejudice.[19]

From 1880 on affairs went noticeably worse for Fletcher, Suits & Co. With the dwindling of San Francisco's whaling fleet, Fletcher himself sought to sell his rocket in the whalemen's own grounds. He went whaling, fishing, and trading in Alaska, but met with no success. He badly burned his already rheumatic hands when a deadly mixture of potassium chlorate and sulfur exploded. Probably he was preparing a new rocket-bomb formula.[20]

In 1881 Fletcher did sell at least one rocket. Charles D. Voy, an independently wealthy naturalist, taxidermist, and "capitalist" from San Francisco bought a repainted, secondhand model for sixteen dollars from Fletcher for the Smithsonian Institution in Washington.[21] Voy also wrote an interesting, illustrated article on the rocket for *La Nature* magazine of Paris. In a letter to Spencer F. Baird, the secretary of the Smithsonian, Voy cites an instance in which a rocket was fired entirely through the body of a whale and toggled itself on the other side. He also said that during a series of experiments with the bombs on the beach, one of them "carried a

FIG. 32.   AN ORIGINAL CALIFORNIA WHALING ROCKET, CA. 1881

The last surviving example of this rocket, disassembled. It is now on display at the National Air and Space Museum, Smithsonian Institution.

(Courtesy of Smithsonian Institution, Washington, D.C.)

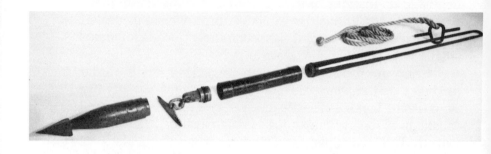

FIG. 33.   CALIFORNIA WHALING ROCKET, CA. 1880

The movable flap automatically protected the face of the operator after the rocket-harpoon was fired. The wood engraving is by Smeeton-Tilly, after a sketch by Gilbert, and was published in *La Nature* (Paris, France) 9 (December 1880):36.

(Photo courtesy of Smithsonian Institution, Washington, D.C.)

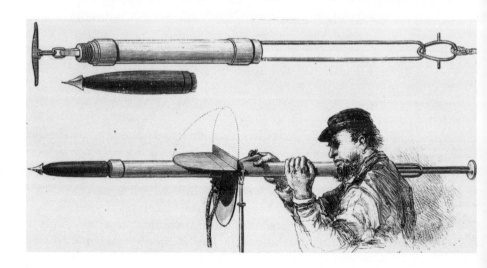

whale-line almost 60 fathoms, which shows what power they have, since a bomb and 20 fathoms of line weigh about 55 pounds."[22] The Smithsonian rocket was later displayed at the Louisiana Purchase Exposition at St. Louis in 1904. Though the rocket launcher is missing, the harpoon specimen is probably the most complete example of the California Whaling Rocket extant. Another sample, incidentally, was displayed at the Great International Fisheries Exhibition at London in 1883.[23]

Only in 1891 do we hear of any other possible employment of the rocket. The late Reginald B. Heggarty, former curator of the Melville Whaling Room, New Bedford Free Public Library, first heard of it as a young boy when he listened to his father's yarns of his whaling days out of San Francisco in the 1880s and 1890s. The father, William Heggarty, seems either to have used or to have heard of the harpoon while whaling in *Alice Knowles,* skippered by Ezra B. Lapham. Years before, Lapham had purchased a rocket for the bark *Progress.* Even if he or his crew no longer used the harpoon, it had left a lasting impression.[24]

By the early 1890s, Fletcher had become foreman of the California Fireworks Co. on Front Street (successors to Church & Co., who had made the powder for his rockets), but there is no evidence that the California Whaling Rocket survived that late or that it was still for sale. On the contrary, it seems that more than a decade earlier the short-lived Fletcher, Suits & Co. had dissolved entirely and that their single product ceased to be manufactured.[25]

The originators of this experiment had gone their separate ways. Lamont remained in the Bay area and died in Oakland, California, in 1926 at age eighty-nine. He had remained a machinist, as did Suits, though both worked at different foundries. Suits died in San Francisco about 1890.[26] The shadowy Fletcher continued to drift. Sporadically, he mended shoes, and he also briefly tended bar in a Barbary Coast saloon. By the mid-90s he had settled permanently back in the east. In New York City the amorous "widower" John Nelson Fletcher, who had been separated since 1880, married a twenty-year-old girl from Hoboken, New Jersey.[27] The former Lena Suits Fletcher, whom he had never bothered to divorce, was still living in Oakland at the time.[28] From about 1895 on, he took up

FIG. 34.   CALIFORNIA WHALING ROCKET

Frank H. Winter of the Smithsonian Institution is holding the example of the California Whaling Rocket which is presently on exhibit in the Rocketry and Spaceflight Gallery of the National Air and Space Museum in Washington, D.C.

(Courtesy of Richard B. Farrar.)

residence as John Baird in New Jersey and became a flagman with the Central Railroad of New Jersey. On February 20, 1903, he died in Newark and was buried under his alias.[29]

With the calamitous earthquake and fire that swept San Francisco three years later, in 1906, the essential records and the buildings where the California Whaling Rocket was born likewise passed into oblivion.[30] An example of the harpoon,

"So Ends."

however, is on display in the National Air and Space Museum at the Smithsonian Institution.

The rocket-harpoon did not become Roys's true legacy to the industry he loved. Nonetheless, his contributions to whaling, as we have learned, were substantial. He realized, for instance, that whale stocks were not a limitless resource. Roys was first to call for formal governmental study of cetaceans in their natural habitats and a search for new, untapped herds. More important, he proved the feasibility of harvesting mighty rorquals: fins, minkes, Bryde's, humpbacks, and seis, and even the gigantic blues—largest of all earthly animals. Roys conceived the idea of shore processing stations, adjacent to the whaling grounds, from which fast steam whale catchers could be dispatched. The men aboard were equipped with guns instead of the hand-thrown harpoons used by their predecessors. Roy's whale compensator concept was adapted into modern whale catchers, where it is called the "accumulator": a system of springs which cushions and reduces tension on the whale line. The shore station freed the ships from trying out oil on board, enabling them to cruise whenever conditions permitted. Ashore, Roys's experiments proved that substantial quantities of oil could be extracted from the portions of the whale previously discarded, such as the bones, flesh, and entrails. Steam pressure kettles did the work more efficiently than old-fashioned try-pots. There is evidence that Roys's work heavily influenced Svend Foyn—called the Father of Modern Whaling—who incorporated these methods into the system of modern whaling that continues to this very day.[10]

Foyn's work was continued by Capt. Carl Anton Larsen, another Norwegian. In 1892 C. A. Larsen took the whaler *Jason* on a sealing and exploration voyage into the Antarctic Ocean, along the western shore of the Weddell Sea. The following year he returned to the Antarctic, and he soon realized that the vast untapped herds of rorqual whales there waited to be exploited. Thus he filled one of Roys's unsatisfied dreams, for the old Yankee captain had long hoped to explore the rich, yet treacherous, Antarctic Ocean. Eventually—after several more expeditions—Larsen sought a place to establish a shore station close to these Antarctic stocks and found the ideal base at the subantarctic isle of South Georgia. He discovered fantastic numbers of humpbacks literally in his own backyard—at the entrance of the sheltered cove where he maintained his base—and killed them with wasteful abandon. Soon the rush was on, and practically every square mile of usable space in the Falkland Islands Dependencies was being utilized for shore whaling stations. Naturally, the only place left to turn was the sea, and the idea of floating whale-processing factories was conceived. Although not really a new idea—having been used in the Arctic experimentally as early as 1903—Larsen brought it to its potential in 1922 with the factory ship *Sir James Clark Ross,* which he outfitted with five catcher ships and took down to the icy fringes of the Antarctic to hunt whole new herds of whales, processing them right on the grounds. The final era of whaling was born.[32]

Unfortunately, today's pelagic whalers are too efficient. Japan and the Soviet Union both have large fleets of swift and powerful catcher ships, on which bow-mounted, updated versions of the Foyn gun have been installed. Guided by helicopters and utilizing electronic devices borrowed from the military, these killing machines confuse, terrorize, and home in on thousands of helpless, majestic whales each season. With their grisly catches—hideously bloated with compressed air—taken in tow, the killers return to the enormous factory ships, some of which measure up to 30,000 tons, and which are capable of processing a 60-foot leviathan right on board in a matter of minutes. Ironically, the very rorquals that Roys sought have been harvested in the hundreds of thousands with such zeal that even they are endangered and promise to be exhausted. With no new herds or species to turn their guns on, pelagic hunters have nowhere to go. Hopefully, modern-day successors to Roys's boundless intellect will find ready and inexpensive substitutes for whale-derived products, thus saving one of mankind's most precious natural resources from hope-

"So Ends."

less extermination. The late Smithsonian mammalogist Remington Kellogg put it quite simply, "Whales once roamed the oceans of the world in millions, but today they may be nearing the same fate that doomed vast herds of bison." Just what would Roys have to say about this sorry state of affairs?

Appendixes

Notes

Glossary

Gazetteer

Index

APPENDIX A

Significant Events in the Life of
Capt. Thomas Welcome Roys

1816   Born to Philander and Tamimer Roys on a farm near Pultneyville, Wayne County, New York.

1833   Begins career as whaleman, serving as greenhand in Sag Harbor, Long Island, whaler *Hudson*.

1835   Ships over in *Hudson*.

1836   Promoted to boatsteerer in *Hudson*.

1837   Signs on Sag Harbor whaler *Gem* as a boatsteerer.

1839   Becomes chief officer of *Gem*.

1840   Sails again in *Gem* as chief officer.

1841   Made captain of Sag Harbor whaler *Crescent*.

1843   Marries Ann Eliza Green, daughter of Capt. Henry Green, under whom he first served in *Hudson*.
Engaged as captain of the Sag Harbor whaler *Josephine*. During this voyage, first learned of vast, untapped stocks of whales in Arctic Ocean north of the forbidding Bering Strait.

1847   Assumes command of the Sag Harbor whaler *Superior*.
Wife dies soon after giving birth to their son, Philander.

1848   Over objections of mates and crew, takes *Superior* through Bering Strait, fills his ship in less than a month, and opens the fabled Arctic whaling grounds; saving the industry from decline. Here, for some years to come, whalers slaughtered docile bowhead whales which Roys had found.

1849   Signs on as captain of the Cold Spring Harbor, Long Island, whaleship *Sheffield*, one of the largest vessels in the industry. Returns to the Arctic, assisting briefly in the search for missing British explorer Sir John Franklin. Takes perhaps over $100,000 in oil and baleen for the voyage: fine work by any standards. During this period, writes the natural history "Descriptions of Whales," which he presents upon his return in 1854 to "Father of Oceanography," Lt. Matthew Maury, U.S.N.

1855   Receives command of New London, Connecticut, whaler *Hannibal*, plans to take her to Hudson Bay, Canada. Kills a blue whale, largest of all leviathans, giving him idea that larger guns might be employed against rorquals, the largest of whales, a previously untapped resource. Conservative owners of *Hannibal* think him insane for such an idea, and when he orders a double-barreled whale gun, have him removed from the ship.

1856   With assistance of several friends buys the Sag Harbor whaler *William F. Safford,* outfitting her with special harpoon guns of his own design for exploratory voyage taking him from fringes of the Arctic to the Antarctic in quest of rorqual whales. Loses his left hand when one of the guns misfired.

1857   Receives his first patent, in Great Britain, for explosive shells and, after adopting Congreve rockets (vs. bore-type guns used in his previous experiments), receives two subsequent patents for rocket whaling apparatus.

Thinking *Safford* had been lost at sea with the mate in command, Roys is assisted by a friend in purchasing a second ship, *Pacific.* *Safford* returns safely, and experiments with the new rocket whaling guns continue for several years—constantly hampered by defective fuses, unreliable powder charges, and manufacturing difficulties. The voyages end in financial failure.

1860   Roys marries Marie Salliord of Lorient, France. Returns with bride to Long Island, New York.

1861   Receives first U.S. patent, for "Improvement in Harpoon-Guns." Joins in partnership with Gustavus A. Lilliendahl, wealthy New York City pyrotechnics manufacturer; work together for half a dozen years trying to perfect rocket method of whaling.

1862   Lilliendahl buys whaleship *Reindeer.* Roys becomes master and fits out for rocket whaling experiments.

1863   Sails to Iceland in *Reindeer* to test whaling rockets.

1864   Ditto.

Thomas Welcome Roys, Jr., born.

1865   Establishes first shore-based whaling station in Iceland, near vast stocks of rorquals offshore. Whales could be taken easily nearby, towed inshore, and processed using unique bone grinders, presses, and steam kettles; infinitely more efficient than old method of cutting in and boiling out blubber aboard ship in great kettles. A small steamer, *Visionary,* is utilized to tow whaleboats out to grounds and dead whales into station. This begins progression from old to modern whaling methods.

1866   Another son, Willis, born.

Steamers *Sileno, Staperaider,* and *Vigilant* outfitted for the Roys-

Appendix A

Lilliendahl experiments at Iceland. (*Reindeer* had been retired, and *Visionary* was wrecked.)

Roys invents and patents method for raising sunken whales.

Roys leaves Iceland at end of season and severs relations with partner Lilliendahl, who continues alone for another year. The break probably caused by financial difficulties.

1867   Roys tries brief stint manufacturing rocket-harpoons in New York City.

1868   A daughter, Matilda, born.

Turns up in British Columbia, western Canada, as master of the whaling steamer *Emma,* trying again to promote and perfect his rocket whaling device.

1869   Cruises again in *Emma.*

1870   Demonstrates rocket-harpoons in Honolulu; makes several brief, "plum puddin' " cruises in whaler *Anne* to engender interest in his weapons.

1871   Takes command of the whaling brig *Byzantium* out of Victoria, British Columbia, on one last experimental voyage. The ship is wrecked and Roys's venture ends in financial disaster.

Shortly after leaving British Columbia for San Francisco, Roys writes his memoirs—eventually given in manuscript form to the Suffolk County Whaling Museum, Sag Harbor, New York.

1872   Involved in manufacturing and improving his rocket-harpoons in San Francisco.

1873   Thought to have returned for a while to New York City. By now, his wife, Marie, had run off with one of Roys's former shipmates, and from this time on he lives a shadowy existence.

1876   Surfaces inexplicitly in San Diego, California, joins a ship, and contracts yellow fever.

1877   Destitute and wandering of mind, the old captain is put ashore at Mazatlán, Mexico, where he dies on January 29.

APPENDIX B

Known Patents of Whaling Devices Invented by Thomas Welcome Roys

Year	Patent No.	Title
		FRANCE
1864	65,221	"Improvements of implements for the killing and capture of whales"
1866	73,901	"Compensator applicable to the hoisting or lifting tackle, for recovering sunken whales or other submerged bodies"
		GREAT BRITAIN
1857	1,402	"Explosive Shells"
1857	2,301	"Apparatus applicable to the Capture of Whales, &c."
1857	2,340	Ditto.
1859	965	"Rocket Guns"
1861	450	"Rocket Guns and Harpoons"
1865	550	"Rocket and Harpoon Guns"
		NETHERLANDS
1866	1,628	"Compensator applicable to the hoisting or lifting tackle, for recovering sunken whales or other submerged bodies"
		NORWAY
1866		"Compensator for raising sunken whales"
		UNITED STATES OF AMERICA
1861	31,190	"Improvement in Harpoon-Guns"
1862	35,474	"Improved Rocket-Harpoon"
1862	35,476	"Improved Apparatus for Raising Sunken Whales to the Surface of the Water"

Appendix B

1866	53,684	"Improved Tackle for Raising Sunken Whales and Other Bodies"
1866	54,211	"Improvement in Rocket-Harpoons"
1879	214,707	"Improvement in Bomb-Lances" (Filed after Roys's death by his son Philander)

APPENDIX C

Voyages of American Ships Reported
(All San Francisco, Calif., vessels, unless noted)

Vessel's Name	Rig	Tons	Captain	Where Bound	Sailed
Alaska	Schr	139	James McKenna	No. Pacific	3/28/
Byzantium	Brig		Thos. W. Roys	Br. Columbia	187
Coral	Bark	362	L. C. Owen	No. Pacific	3/4/7
Daisy Whitelaw	Stmr	44	T. Whitelaw	S. Francisco area	188
Dawn	Bark	260	W. H. Kelley	No. Pacific	3/16/
Favorite	Stmr			Alaska	c. 188
Francis Palmer	Bark	195	T. W. Williams	No. Pacific	4/8/7
Hidalgo	Brig	175	L. H. Williams	No. Pacific	4/2/7
Legal Tender	Bark			Arctic	6/79
Leo	Schr		F. A. Baker		
Mount Wollaston	Bark		E. F. Nye		1879
Newton Booth	Schr		J. Caughill	Calif. Coast	
Progress	Bark		E. B. Lapham		1878
Rainbow	Bark	351	B. Cogan	No. Pacific	1/21/7
Rainbow	Bark	351	B. Cogan	No. Pacific	11/11/
Reindeer	Bark	158	Thos. W. Roys	Iceland	1862–
Rocket	Stmr	5½		Calif. Coast	1878
Sea Breeze	Bark	323	W. M. Barnes	Pacific	10/2/
Siberia	Aux. Brig		E. E. Smith	Russia	3/15/
Wm. F. Safford	Brig	175	Thos. W. Roys	Atlantic	5/5/5

Sources:
National Air and Space Museum, Smithsonian Institution (Notes collected by Frank H. Winter, Historian).
Reginald B. Hegarty, *Returns of Whaling Vessels Sailing from American Ports, 1876–1928.* (New Bedford, Mass., 1959).

rived	*Sperm Oil (Bbls.)*	*Whale Oil (Bbls.)*	*Whale-bone (Lbs.)*	*Walrus Ivory (Lbs.)*	*Walrus Oil (Bbls.)*	*Remarks*
*/3/79	400	6000		1200		Reputed to have carried whaling rockets. No details.
:ecked						Sailed from Br. Columbia.
*/28/80		3500	37000		100	
						Took a 73-foot, 90-ton finback off San Francisco.
*/17/79		850	4000	4000		
						Owned by North West Company, near Sitka, Alaska.
*/17/79		500	3500	1500		
*/11/79		120		1000		Reputed to have carried whaling rockets. No details.
						Reportedly cleared with "a number of [rocket] guns and shots." Possibly supply ship.
						No details available.
						Carried 15 rocket-harpoons, 2 launchers. No other details.
						Reputed to have carried whaling rockets. No details.
						Reputed to have carried whaling rockets. No details.
10/78	370	5250	300		500	From New Bedford, Mass.
*/7/81	10	600	30000			
						Roys-Lilliendahl experimental voyages. Sailed from New York City.
						Experimental vessel of Fletcher & Suits, Roys's successors. Took 35 whales.
*/9/78	475	3025	1150			Reputed to have carried whaling rockets. No details. From New Bedford, Mass.
2/79						Registered in Russia, but American owned.
1860						Roys developed rocket-harpoon on this ship in 1857. Was experimental voyage.

NOTES

Preface

1. Arne Odd Johnsen, *Finnmarksfangstens historie, 1864–1905*, Den moderne hvalfangsts historie, vol. 1 (Oslo, 1959), p. 66 (Our translation.)

1 / *Learning the Ropes*

1. Thomas W. Roys to Matthew F. Maury, January 19, 1851, in Maury, *Explanations and Sailing Directions to Accompany the Wind and Current Charts,* 7th ed. (Washington, D.C., 1855), p. 278.

2. Thomas W. Roys, "Descriptions of Whales" (1854), pp. 23–24, The Mariners Museum, Newport News, Va.

3. Dorothy S. Facer, Wayne County (N.Y.) Historian, to Frederick P. Schmitt, April 9, 1969.

4. "Passing of a Real Pioneer," *Butler County Press* (David City, Neb.), June 23, 1932, p. 1.

5. *Commercial Press* (Pultneyville, N.Y.), September 1869, p. 3.

6. Town of Williamson, N.Y., Records of Lakeview Cemetery, in Department of History, Wayne County, Lyons, N.Y.

7. U.S. Census Office, 7th Census, 1850, for Wayne County, N.Y.

8. *Butler County Press,* June 23, 1932, p. 1.

9. Thomas W. Roys, "The Voyages of Thomas Welcome Roys" (n.d.), p. 5, Suffolk County Whaling Museum, Sag Harbor, N.Y.

10. Ibid., pp. 5–6.

11. Ibid., p. 6.

12. Ibid.

13. James Truslow Adams, *History of the Town of Southampton* (Bridgehampton, N.Y., 1918), pp. 324–25.

14. Ibid.

15. Roys, "Voyages," pp. 6–7.

16. Adams, *History of Southampton,* pp. 326–27.

17. Roys, "Voyages," p. 7.

18. Adams, *History of Southampton,* pp. 326–27.
19. Roys, "Voyages," p. 7; Adams, *History of Southampton,* pp. 328–29.
20. Roys, "Voyages," pp. 7–8.
21. Ibid., pp. 8–9.
22. Ibid., p. 9.
23. Ibid., pp. 9–10.
24. Ibid., p. 10.
25. Ibid., pp. 10–11.
26. Ibid., p. 11.
27. Ibid., pp. 12–13.
28. Ibid., p. 13.
29. Adams, *History of Southampton,* pp. 330–31.
30. *Corrector* (Sag Harbor, N.Y.), August 26, 1843, p. 3.

2 / *The Rise to Success*

1. James Truslow Adams, *History of the Town of Southampton* (Bridgehampton, N.Y., 1918), pp. 332–33; Dennis Wood, "Whaling Vessels from the United States: 1831–1873" (n.d.), 1:70, Melville Whaling Room, New Bedford (Mass.) Free Public Library.
2. Thomas W. Roys, "The Voyages of Thomas Welcome Roys" (n.d.), pp. 13–14, Suffolk County Whaling Museum, Sag Harbor, N.Y.
3. Ibid., pp. 14, 75.
4. Ibid., p. 14; Charles M. Scammon, Papers and Correspondence, PK 206 (Scrapbooks), 1:102–3, Bancroft Library, University of California, Berkeley.
5. Roys, "Voyages," pp. 14–15.
6. Ibid., pp. 15–16.
7. Ibid.
8. Ibid., pp. 16–17.
9. Ibid., pp. 17–18.
10. Ibid., p. 18.
11. Ibid., pp. 18–19.
12. Ibid., p. 19.
13. Wood, "Whaling Vessels," 1:70.
14. Roys, "Voyages," p. 19.
15. Wood, "Whaling Vessels," 1:70.
16. Frederick P. Schmitt and Frank H. Winter, "First Whaler Through

the Bering Strait," *Compass* 44 (Summer 1974):24–27.

17. Thomas W. Roys, "Descriptions of Whales" (1854), pp. 25–26, The Mariners Museum, Newport News, Va.; "Yankee Whaling Enterprise" and "New Cruising Ground for Whale Ships," *The Friend* (Honolulu, Hawaii), November 1, 1848, p. 1. See also Scammon, Papers, 1:102–3.

18. Roys, "Descriptions," pp. 25–26. *The Friend,* November 1, 1848, p. 1; Scammon, Papers, 1:102–3.

3 / *A Bold Voyage into the Unknown*

1. Dennis Wood, "Whaling Vessels from the United States: 1831–1873" (n.d.), 2:619, Melville Whaling Room, New Bedford (Mass.) Free Public Library.

2. Arthur C. Watson, *The Long Harpoon* (New Bedford, Mass., 1929), p. 52; Charles M. Scammon, Papers and Correspondence, PK 206 (Scrapbooks), 1:102–3, Bancroft Library, University of California, Berkeley.

3. Thomas W. Roys, "The Voyages of Thomas Welcome Roys" (n.d.), pp. 19–20, Suffolk County Whaling Museum, Sag Harbor, N.Y.

4. *Corrector* (Sag Harbor, N.Y.), August 11, 1847, p. 3; U.S. Census Office, 10th Census, 1880, for Wayne County, N.Y.

5. Wood, "Whaling Vessels," 2:619.

6. Roys, "Voyages," p. 20.

7. Ibid.; Wood, "Whaling Vessels," 2:619.

8. Scammon, Papers, 1:102–3.

9. Thomas Roys, "Descriptions of Whales" (1854), p. 26, The Mariners Museum, Newport News, Va.

10. Roys, "Voyages," p. 20.

11. Ibid.; "Yankee Whaling Enterprise" and "New Cruising Ground for Whale Ships," *The Friend* (Honolulu, Hawaii), November 1, 1848, p. 1.

12. Roys, "Descriptions of Whales," p. 26.

13. Roys, "Voyages," pp. 20–21.

14. Ibid., p. 21.

15. Roys, "Descriptions of Whales," p. 26.

16. Roys, "Voyages," p. 21.

17. Roys, "Descriptions of Whales," p. 26.

18. Roys, "Voyages," p. 21.

19. Roys, "Voyages," pp. 21–22.

Notes

20. *The Friend,* November 1, 1848, p. 1.

21. *Balaena mysticetus Roysii.* See Charles M. Scammon, *The Marine Mammals of the North-western Coast of North America* (San Francisco and New York, 1874), pp. 60–61; Charles M. Scammon, "On the Cetaceans of the Western Coast of North America," *Proceedings of the Academy of Natural Sciences of Philadelphia* (1869), 1:35–36, 289. See also Avenir G. Tomilin, *Kitoobrazyne* (Moscow, 1957) (Sergei I. Ognev, Zveri SSR i Prilezhashchikh stran, v. 9). Translated as *Cetacea* by Israel Program for Scientific Translations (Jerusalem, 1967). (Sergei I. Ognev, ed., Mammals of the U.S.S.R. and adjacent countries, v. 9), pp. 14 ff. It should be noted that present-day cetologists have not been able to confirm the existence of this subspecies because of the scarcity of bowhead whales, which are considered endangered animals.

22. Alexander Starbuck, *History of the American Whale Fishery* (Washington, D.C., 1878), p. 98. See also William M. Davis, *Nimrod of the Sea* (New York, 1874), pp. 388–90.

23. Scammon, *Marine Mammals,* p. 60.

24. Capt. Hartson H. Bodfish, *Chasing the Bowhead* (Cambridge, Mass., 1936), p. 89.

25. Starbuck, *History of the American Whale Fishery,* pp. 448–49.

26. Bodfish, *Chasing the Bowhead,* p. 89.

27. Richard C. Kugler, Director, Old Dartmouth Historical Society and Whaling Museum, New Bedford, Mass., to Frederick P. Schmitt, September 23, 1971; Watson, *The Long Harpoon,* pp. 54–56.

28. Tomilin, *Cetacea,* pp. 27–35; Frederick P. Schmitt, "Oh, What a Wild One He Must Have Been!" *Yankee* 36 (June 1972):102–7.

29. Roys, "Descriptions of Whales," p. 27.

30. *The Friend,* November 1, 1848, p. 1.

31. From some general notes provided by George E. Levey, former curator, Suffolk County Whaling Museum, Sag Harbor, N.Y.

32. *Whalemen's Shipping List and Merchant's Transcript* (New Bedford, Mass.), February 6, 1849, p. 2.

33. Roys, "Voyages," p. 22.

34. Wood, "Whaling Vessels," 2:619.

35. Roys, "Descriptions of Whales," p. 27.

36. Ibid., pp. 28–29.

37. Roys, "Voyages," p. 24.

38. Quoted ibid., p. 23.

39. *Nautical Magazine and Naval Chronicle* (London) 21 (June 1852): 327.

4 / *Return to Whalers' Utopia*

1. Charles M. Scammon, Papers and Correspondence, PK 206 (Scrapbooks), 1:102–3, Bancroft Library, University of California, Berkeley.

2. Walter Restored Jones to Lady Jane Franklin, July 31, 1849, Records of the Admiralty, Public Record Office, London, ADM 7 / 189:5940.

3. Frederick P. Schmitt, *Mark Well the Whale!* (Port Washington, N.Y., 1971), pp. 20–21.

4. Scammon, Papers, 1:102–3.

5. Isaac M. Jessup, journal of a voyage in ship *Sheffield*, August 17, 1849, to June 16, 1850 (manuscript), entry for August 17, 1849, G. W. Blunt White Library, Mystic Seaport, Mystic, Conn.

6. Ibid., August 17, August 18, 1849. See also various entries, August 19–27, 1849.

7. Ibid., September 2, 1849.

8. Ibid., October 14, November 4, November 6, 1849. See also various entries, October 14 through November 6, 1849.

9. Ibid., November 23, December 1, 1849. See also various entries, November 20 through December 21, 1849.

10. Ibid., December 24, 1849. See also entry for December 23, 1849.

11. Ibid., December 29, 1849; January 17, February 8, 1850. See also various entries, December 29, 1849, through February 8, 1850.

12. Ibid., February 11, 1850. See also entry for February 9, 1850.

13. Depositions of various crew members relating attempted mutiny aboard ship *Sheffield*, dated February 1850, Jones Collection, Whaling Museum Society, Cold Spring Harbor, N.Y.

14. Deposition of Thomas W. Roys, master, Henry J. Green, first officer, and Samuel W. Roys, second officer, relating attempted mutiny, ship *Sheffield*, dated February 10, 1850, Jones Collection. See also, Thomas Welcome Roys to Benjamin H. Foster, March 31, 1850, Morse Whaling Collection, John Hay Library, Brown University, Providence, R.I.

15. Jessup, journal, February 23, 1850. See also entries for February 21 and 22, 1850.

16. Ibid., February 22 and 23, 1850.

17. Harry D. Sleight, *The Whale Fishery on Long Island* (Bridgehampton, N.Y., 1931), pp. 129–34, contains an excellent account of Sag Harbor whalemen who migrated to the gold fields of California.

18. Jessup, journal, February 26, 1850.

19. Ibid., March 1 and 3, 1850.

Notes

20. Ibid., April 1 and 2, 1850.

21. James Truslow Adams, *History of the Town of Southampton* (Bridgehampton, N.Y., 1918), p. 367.

22. Jessup, journal, April 3, 1850.

23. Ibid., April 28, May 7, 1850. See also various entries, April 5 through June 15, 1850.

24. Walter Restored Jones to Lady Jane Franklin, July 31, 1849, Public Record Office.

25. Thomas W. Roys, "Descriptions of Whales" (1854), p. 19, The Mariners Museum, Newport News, Va. Additional information on the migration of bowhead whales can be found in Avenir G. Tomilin, *Kitoobraznye* (Moscow, 1957) (Sergei I. Ognev, Zveri SSR i Prilezhashchikh stran, v. 9). Translated as *Cetacea* by Israel Program for Scientific Translations (Jerusalem, 1967). (Sergei I. Ognev, ed., Mammals of the U.S.S.R. and adjacent countries, v. 9), p. 28.

26. Thomas W. Roys, "The Voyages of Thomas Welcome Roys" (n.d.), p. 24, Suffolk County Whaling Museum, Sag Harbor, N.Y.

27. Roys, "Descriptions of Whales," pp. 20–21.

28. *Long Islander* (Huntington, N.Y.), April 11, 1851, p. 2.

29. Roys, "Voyages," pp. 24–25.

30. Ibid., pp. 25–26.

31. Dennis Wood, "Whaling Vessels from the United States: 1831–1873" (n.d.), 2:613, Melville Whaling Room, New Bedford, (Mass.) Free Public Library.

32. Roys, "Voyages," pp. 26–27; *Long Islander,* April 11, 1851, p. 2.

33. Roys, "Voyages," p. 27.

34. *Long Islander,* April 11, 1851, p. 2.

35. Roys, "Voyages," p. 27.

36. Wood, "Whaling Vessels," 2:613.

37. *Corrector* (Sag Harbor, N.Y.), April 12, 1851, p. 3.

38. Roys, "Voyages," p. 27.

39. Scammon, Papers, 1:102–3.

40. Roys, "Descriptions of Whales," p. 28.

41. Ibid., p. 29.

42. Walter Restored Jones to Lady Jane Franklin, July 31, 1849, Public Record Office.

43. Walter Restored Jones to Lady Jane Franklin, September 13, 1849, Records of the Admiralty, Public Record Office, London, ADM 7 / 189: 5940.

44. Roys, "Voyages," pp. 27–28.

45. Roys claimed that the disappearance occurred on San Cristobal (Makira) Island ("Voyages," p. 28), but other authors (see note following) maintain Boyd vanished on Guadalcanal Island.

46. For a more complete account of Ben Boyd's life and exploits see Max Colwell, *Whaling Around Australia* (London, 1969), pp. 70–83, 91; William John Dakin, *Whalemen Adventurers* (Sydney, 1963), pp. 90, 98–106; and L. S. Rickard, *The Whaling Trade in Old New Zealand* (Auckland, 1965), pp. 123–25, 134.

47. Roys, "Voyages," p. 28.

48. Dakin, *Whalemen Adventurers,* p. 106.

49. Roys, "Voyages," pp. 28–29.

50. Scammon, Papers, 1:102–3.

51. Wood, "Whaling Vessels," 2:613.

52. Schmitt, *Mark Well the Whale!* p. 122.

5 / *The Professional Whaleman*

1. For further reading, see William A. Herdman, *Founders of Oceanography and Their Work* (New York, 1923); Robert C. Cowen, *Frontiers of the Sea* (Garden City, N.Y., 1960).

2. J. L. McHugh, "Pathfinder of the Seas," *Sea Frontiers* 4 (May 1958):101–7. For further reading, see Charles Lee Latham, *Matthew Fontaine Maury: The Pathfinder of the Seas* (Annapolis, 1927); Frances L. Williams, *Matthew Fontaine Maury, Scientist of the Sea* (New Brunswick, N.J., 1963).

3. Matthew F. Maury, *Explanations and Sailing Directions to Accompany the Wind and Current Charts,* 7th ed. (Washington, D.C., 1855), pp. 277–78.

4. Matthew F. Maury to Thomas W. Roys, October 3, 1849, record group 78, Naval Observatory letters sent, vol. 4, National Archives, Washington, D.C.

5. Maury, *Explanations,* pp. 277–78.

6. Matthew F. Maury to Thomas W. Roys, February 9, March 1, and March 29, 1854, record group 78, Naval Observatory letters sent, vol. 10, National Archives, Washington, D.C.

7. Maury to Roys, February 9, 1854, National Archives.

Notes

8. Thomas W. Roys, "Descriptions of Whales" (1854), pp. 1–24, The Mariners Museum, Newport News, Va.

9. Maury to Roys, February 9, 1854, National Archives.

10. Roys, "Descriptions," p. 2. See also note 21, chapter 3, above.

11. Phillip Hershkovitz, *Catalog of Living Whales* (Washington, D.C., 1966), p. 194. See also note 21, chapter 3.

12. Charles M. Scammon, *The Marine Mammals of the North-western Coast of North America* (San Francisco and New York, 1874), pp. 52–65, 305–6.

13. "The 'Killer Whale,'" *Annual of Scientific Discovery* (London, 1855), pp. 369–70.

14. Thomas W. Roys, "Voyages of Thomas Welcome Roys" (n.d.), pp. 57–58, Suffolk County Whaling Museum, Sag Harbor, N.Y.

15. Thomas W. Roys to Matthew F. Maury, October 19, 1860, record group 78, Naval Observatory letters received, National Archives, Washington, D.C.

16. McHugh, "Pathfinder of the Seas," pp. 101–7.

17. Roys, "Descriptions of Whales," pp. 21–22.

18. Roys, "Voyages," pp. 66, 90.

19. Frederick P. Schmitt, "Whaling's Last Refrain?" *Sea Frontiers* 19 (September-October 1973):306–12.

Chapter 6 / Chasing the Mighty Rorquals

1. Thomas W. Roys, "Voyages of Thomas Welcome Roys" (n.d.), pp. 77–78, Suffolk County Whaling Museum, Sag Harbor, N.Y. For further research on this chapter, see also Rogers Bishop, journal of a voyage in ship *Hannibal*, May 21, 1855, to December 26, 1855, combined with journal of a voyage in brig *William F. Safford*, May 5, 1856, to August 16, 1857, private collection of Mrs. Jean Gann, Hampton Bays, N.Y. A transcript is in the possession of the authors. This journal was discovered when this book was in press.

2. Thomas W. Roys, "Descriptions of Whales" (1854), pp. 21–22, The Mariners Museum, Newport News, Va.

3. Thomas W. Roys to Matthew F. Maury, October 19, 1860, record group 78, Naval Observatory letters received, National Archives, Washington, D.C.; Roys, "Voyages," pp. 29–30.

4. Roys to Maury, October 19, 1860, National Archives.

5. Robert G. Albion, *Square Riggers on Schedule* (Princeton, N.J., 1938), p. 300.

6. Dennis Wood, "Whaling Vessels from the United States: 1831–1873" (n.d.), 3:550, Melville Whaling Room, New Bedford, (Mass.) Free Public Library.

7. Roys to Maury, October 19, 1860, National Archives; Roys, "Voyages," p. 30.

8. *The Times* (St. John's, Newfoundland), August 29, 1855, p. 2.

9. Roys, "Voyages," p. 30.

10. This was a large, all-brass shoulder gun developed by Robert Brown of New London, Conn., about 1852. It was made to discharge harpoons, lances, and bombs. The gun weighed almost thirty-five pounds.

11. Roys to Maury, October 19, 1860, National Archives.

12. Ibid.; Roys, "Voyages," p. 30.

13. Roys to Maury, October 19, 1860, National Archives; Roys, "Voyages," p. 30.

14. Roys to Maury, October 19 , 1860, National Archives; Roys, "Voyages," pp. 30–31.

15. Roys, "Voyages," p. 31.

16. Permanent registers, brig *William F. Safford,* April 29, 1856, and May 29, 1856, Sag Harbor, N.Y., record group 41, Bureau of Marine Inspection and Navigation, National Archives, Washington, D.C.

17. Frederick P. Schmitt, "Satan's Ships," *Long Island Forum* 37 (June 1974):110–14.

18. Roys, "Voyages," p. 93.

19. Roys to Maury, October 19, 1860, National Archives.

20. George Brown Goode, *The Fisheries and Fishery Industries of the United States,* section 5: History and Methods of the Fisheries (Washington, D.C., 1887), 2: 253, 255; Clifford W. Ashley, *The Yankee Whaler* (Boston, 1926), p. 87.

21. Roys to Maury, October 19, 1860, National Archives.

22. Wood, "Whaling Vessels," 3:616.

23. Roys, "Voyages," p. 93.

24. Roys to Maury, October 19, 1860, National Archives; Arne Odd Johnsen, *Finnmarksfangstens historie, 1864–1905* Den moderne hvalfangst historie, vol. 1 (Oslo, 1959), p. 66 (our translation).

25. Roys to Maury, October 19, 1860, National Archives; Roys, "Voyages," p. 31; and Johnsen, *Finnmarksfangstens historie, 1864–1905,* p. 67.

26. Roys, "Voyages," p. 93.

Notes

27. Roys to Maury, October 19, 1860, National Archives.

28. Roys, "Voyages," pp. 31, 93; Wood, "Whaling Vessels," 3:616.

29. *Examiner* (Cork, Ireland), September 17, 1856, p. 2.

30. Roys to Maury, October 19, 1860, National Archives.

31. *Dictionary of National Biography* (London, 1917), 21:166–70.

32. Roys to Maury, October 19, 1860, National Archives; Roys, "Voyages," pp. 31–32.

33. Roys, "Voyages," p. 32.

34. Ibid., pp. 32–33; Roys to Maury, October 19, 1860, National Archives.

35. British Patent Specification 2301 / 1857; see also, 1402 / 1857, 2340 / 1857, The Patent Office, Orpington, Kent, England.

36. Roys to Maury, October 19, 1860, National Archives.

37. Ibid.; Roys, "Voyages," p. 33.

38. Wood, "Whaling Vessels," 3:616; Roys, "Voyages," p. 33.

39. Roys to Maury, October 19, 1860, National Archives. See also, Roys, "Voyages," p. 33.

40. For further reading see Frank H. Winter, "Sir William Congreve: A Bi-Centennial Memorial," *Spaceflight* 14 (September 1972):333–34.

41. Roys to Maury, October 19, 1860, National Archives.

42. Roys, "Voyages," p. 33.

43. Ibid., pp. 33, 93.

44. Roys to Maury, October 19, 1860, National Archives.

45. Roys, "Voyages," pp. 33, 93.

46. Ibid., p. 34.

47. Wood, "Whaling Vessels," 3:616; *Corrector* (Sag Harbor, N.Y.), February 5, 1859, p. 3.

48. Roys to Maury, October 19, 1860, National Archives.

49. Ibid.

50. Wood, "Whaling Vessels," 3:616.

51. Roys to Maury, October 19, 1860, National Archives.

52. Ibid.

53. Roys, "Voyages," p. 34.

54. Roys to Maury, October 19, 1860, National Archives.

55. Roys, "Voyages," p. 34.

56. Roys to Maury, October 19, 1860, National Archives.

57. Ibid.

58. Ibid.

59. British Patent Specification 965 / 1859, The Patent Office.

60. Roys to Maury, October 19, 1860, National Archives.

7 / Intermezzo

1. Jeannette Edwards Rattray, *The Perils of the Port of New York* (New York, 1973), p. 228.

2. Thomas W. Roys to Benjamin H. Foster, October 28, 1850, Morse Whaling Collection, John Hay Library, Brown University, Providence, R.I.

3. Roys to Foster, October 10, 1851, and March 1, 1852, Morse Whaling Collection.

4. U.S. Census Office, 10th Census, 1880, for Pultneyville, Wayne County, N.Y.

5. Colored photographic portraits of Thomas W. and Marie S. Roys, ca. 1863, on display in Suffolk County Whaling Museum, Sag Harbor, N.Y.; U.S. Census Office, 9th Census, 1870, for Town of Southold, Suffolk County, N.Y.; Harry D. Sleight, *The Whale Fishery on Long Island* (Bridgehampton, N.Y., 1931), p. 144; Dr. Clarence A. Wood, " 'Blubber Row,' Southold Town," *Long Island Forum* 12 (July 1949):125–26.

6. U.S. Patent 31,190, January 22, 1861, Patent Office, Washington, D.C. A working model of the launcher / gun is on display in the Suffolk County Whaling Museum, Sag Harbor, N.Y. For an earlier version, see British Patent Specification 450 / 1861, The Patent Office, Orpington, Kent, England.

7. U.S. Patent 31,190, January 22, 1861, Patent Office.

8. Ibid.

9. Arne Odd Johnsen, *Finnmarksfangstens historie, 1864–1905,* Den moderne hvalfangsts historie, vol. 1, (Oslo, 1959) pp. 66–72, 646–47 (our translation).

10. Thomas W. Roys to Thomas Nye, undated letter ca. 1859–60, quoted in Johnsen, *Finnmarksfangstens historie, 1864–1905*, p. 647; "Old Whaling Gun Believed Father of Modern 'Bazooka,' " *Standard-Times* (New Bedford, Mass.), February 3, 1946, p. 8.

11. Thomas W. Roys to Matthew F. Maury, October 19, 1860, record group 78, Naval Observatory letters received, National Archives, Washington, D.C.

12. Capt. Theron B. Worth to Thomas Nye, January 11, 1860, in private collection of Mr. Edouard A. Stackpole, Nantucket, Mass.; *Standard-Times* (New Bedford, Mass.), February 3, 1946, p. 8.

13. *Standard-Times* (New Bedford, Mass.), February 3, 1946, p. 8.

14. Thomas W. Roys, "Voyages of Thomas Welcome Roys" (n.d.), p. 35, Suffolk County Whaling Museum, Sag Harbor, N.Y. See also Rev. Alfred

Notes

Rodman Hussey, "Life of Charles W. Morgan," *The Log* (of Mystic Seaport), 18 (summer 1966):72–74.

15. Roys, "Voyages," p. 35.

16. *Whalemen's Shipping List and Merchant's Transcript* (New Bedford, Mass.), various issues, June 18 to August 13, 1861.

8 / Enter Mr. G. A. Lilliendahl

1. British Patent Specification 2301 / 1858, The Patent Office, Orpington, Kent, England.

2. Frank H. Winter and Mitchell R. Sharpe, "Edward Mourrier Boxer, Rocketeer," *Spaceflight* 16 (November 1974):427–29; Frank H. Winter and Mitchell R. Sharpe, "The California Whaling Rocket and the Men Behind It," *California Historical Quarterly* 50 (December 1971):349.

3. Frank H. Winter, "Sir William Congreve: A Bi-Centennial Memorial," *Spaceflight* 14 (September 1972):333–34.

4. Ibid. *Algemeene konst en letter-bode* (Haarlem, Netherlands, 1822), p. 43; Basil Lubbock, *The Arctic Whalers* (Glasgow, 1937), p. 227; Arne Odd Johnsen, *Finnmarksfangstens historie, 1864–1905*, Den moderne hvalfangsts historie, vol. 1 (Oslo, 1959) pp. 76–77 (our translation).

5. Cornelis de Jong, *Geschiedenis van de oude Nederlandse walvisvaart, Deel een, Grondslagen, ontstaan en opkomst, 1612–1642* (Pretoria, South Africa, 1972), pp. 155–56.

6. Winter and Sharpe, "The California Whaling Rocket and the Men Behind It," p. 361.

7. Thomas W. Roys to Obed N. Swift, December 26, 1860 (printed form letter), Kendall Whaling Museum, Sharon, Mass.

8. "G. A. Lilliendahl Died in Mexico," *The Evening Journal* (Jersey City, N.J.), December 5, 1907, p. 5; "Lilliendahl's Death Ends a Busy Life," ibid., December 9, 1907, p. 3.

9. *The Evening Journal,* December 55, 1907, p. 5; ibid., December 9, 1907, p. 3; "Fetes at New York to Commemorate the Laying of the Atlantic Telegraph Cable," *Illustrated London News*, September 25, 1858, p. 298.

10. *The Evening Journal*, December 5, 1907, p. 5; ibid., December 9, 1907, p. 3.

11. Ibid., December 9, 1907, p. 3.

12. British Patent Specification 450 / 1861, The Patent Office.

13. U.S. Patent 35,474, June 3, 1862, U.S. Patent 35,475, June 3, 1862, and U.S. Patent 35,476, June 3, 1862, Patent Office, Washington, D.C.

14. U.S. Patent 35,977, July 22, 1862, Patent Office.

15. Thomas W. Roys, "Voyages of Thomas Welcome Roys" (n.d.), p. 35, Suffolk County Whaling Museum, Sag Harbor, N.Y.; U.S. Patent Office, instrument dated June 4, 1862, recorded June 13, 1862, Liber O-6, p. 172, for sale of Roys's patent to Lilliendahl, Patent Office, Washington, D.C.

16. Permanent register, bark *Reindeer,* New York, N.Y., May 15, 1862, record group 41, Bureau of Marine Inspection and Navigation, National Archives, Washington, D.C. According to this document, *Reindeer* was built at Columbia, Maine, in 1857 and was formerly registered in Newport, R.I. She was 100 feet long and had a 25¼ foot beam.

17. Roys, "Voyages," pp. 35–36.

18. Ibid., p. 36; Peter Duignan and Clarence Clendenen, *The United States and the African Slave Trade 1619–1862* (Stanford, Calif., 1963), p. 51.

9 / Beginning the Inventive Years

1. *Nordanfari* (Akureyri, Iceland), August 1863, pp. 67–68, translated by Gunnar Sveinsson; Thomas W. Roys, "Voyages of Thomas Welcome Roys" (n.d.), pp. 36–37, Suffolk County Whaling Museum, Sag Harbor, N.Y.

2. Roys, "Voyages," p. 77; Charles M. Scammon, *The Marine Mammals of the North-western Coast of North America* (San Francisco and New York, 1874), p. 70.

3. "Lilliendahl's Death Ends a Busy Life," *The Evening Journal* (Jersey City, N.J.), December 9, 1907, p. 3; Bernard Fried, Department of Biology, Lafayette College, Easton, Pa., to Frederick P. Schmitt, December 28, 1970.

4. Roys, "Voyages," p. 37; *Evening Journal,* December 9, 1907, p. 3.

5. *Corrector* (Sag Harbor, N.Y.), various issues, 1856–59; *Nordanfari,* August 1863, pp. 67–68.

6. Arne Odd Johnsen, *Finnmarksfangstens historie, 1864–1905,* Den moderne hvalfangsts historie, vol. 1 (Oslo, 1959), p. 80 (our translation).

7. Civil War Pension Records, Gustavus A. Lilliendahl, application no. 1,362,728, record group 15, Veterans Administration, National Archives, Washington, D.C.; *Evening Journal,* December 9, 1907, p. 3.

8. *Nordanfari,* September 1864, p. 37, translated by Gunnar Sveinsson; Ole Smith, prefect of the district of Seydisfjördur, to the Governor of North and East Iceland, November 12, 1864, N.M. XV, 23 (Copybook of Nordur-Múlasýsla 1863–65), 763 / 1864, Official Archives of Iceland, Reykjavik (our

Notes

translation). Roys, "Voyages," p. 77. Roys claims here to have killed thirty-three whales for the season, perhaps to impress financial backers.

9. U.S. Patent Office, instrument dated April 15, 1864, recorded April 19, 1864, Liber F-7, p. 291, Patent Office, Washington, D.C.

10. Roys, "Voyages," p. 77.

11. *Whalemen's Shipping List and Merchant's Transcript* (New Bedford, Mass.), September 6, 1864, p. 2.

12. Ole Smith, November 12, 1864, Official Archives of Iceland.

13. Ibid.; Department of Justice, Copenhagen, to Ole Smith, November 21, 1864, section Nordur og Austur Amt file, Fridrikshafn, for May 13, 1865, Official Archives of Iceland, Reykjavik (our translation).

14. Department of Justice, Copenhagen, to Ole Smith, February 22, 1865, section Nordur og Austur Amt file for Fridrikshafn, May 13, 1865, Official Archives of Iceland, Reykjavik (our translation); Carl Normann, "Hval-, hvalros- og saelhunde-fangstens historie og udvikling," *Tidsskrift for søvaesen* (Copenhagen, 1867), 2:246 (our translation).

15. Roys, "Voyages," p. 77.

16. Broadside entitled "Masters of Vessels!" concerning ineptitude of William Henry Royce (*sic*) and others, n.d., Old Dartmouth Historical Society and Whaling Museum, New Bedford, Mass.; *Corrector* (Sag Harbor, N.Y.) and *Express* (Sag Harbor, N.Y.), various issues, 1856–61; Isaac M. Jessup [to his father], March 18, 1865, in private collection of Mr. Thomas G. Lytle, Norwalk Conn.; Captain (no forename given) Tvede, "Den amerikanske hvalfanger-virksomhed under Island i 1865–66," *Tidsskrift for fiskeri* (Copenhagen, 1868), 2:55–56 (our translation); "Passing of a Real Pioneer," *Butler County Press* (David City, Neb.), June 23, 1932, p. 1; Mrs. Fred Cornwall, Pultneyville, N.Y., to Frederick P. Schmitt, May 16, 1969; and John F. Leavitt, *The Charles W. Morgan* (Mystic, Conn., 1973), p. 91.

17. *Nordanfari,* May 30, 1865, p. 40, translated by Gunnar Sveinsson.

18. Roys, "Voyages," pp. 37–38, 95; Tvede, "Den amerikanske hvalfanger-virksomhed under Island i 1865–66," 2:60. Roys notes in his "Voyages" (p. 95) that Lilliendahl also supplied rockets from this defective lot to five ships of the firm of Swift and Perry of New Bedford, Mass.

19. Roys, "Voyages," p. 38; Ole Smith to the Department of Justice, Copenhagen, June 6, 1865, N.M. XV, 23 (Copybook of Nordur-Múlasýsla 1863–65), 952 / 1865, Official Archives of Iceland, Reykjavik (our translation).

20. Johnsen, *Finnmarksfangstens historie, 1864–1905,* pp. 72–73.

21. Harald V. Fiedler, ed., "Utdrag af Captltnt O. Hammers dagbog . . . , *Tidsskrift for fiskeri* (Copenhagen, 1868), 2:260 (our translation).

22. Ibid., 2:265.
23. Roys, "Voyages," p. 43.
24. Ibid., p. 43.
25. Ibid., pp. 43–44.
26. Ibid., pp. 44–45.
27. Ibid., pp. 45–46.
28. *Pjódólfr* (Reykjavik, Iceland), November 2, 1865, p. 1, translated by Gunnar Sveinsson; Tvede, "Den amerikanske hvalfanger-virksomhed under Island i 1865–66," 2:54; Johnsen, *Finnmarksfangstens historie, 1864–1905*, pp. 72–73.
29. *Pjódólfr*, November 2, 1865, p. 1; Normann, "Hval-, hvalros- og saelhunde-fangstens historie og udvikling," 2:54–55; Tvede, "Den amerikanske hvalfanger-virksomhed under Island i 1865–66," 2:54–56, 65; Roys, "Voyages," p. 38; Johnsen, *Finnmarksfangstens historie, 1864–1905*, p. 73.
30. Roys, "Voyages," p. 38; Tvede, "Den amerikanske hvalfanger-virksomhed under Island i 1865–66," 2:54–55.

10 / Defeated Again

1. Captain (no forename given) Tvede, "Den amerikanske hvalfanger-virksomhed under Island i 1865–66," *Tidsskrift for fiskeri* (Copenhagen, 1868), 2:58 (our translation); Thomas W. Roys, "Voyages of Thomas Welcome Roys" (n.d.), pp. 39–40, Suffolk County Whaling Museum, Sag Harbor, N.Y.; Arne Odd Johnsen, *Finnmarksfangstens historie, 1864–1905*, Den moderne hvalfangsts historie, vol. 1 (Oslo, 1959), p. 74 (our translation). The spelling of Roys's steamers *Staperaider* and *Sileno* varies in these accounts. His own spelling has been retained throughout.
2. Apparently she never sailed; see Johnsen, *Finnmarksfangstens historie, 1864–1905*, p. 74.
3. *Corrector* (Sag Harbor, N.Y.), March 10, 1866, p. 1.
4. Tvede, "Den amerikanske hvalfanger-virksomhed under Island i 1865–66," 2:58–59. Ole Smith, prefect of the district of Seydisfjördur, to the Ministry of Justice, Copenhagen, November 19, 1866, N.M. XV, 24 (Copybook of Nordur-Múlasýsla 1866–68), 144 / 1866, Official Archives of Iceland, Reykjavik (our translation).
5. Ole Smith, prefect of the district of Seydisfjördur, to the Ministry of Justice, Copenhagen, May 24, 1866, N.M. XV, 24 (Copybook of Nordur-

Notes

Múlasýsla 1866–68), 81 / 1866, Official Archives of Iceland, Reykjavik (our translation).

6. Ole Smith to Ministry of Justice, November 19, 1866, Official Archives of Iceland; *Nordanfari* (Akureyri, Iceland), December 24, 1866, pp. 71–72, translated by Gunnar Sveinsson; Tvede, "Den amerikanske hvalfanger-virksomhed under Island i 1865–66," 2:62.

7. Ole Smith to Ministry of Justice, November 19, 1866, Official Archives of Iceland.

8. Tvede, "Den amerikanske hvalfanger-virksomhed under Island i 1865–66," 2:62.

9. Ole Smith to Ministry of Justice, November 19, 1866, Official Archives of Iceland; Tvede, "Den amerikanske hvalfanger-virksomhed under Island i 1865–66," 2:61–62.

10. Ole Smith to Ministry of Justice, November 19, 1866, Official Archives of Iceland.

11. Ibid.

12. Harald V. Fiedler, ed., "Utdrag af Captltnt O. Hammers dagbog . . . ," *Tidsskrift for fiskeri* (Copenhagen, 1869), 3:87 (our translation).

13. Tvede, "Den amerikanske hvalfanger-virksomhed under Island i 1865–66," 2:57.

14. Ibid.; Roys, "Voyages," p. 40.

15. Roys, "Voyages," pp. 40–41.

16. Tvede, "Den amerikanske hvalfanger-virksomhed under Island i 1865–66," 2:59–60.

17. Ibid., 2:60–61.

18. Ibid., 2:63; Ole Smith to Ministry of Justice, November 19, 1866, Official Archives of Iceland.

19. Harald V. Fiedler, ed., "Utdrag af Captltnt O. Hammers dagbog . . . ," *Tidsskrift for fiskeri* (Copenhagen, 1868), 2:289 (our translation). Roys talked to Captain Hammer about the risk of the harpoon "glancing off the whale."

20. Roys, "Voyages," p. 77.

21. U.S. Patent 54,211, April 24, 1866, Patent Office, Washington, D.C.; British Patent Specification 550 / 1865, The Patent Office, Orpington, Kent, England.

22. Frank H. Winter and Mitchell R. Sharpe, "The California Whaling Rocket and the Men Behind It," *California Historical Quarterly* 50 (December 1971):335.

23. Tvede, "Den amerikanske hvalfanger-virksomhed under Island i 1865–66," 2:60, 63.

24. Ambrose W. Landre, July 15, 1866, quoted in *Whalemen's Shipping List and Merchant's Transcript* (New Bedford, Mass.), August 21, 1866, p. 2.

25. Tvede, "Den amerikanske hvalfanger-virksomhed under Island i 1865–66," 2:63.

26. Roys, "Voyages," pp. 39–40.

27. Johnsen, *Finnmarksfangstens historie, 1864–1905*, pp. 77–78.

28. Tvede, "Den amerikanske hvalfanger-virksomhed under Island i 1865–66," 2:65–66.

29. *Ibid.*, 2:66.

30. Roys, "Voyages," p. 40.

31. U.S. Patent 53,684, April 3, 1866, Patent Office.

32. Tvede, "Den amerikanske hvalfanger-virksomhed under Island i 1865–66," 2:67.

33. Ibid., 2:68.

34. *Nordanfari*, December 24, 1866, pp. 71–72, translated by Gunnar Sveinsson; Roys, "Voyages," p. 40.

35. Ole Smith to Ministry of Justice, November 19, 1866, Official Archives of Iceland (our translation).

36. Ole Smith, prefect of the district of Seydisfjördur, to the Ministry of Justice, Copenhagen, November 8, 1867, N.M. XV, 24 (Copybook of Nordur-Múlasýsla 1866–68), 357 / 1867, Official Archives of Iceland, Reykjavik (our translation); Roys, "Voyages," pp. 41, 94.

37. Harald V. Fiedler, ed., "Utdrag af Captltnt O. Hammers dagbog...," *Tidsskrift for fiskeri*, 2 (1868), 3 (1869), and 4 (1870); R. Hammer, *Kaptajnlöjtnant O. C. Hammer, en livsskildring* (Copenhagen, 1928), p. 224 (both our translations).

38. *Nordanfari*, May 31, 1867, p. 43, translated by Gunnar Sveinsson; Ole Smith to the Ministry of Justice, November 8, 1867, Official Archives of Iceland.

39. Ole Smith to the Ministry of Justice, November 8, 1867, Official Archives of Iceland.

40. Capt. Christen Julius Klitgaard. *Fifty Years as Master Mariner* (New York, 1930), pp. 182–85.

41. Ole Smith to the Ministry of Justice, November 8, 1867, Official Archives of Iceland (our translation).

42. Johnsen, *Finnmarksfangstens historie, 1864–1905*, p. 78.

43. *Nordanfari*, February 15, 1868, pp. 6–7, and July 4, 1868, p. 31.

44. "G. A. Lilliendahl Died in Mexico," *The Evening Journal* (Jersey

Notes

City, N.J.), December 5, 1907, p. 5; "Lilliendahl's Death Ends a Busy Life," ibid., December 9, 1907, p. 3; *Manual of the One Hundred and Third Session of the Legislature of New Jersey, 1879* (Trenton, 1879), p. 104.

45. Gunnar Sveinsson, Pjódskjalasafn Islands, Reykjavik, Iceland, to Frank H. Winter, January 9, 1970.

46. Johnsen, *Finnmarksfangstens historie, 1864–1905*, pp. 79–83 (our translation).

11 / Competition Arrives

1. Harald V. Fiedler, ed., "Utdrag af Captltnt O. Hammers dagbog . . . ," *Tidsskrift for fiskeri* (Copenhagen, 1868), 2:277–78 (our translation).

2. Ibid. (1869), 3:100.

3. Sigurd Ristling, "Svend Foyn," in *Norsk biografisk lexsikon,* Edv. Bull and Einar Jansen, eds. (Oslo, 1929), 4:215–19; Arne Odd Johnsen, *Svend Foyn og hans dagbok* (Oslo, 1943) (our translation throughout); Johnsen, "Causation Problems of Modern Whaling," *Norsk hvalfangst-tidende* [Norwegian Whaling Gazette] 36 (August 1947):281–94; Johnsen, *Finnmarksfangstens historie, 1864–1905*, Den moderne hvalfangsts historie, vol. 1 (Oslo, 1959), pp. 131–270 (our translation).

4. Johnsen, *Svend Foyn og hans dagbok;* Johnsen, "Causation Problems of Modern Whaling;" Johnsen, *Finnmarksfangstens historie, 1864–1905*, pp. 131–270; Cornelis de Jong, "Het Haugiaanse reveil en de kapitalistische ontwikkeling van Noorwegen," *De Economist* (Haarlem, Netherlands) 100 (1951):845–48 (our translation).

5. Johnsen, *Svend Foyn og hans dagbok,* pp. 59–60; Johnsen, *Finnmarksfangstens historie, 1864–1905*, pp. 168–72.

6. Johnsen, *Svend Foyn og hans dagbok,* pp. 60–61.

7. Ibid., p. 220.

8. Arne Odd Johnsen, "The Shell Harpoon: A Short Account of the Way in which Svend Foyn Solved the Projectile Problem," *Norsk hvalfangst-tidende* 29 (September 1940):222–41; Johnsen, *Svend Foyn og hans dagbok,* pp. 63, 220.

9. Johnsen, *Svend Foyn og hans dagbok,* p. 232.

10. Ibid., p. 250.

11. Fiedler, "Utdrag af Captltnt O. Hammers dagbog . . ." (1870), 4:80, 89, and (1871), 5:236.

12. Risting, "Svend Foyn," 4:215–19; Johnsen, *Svend Foyn og hans dagbok*, pp. 35–36.

13. Fiedler, "Utdrag af Captltnt O. Hammers dagbog . . ." (1869), 3:100.

14. R. Hammer, *Kaptajnlöjtnant O. C. Hammer, en lirsskildring* (Copenhagen, 1928); T. A. Topsøe-Jensen and Emil Marquard, *Officerer i den Dansk-Norske søetat 1660–1814 og den Danske søetat 1814–1932* (Copenhagen, 1935), 1:524–25 (both our translation); Johnsen, *Finnmarksfangstens historie, 1864–1905*, pp. 83–86.

15. Captain (no forename given) Tvede, "Den amerikanske hvalfanger-virksomhed under Island i 1865–66," *Tidsskrift for fiskeri* (Copenhagen, 1868), 2:50–69 (our translation). Hammer, *Kaptajnlöjtnant O. C. Hammer, en lirsskildring*, pp. 197–200.

16. Carl Normann, "Hval-, hvalros- og saelhunde-fangstens historie og udvikling," *Tidsskrift for søvaesen* (Copenhagen, 1867), 2:246 (our translation); Tvede, "Den amerikanske hvalfanger-virksomhed under Island i 1865–66," 2:50–69.

17. *Pjódólfr* (Reykjavik, Iceland), May 7, 1866, pp. 105–6, translated by Gunnar Sveinsson; Fiedler, "Utdrag af Captltnt O. Hammers dagbog . . ." (1868), 2:277; Johnsen, *Finnmarksfangstens historie, 1864–1905*, pp. 84–85.

18. Fiedler, "Utdrag af Captltnt O. Hammers dagagbog . . ." (1868), 2:287–88.

19. L. Loizillon, "Harpon à fusée employé à là pêche de la baleine en Islande," *Revue maritime et coloniale* (Paris), 28 (December 1866): 863–66 (our translation); Tvede, "Den amerikanske hvalfanger-virksomhed under Island i 1865–66," 2:66–67; Fiedler, "Utdrag af Captltnt O. Hammers dagbog . . ." (1869), 3:87–88, 94.

20. Gaetano Amici, a Copenhagen pyrotechnician of Italian descent, had doubts probably from the beginning about whether the rocket-harpoon would kill fin whales effectively. See Johnsen, *Finnmarksfangstens historie, 1864–1905*, pp. 86–89, for illustrations of Amici's patent drawings. Nothing is known of the practical application of Amici's devices in actual whaling service; perhaps they were never used, for whaling people and authorities disliked the utilization of poison against whales, for good reason. For still

Notes

further reading, see "Gaetano Amici," *Salmonsens konversations leksikon* (Copenhagen, 1928), 23:521.

21. Fiedler, "Utdrag af Captltnt O. Hammers dagbog . . ." (1868), 2:269.

22. Normann, "Hval-, hvalros- og saelhunde-fangstens historie og udvikling," 2:246; Fiededler, "Utdrag af Captltnt O. Hammers dagbog . . ." (1869), 3:86.

23. Fiedler, "Utdrag af Captltnt O. Hammers dagbog . . ." (1869), 3:87–88, 94.

24. Normann, "Hval-, hvalros- og saelhunde-fangstens historie og udvikling," 2:246; Johnsen, *Finnmarksfangstens historie, 1864–1905*, p. 85.

25. Loizillon, "Harpon à fusée employé à là pêche de la baleine en Islande," p. 866.

26. Capt. Christen Julius Klitgaard, *Fifty Years as Master Mariner* (New York, 1930), p. 185. *Nordanfari* (Akureyri, Iceland), July 4, 1868, p. 31, translated by Gunnar Sveinsson; Johnsen, *Finnmarksfangstens historie, 1864–1905*, p. 85.

27. Johnsen, *Svend Foyn og hans dagbok*, pp. 229–30, and *Finnmarksfangstens historie, 1864–1905*, pp. 85–88.

28. Johnsen, *Finnmarksfangstens historie, 1864–1905*, p. 90; Cornelis de Jong, "Twee scheepsjournalen van C. J. Bottemanne als laatste Nederlandse commandeur ter walvisvangst," *Economisch-historisch jaarboek*, vol 30 (The Hague, 1965), p. 92; Judicial Register, Nordur-Múlasýsla [county], record of maritime court held in Seydisfjördur on September 23, 1865, N.M. III, 9:34, Official Archives of Iceland, Reykjavik (both our translation).

29. Johnsen, *Finnmarksfangstens historie, 1864–1905*, p. 91. There was a revival of Dutch whaling in 1946, when the ex-tanker *Willem Barendsz* (12,500 tons) was converted to a whaling factory ship and sent to the Antarctic. In 1955 she was replaced by the brand-new factory ship *Willem Barendsz II* (26,570 tons). The last season for *Barendsz II* was 1965–66, when she was sold to South African interests and was converted to a factory ship for processing sardines into fishmeal and oil.

30. De Jong, "Twee scheepsjournalen van C. J. Bottemanne als laatste Nederlandse commandeur ter walvisvangst," p. 116, n. 27.

31. Fiedler, "Utdrag af Captltnt O. Hammers dagbog . . ." (1869), 3:53–54, (1871), 5:68, and (1872), 6:87–88.

32. Johnsen, *Finnmarksfangstens historie, 1864–1905*, p. 91.

THomas Welcome Roys

12 / One Last Try

1. *Whalemen's Shipping List and Merchant's Transcript* (New Bedford, Mass.), February 19, 1867, and subsequent issues.

2. *Commercial Press* (Pultneyville, N.Y.), September 1869, p. 3; October 1869, p. 3.

3. Mrs. Fred Cornwall, Pultneyville, N.Y., to Frederick P. Schmitt, September 18, 1970. See also *Commercial Press*, August 1869, p. 3.

4. "Passing of a Real Pioneer," *Butler County Press* (David City, Neb.), June 23, 1932, p. 1.

5. U.S. Patent Office, instrument dated December 20, 1867, recorded December 23, 1867, Liber B-10, p. 191, Patent Office, Washington, D.C. The agreement encompassed patents 35,474 (Improved Rocket-Harpoon) of June 3, 1862; 53,684 (Improved Tackle for Raising Sunken Whales and Other Bodies) of April 3, 1866; and 54,211 (Improvement in Rocket-Harpoons) of April 24, 1866.

6. Thomas W. Roys, "Voyages of Thomas Welcome Roys" (n.d.), p. 41, Suffolk County Whaling Museum, Sag Harbor, N.Y.

7. *British Colonist* (Victoria, B.C.), July 27, 1868, p. 3; *Colonist* [magazine] (Victoria, B.C.), January 13, 1963, p. 7.

8. *British Colonist*, August 24, 1868, p. 3; August 28, p. 3.

9. Quoting *British Colonist*, July 1, 1868, p. 3: "The steamer *Holmes,* Capt. Ross [*sic*], has cleared for a whaling cruise in the Gulf of Georgia and surrounding waters." "Ross" could be a misspelling for "Roys."

10. Port of Victoria registry book, December 17, 1867, folio 7, Provincial Archives, Victoria, B.C.

11. *British Colonist*, August 20, 1868, p. 3.

12. Ibid., August 24, 1868, p. 3. Ibid., August 28, 1868, p. 3; September 5, 1868, p. 3; September 16, 1868, p. 3; December 5, 1868, p. 3.

13. Passenger manifests, December 7, 1868, arrival of ship *Robert Cowan* from Victoria, B.C., in Hawaii State Archives, Honolulu; *British Colonist*, October 7, 1868, p. 3; October 23, 1868, p. 3; January 7, 1869, p. 3; January 25, 1869, p. 3.

14. *British Colonist*, November 14, 1868, p. 3. Ibid., August 28, 1868, p. 3; February 9, 1869, p. 3; February 24, 1869, p. 3; March 4, 1869, p. 3.

Notes

15. Ibid., March 4, 1869, p. 3. Ibid., March 9, 1869, p. 3; Roys, "Voyages," p. 41.

16. *British Colonist,* March 13, 1869, p. 3; March 31, 1869, p. 3; April 23, 1869, p. 3; and Roys, "Voyages," pp. 41–42.

17. *British Colonist,* May 3, 1869, p. 3; May 10, 1869, p. 3; May 21, 1869, p. 3.

18. Ibid., June 14, 1869, p. 3. Ibid., June 4, 1869, p. 3; and June 9, 1869, p. 3; and Roys, "Voyages," p. 42.

19. *British Colonist,* July 22, 1869, p. 3, and August 6, 1869, p. 3. Ibid., July 27, 1869, p. 3; September 12, 1869, p. 3; September 17, 1869, p. 3; November 9, 1869, p. 3; December 14, 1869, p. 3; December 21, 1869, p. 3; and passenger manifests, July 12, 1869, arrival of brig *Byzantium* from Burrard Inlet, B.C., in Hawaii State Archives.

20. *Pacific Commercial Advertiser* (Honolulu, Hawaii), February 26, 1870, p. 3. Ibid., March 5, 1870, p. 3. Harbor master's records, entries and clearances of whaling vessels, Port of Honolulu, Hawaiian Islands, March 29, 1870, in Hawaii State Archives; and Roys, "Voyages," p. 42.

21. *Pacific Commercial Advertiser,* April 9, 1870, p. 3. Ibid., April 16, 1870, p. 3.

22. *British Colonist,* June 1, 1870, p. 3, and June 4, 1870, p. 3. Ibid., June 3, 1870, p. 3; June 12, 1870, p. 3; September 14, 1870, p. 3; November 26, 1870, p. 3; December 10, 1870, p. 3.

23. *British Colonist,* May 23, 1871, p. 3. Ibid., May 11, 1871, p. 3; May 31, 1871, p. 3; October 25, 1871, p. 3; and Port of Victoria registry book, May 20–21, 1869, folios 20 and 36, Provincial Archives. See also *Journal of Commerce* (San Francisco), August 8, 1878, for a biography of Capt. Rufus Calhoun.

24. Roys, "Voyages," p. 42. *British Colonist,* July 24, 1871, p. 3; August 8, 1871, p. 3; September 2, 1871, p. 3; September 30, 1871, p. 3.

25. Roys, "Voyages," p. 42.

26. *Standard* (Victoria, B.C.), October 25, 1871, p. 3; November 6, 1871, p. 3; November 11, 1871, p. 3; and *British Colonist,* October 25, 1871, p. 3; November 7, 1871, p. 3; November 22, 1871, p. 3. See also E. W. Wright, ed., *Lewis & Dryden's Marine History of the Pacific Northwest* (New York, 1961), p. 199.

27. *British Colonist,* November 7, 1871, p. 3. Ibid., October 25, 1871, p.

3, and November 10, 1871, p. 3; *Weekly Intelligencer* (Seattle, Wash.),
November 20, 1871, p. 2; passenger arrivals, November 24, 1871, San
Francisco (Calif.) Historical Records, Colma, Calif.; Roys, "Voyages," pp.
42–43, 90–91.

28. Roys, "Voyages," p. 47.

13 / *"So Ends."*

1. Alexander Starbuck, *History of the American Whale Fishery* (Washington, D.C., 1878,) pp. 696–97; Reginald B. Hegarty, *Returns of Whaling Vessels Sailing from American Ports . . . 1876–1928* (New Bedford, Mass., 1959), pp. 14–16; Frank H. Winter and Mitchell R. Sharpe, "The California Whaling Rocket and the Men Behind It," *California Historical Quarterly* 50 (December 1971):349–62. Much of chapter 13 is based on this article.

2. U.S. Patent Office, instruments dated June 17, 1872, and June 21, 1873, recorded December 14, 1877, Liber B-10, p. 191, and Liber P-22, p. 365, Patent Office, Washington, D.C.; *San Francisco Directory* (San Francisco, 1872), 95:310.

3. U.S. Patent Office, instruments dated June 17, 1872, and June 21, 1873, Patent Office; *San Francisco Examiner,* December 28, 1926, p. 4; U.S. Census Office, 10th Census, 1880, for San Francisco, Calif., sec. 12.

4. Winter and Sharpe, "The California Whaling Rocket and the Men Behind It," p. 351.

5. U.S. Census Office, 9th Census, 1870, Town of Southold, Suffolk County, N.Y.; *Trow's New York City Directory* (New York, N.Y., 1873–74 ed.), p. 1122; Charles M. Scammon, *The Marine Mammals of the Northwestern Coast of North America* (San Francisco and New York, 1874), p. 60.

6. *Long Island Democrat* (Jamaica, N.Y.), March 27, 1877, p. 3; E. G. Kelton, U.S. Consul, Mazatlán, Mexico, to William Hunter, Second Assistant Secretary of State, March 18, 1878, in *File Microcopies of Records in the National Archives,* no. 159, roll 4 (*Despatches from United States Consuls in Mazatlán, 1826–1906,* vol. 4, January, 1870–November 29, 1885) (Washington, D.C., 1949); *Express* (Sag Harbor, N.Y.), December 12, 1924; Mrs. David M. Byington (a descendant of Thomas W. Roys), Aurora, Col., to Frederick P. Schmitt, August 28, 1971; Death certificate for Thomas W. Roys, January 29, 1877, "Defunciones—1877," 4:24, Civil Registry, Mazatlán, Sinaloa, Mexico; Winter and Sharpe, "The California Whaling Rocket and the Men Behind It," p. 351.

7. Power of attorney, Marie S. Roys to Philander B. Roys, New York,

Notes

N.Y., July 25, 1878; petition for administration of Philander B. Roys for the estate of Thomas W. Roys, July 27, 1878, and administrator's bond of Philander B. Roys as administrator for the estate of Thomas W. Roys, July 27, 1878, no. 1878:01265—all in County Clerk's Office, County of Wayne, Lyons, N.Y.; application for patent for rocket-harpoon invented by Thomas W. Roys, "dec'd," by Philander B. Roys, administrator, to Hawaiian Minister of the Interior, February 14, 1879, Sanford Dole Collection, Hawaii State Archives, Honolulu, Hawaii; U.S. Patent 214,707, April 22, 1879, Patent Office, Washington, D.C.

8. Civil War pension claim of John Nelson Fletcher, alias John Baird, pension no. 116,904, record group 15, Veterans Administration, National Archives, Washington, D.C.; Certificate of marriage, John Baird to Josephine Hawkins, October 11, 1891, no. HD 12175-91, Office of the City Clerk, New York, N.Y.

9. North Carolina Department of Archives and History, Raleigh, N.C., to Frank H. Winter, November 12, 1969; *Confederate Papers Relating to Citizens or Business Firms,* roll 996, microcopy 346, and *Compiled Service Records of Confederate Soldiers . . . of North Carolina,* roll 122, microcopy 270, National Archives, Washington, D.C.

10. Various Baltimore city directories, 1867–72, passim; *San Francisco City Directory,* 1875, p. 974, and 1876, p. 311.

11. *San Francisco City Directory,* 1875, pp. 439, 696; *Journal of Commerce* (San Francisco), March 27, 1884, p. 2.

12. Civil War pension claim of John Nelson Fletcher, National Archives; *Mining & Scientific Press* (San Francisco), December 28, 1878, p. 401, and April 5, 1879, p. 209.

13. *Mining & Scientific Press,* April 5, 1879, p. 209.

14. Ibid.; Records of Steam Vessels, 1875–98, San Francisco Customs District, 27, and Index of Conveyances of Vessels, 1877–92, 212, record group 36, Bureau of Customs, National Archives, Washington, D.C.

15. *Mining & Scientific Press,* April 5, 1879, p. 209. *Whalemen's Shipping List and Merchant's Transcript* (New Bedford, Mass.), May 13, 1879, p. 2.

16. *Whalemen's Shipping List and Merchant's Transcript,* May 13, 1879, p. 2. *Mining & Scientific Press,* April 5, 1879, p. 209; *Daily Alta* (San Francisco), July 4, 1880, p. 1, and July 10, 1880, p. 4; *San Francisco Examiner,* July 10, 1880, p. 2; *San Francisco Chronicle,* July 10, 1880, p. 4; *The American Naturalist* 14 (April 1880):292–95.

17. *Bulletin of the U.S. National Museum,* 27, "Descriptive . . . Report Upon the Fisheries" (Washington, D.C., 1884), p. 281; Alaska Historical

Society, Juneau, to Frank H. Winter, March 2, 1970; Lloyd C. M. Hare, *Salted Tories* (Mystic, Conn., 1960), p. 57.

18. *San Francisco Chronicle,* October 6, 1879, p. 2. Ibid., September 23, 1879, p. 2.

19. Charles D. Voy to Spencer F. Baird, January 5, 1881, and February 7, 1881, Official Incoming Correspondence, 1879–82, Smithsonian Archives, Smithsonian Institution, Washington, D.C.; Interview, Frank H. Winter with Reginald B. Hegarty, March 24, 1970, New Bedford, Mass.

20. Civil War pension claim of John Nelson Fletcher, National Archives.

21. Charles D. Voy to Spencer F. Baird, January 5, 1881, and February 7, 1880, Smithsonian Archives; various Oakland, Calif., city directories, 1886–92, passim; *San Francisco Chronicle,* August 29, 1895, p. 8; Accession Card 10081 (California Whaling Rocket), Smithsonian Institution, Washington, D.C.; W. de C. Ravenel, *U.S. Commission of Fish . . . Its Exhibit at the Louisiana Purchase Exposition, St. Louis, Mo., 1904* (Washington, D.C., 1904), p. 37. What appears to be a partial specimen of a California whaling rocket is on display in the Old Dartmouth Whaling Museum at New Bedford, Mass.

22. Charles D. Voy, "Episode d'une Expédition de Pêche à la Baleine," *La Nature* (Paris), 9 (December 1880): 56–57. Our translation; see also English synopsis in *Boston Journal of Chemistry* 15 (February 1881):17.

23. Ravenel, *U.S. Commission of Fish,* p. 37; James Temple Brown, *The Whale Fishery and Its Appliances* (Washington, D.C., 1883), pp. 11, 16, 55–56, 62.

24. Interview, Winter with Hegarty, March 24, 1970; *Whalemen's Shippig List and Merchant's Transcript,* May 13, 1879, p. 2.

25. *San Francisco City Directory,* 1894, p. 555.

26. Various San Francisco city directories, 1876–90, passim; *San Francisco Examiner,* December 28, 1926, pp. 4, 5; *Langley's San Francisco Directory* (San Francisco, 1895), p. 1423; letter from San Francisco Department of Health, San Francisco, Calif., to Frank H. Winter, September 8, 1970.

27. *San Francisco City Directory,* 1881, p. 361, 1884, p. 457, and 1894, p. 555; Civil War pension claim of John Fletcher Nelson, National Archives; Certificate of marriage, John Baird to Josephine Hawkins, October 11, 1891, City Clerk, New York.

28. Civil War pension claim of Mortimer Gilbert, pension no. WO 997–301, record group 15, Veterans Administration, National Archives, Washington, D.C.; *San Francisco Chronicle,* August 17, 1924.

29. Civil War pension claim of John Fletcher Nelson, National Archives;

Notes

Newark City Directory (Newark, N.J., 1899), p. 229; Death certificate, John Baird, February 20, 1903, no. 1974, New Jersey Department of Health, Trenton, N.J.; Fairmont Cemetery Association, Newark N.J., to Frank H. Winter, March 12, 1970.

30. Winter and Sharpe, "The California Whaling Rocket and the Men Behind It," p. 361.

31. See chapters 6 through 11, above.

32. Leonard H. Matthews, ed., *The Whale* (New York, 1968), pp. 194–98; Frederick P. Schmitt, *The Whale's Tale* (Chippenham, Wilts., England, 1975), p. 51.

GLOSSARY

BALEEN

Long, fibrous, hornlike plates, found in rows in the mouths of toothless (suborder Mysticeti) whales. Strain plankton-type food from seawater. Also known as whalebone.

BARE POLES

No sails set.

BARREL

Unit of measure aboard whaleships (31½ gallons).

BEAT

To sail close-hauled to the wind.

BELUGA (*Delphinapterus leucas*)

Small, toothed cetacean, living almost exclusively in the Arctic and northern temperate seas. Also called white whale.

BEND (ON)

Tie or make fast, as with a line or rope.

BILLET

A job or duty aboard ship.

BLUBBER

Fatty outer tissue of a whale, just under skin.

BLUBBER HOLD

The foul-smelling area below decks where blubber was cut up into smaller pieces.

BLUE WHALE (*Balaenoptera musculus*)

A rorqual whale that weighs up to 100 tons, being the largest animal on earth. Roys was first to hunt them on a commercial basis. Almost extinct now. Formerly called sulphur-bottom whale.

BOATSTEERER

A harpooner; he steered the whaleboat while the mate attempted to kill the whale.

BOMB LANCE

A brass tube about fourteen inches long, which was filled with an explosive charge fired from a shoulder gun for the coup de grace.

Glossary

BOTTLENOSED WHALE (*Hyperoodon ampullatus*)	A smaller, toothed cetacean, which is found in the North Atlantic and North Pacific oceans.
BOWER	Main anchor.
BOWHEAD WHALE (*Balaena mysticetus*)	Also called Greenland whale and polar whale. A docile member of the suborder Mysticeti. Roys was the first whaler to fully exploit them in the western Arctic in 1848.
BOWSPRIT	A spar projecting from the bow of a ship.
BREACH	A whale's leap from the water.
BRYDE'S WHALE (*Balaenoptera edeni*)	A large, pelagic species of rorqual whales.
BULWARK	Sides of ship extending above the main deck.
BUNCH BACK WHALE	*See* Roys's whale.
CABLE	Line bent to anchor.
CETACEA	Scientific name of order in which whales are classified.
COOPER	Ship's barrel maker.
CUT IN	Process of stripping blubber from a whale.
DARTING GUN	A combination harpoon and bomb lance.
DAVITS	Supports from which whaleboats were suspended and lowered.
DIRTY	Bad, poor (whalers' slang).
DRAW	When a harpoon pulls out of a whale (whalers' slang).
ENSIGN	National flag.
FASTEN TO	To harpoon a whale.
FINBACK (or FIN) WHALE (*Balaenoptera physalus*)	Large member of the rorquals; closely related to the blue whale.
FLENSE	To cut in (a whale).
FLUE	Barb(s) on a harpoon.
FLUKES	Horizontal tail of a whale.

FLURRY	Death struggle of a harpooned whale.
FORECASTLE (FO'C'SLE)	Deck and crew space in bow.
GAM	Visit; converse (whalers' slang).
GRAY WHALE (*Eschrichtius gibbosus*)	A powerful, fast rorqual now found only in the North Pacific.
GREASY LUCK	Good luck (whalers' slang).
GREENHAND	Neophyte whaleman.
GREENLAND WHALE	*See* bowhead whale.
GROWLER	Small iceberg.
HALYARD	Rope for hoisting sails, flags, etc.
HEAVE TO	Stop.
HUMBUG	To engage in busy work at sea.
HUMPBACK WHALE (*Megaptera novaeangliae*)	Mysticeti whale that was not too popular with old-time whalers because its skin is covered with troublesome barnacles and parasites.
IRON	A harpoon (whalers' slang).
KANAKA	A native of the South Sea islands.
KEDGE (OFF)	Work free of an obstruction by pulling on the anchor(s) with the windlass (winch).
KILLER WHALE (*Orcinus orca*)	The most aggressive and most feared of the toothed whales. Roys wrote one of the first natural history accounts of these interesting creatures. (Also called orca.)
LANCE	Long-handled instrument for killing whales.
LAY	Whaleman's share in the earnings of a voyage.
MINKE WHALE (*Balaenoptera acutorostrata*)	A medium-sized rorqual whale, which is found in polar, temperate, and tropical waters, virtually worldwide.
MYSTICETI	A suborder of cetacea that have baleen (*q.v.*), or whalebone, in mouths instead of teeth. They eat minute marine organisms.

Glossary

NANTUCKET SLEIGHRIDE   A whaleboat being towed at great speed by a harpooned, fleeing leviathan (whalers' slang).

NARWHAL (*Monodon monoceros*)   A small, toothed whale. Males have a long, twisted "tusk," which is actually a modified tooth that can reach nine feet in length. Roys saw these whales in the Arctic.

ORCA   *See* killer whale.

PACK ICE   Large, tight mass of floating ice.

PATENT LOG   Mechanical device for measuring distance through the water.

PELAGIC   Of, or occurring on, the open sea.

PINTLE   Pin for attaching rudder to stern piece.

PLUM PUDDIN' CRUISE   Derogatory term for a short whaling voyage (whalers' slang).

POD   Herd or school of whales.

POLAR WHALE   *See* bowhead whale.

QUADRANT   Early navigational instrument for determining latitude at sea. Preceded the sextant.

RECRUIT   Obtain fresh food and supplies.

RIGHT WHALE (*Eubalaena glacialis*)   One of the first whales to be hunted; it was the "right" whale to catch. Almost extinct in Roys's time, according to his writings. Also known as Biscayan right whale.

RORQUAL   The largest of the whalebone, or baleen (*q.v.*), whales, which are characterized by a number of grooves on their undersides.

ROYAL MAST   An upper mast.

ROYS'S WHALE (*Balaena mysticetus Roysii*)   First identified by Roys as a subspecies of bowhead whale, with a hump, or "bunch," on its spine. Currently, some scientists doubt that it ever existed, because to date no specimens have ever been found for study. It is quite possible that Roys was correct in his observations, but since bowhead whales are now scarce, we may never know for sure.

RUNT Small, sick, or emaciated whale (whalers' slang).

SCREW Propeller.

SCUTTLEBUTT Gossip or rumor aboard ship.

SEI WHALE (*Balaenoptera borealis*) A large rorqual species which was not harvested in large numbers until relatively recent times.

SHIP OVER To sign on for another voyage in the same ship.

SHOOKS Barrel staves.

SKUNK Old slang word meaning to cheat.

SO ENDS A phrase commonly placed at the close of a day's entry in whaling logs and journals.

SOUND Dive swiftly.

SPERM WHALE (*Physeter catodon*) Largest of the toothed whales; aggressive, but prized for its fine oil and its spermaceti, a fine-quality wax found in its skull cavity.

SQUARE AWAY To put sails in order.

STAND OFF To avoid; wait.

STAYS The fore-and-aft standing rigging that supports the masts of a sailing ship.

SULPHUR-BOTTOM WHALE *See* blue whale.

TRY-POT Huge 200-gallon cauldrons in which blubber was "tryed out." *See* also tryworks.

TRYWORKS Brick furnaces on deck, supporting try-pots.

WHALEBOAT Small (about thirty feet long) cedar craft used to pursue whales.

WHALEBONE *See* baleen.

WHALING GROUNDS Parts of the oceans where whales were most commonly found and hunted.

WHITE WHALE *See* beluga.

WINDLASS Barrellike winch for hauling anchors.

GAZETTEER

Countries are listed according to their present names. Many places have changed sovereignty since Roys's time.

The latitudes, longitudes, and distances are approximate.

AMARGURA ISLAND	*See* Fonua'lei Island.
AVACHA, BAY OF	*See* Avachinskaya Guba.
AVACHINSKAYA GUBA, U.S.S.R.	Inlet of the Pacific Ocean on the SE coast of the Kamchatka Peninsula. City of Petropavlovsk-Kamchatskiy (*q.v.*) is on the NE shore.
AZORES	(Between 37° to 40°N and 25° to 31°W) Group of nine islands belonging to Portugal, 900 to 1200 miles W of Lisbon, in the Atlantic Ocean.
BARKLEY SOUND, BRITISH COLUMBIA, CANADA	Inlet of the Pacific Ocean on SW Vancouver Island.
BASSAS DA INDIA, MADAGASGAR (*Malagasy Republic*)	(22°S by 40°E) Volcanic rock and reefs in the Mozambique Channel, Indian Ocean, between Madagascar and the SE African coast.
BJØRN ØYA, NORWAY	(74°N by 19°E) Island in the Arctic Ocean, 450 miles NNW of Hammerfest, Norway.
BONIN ISLANDS, JAPAN	(27°N by 141°E) A Pacific archipelago, 600 miles S of Tokyo.
BURRARD INLET, BRITISH COLUMBIA, CANADA	An arm of the Strait of Georgia (*q.v.*), extending E into mainland British Columbia. The city of Vancouver is on the S side.
CANARY ISLANDS	(Between 27° to 28°N and 15° to 18°W) Archipelago belonging to Spain, about 200 miles off the NW coast of Africa in the Atlantic Ocean.

CAPE FLATTERY, WASHINGTON

Situated at the NW extremity of Washington state, on S side of the entrance to Juan de Fuca Strait.

CAPE VERDE ISLANDS

(Between 15° to 17°N and 23° to 25°W) Nine major Portuguese islands located in the Atlantic Ocean, 400 miles W of Dakar, Senegal, W Africa.

CHATHAM ISLANDS, NEW ZEALAND

(44°S by 176°W) Situated in the S Pacific Ocean, 500 miles ESE of Wellington, N.Z.

CROSS SOUND, ALASKA

Inlet between SE Alaskan mainland and N Chichagof Island.

CROZET ISLANDS, FRENCH SOUTHERN AND ANTARCTIC TERRITORIES

(46°S by 52°E) Five small islands in the subantarctic S Indian Ocean, 1500 miles SE of Cape Town, S Africa.

CUMBERLAND INLET, NORTHWEST TERRITORIES, CANADA

Actually Cumberland *Sound,* an inlet of Davis Strait, NE Canada, opposite Greenland.

CUMSHEWA, BRITISH COLUMBIA, CANADA

A geographical locality, NW Moresby Island, Queen Charlotte Islands.

DAVIS STRAIT

An arm of the N Atlantic Ocean, between SE Baffin Island (Northwest Territories, Canada) and SW Greenland.

DEEP BAY, BRITISH COLUMBIA, CANADA

A small bay N of Nanaimo (*q.v.*) in the Strait of Georgia (*q.v.*).

DESOLATION ISLAND

See Kerguelen Islands.

DIOMEDE ISLANDS, U.S.S.R.–ALASKA

(66°N by 169°W) Two islands lying in the middle of the Bering Strait, N Pacific Ocean, between NE Siberia and Alaska.

DJAILOLO, STRAIT OF, INDONESIA

Passage in the Molucca Islands, connecting the Ceram Sea with the W Pacific Ocean.

DJUPIVOGUR, ICELAND

Village located in the Berufjördur on the E coast of Iceland.

DORDRECHT, NETHERLANDS

Town in S Holland, 12 miles ESE of Rotterdam.

FAEROE ISLANDS, DENMARK

(62°N by 7°W) A group of twenty-one volcanic islands in the N Atlantic Ocean, 300

	miles SE of Iceland and 200 miles NW of the Shetland Islands.
FAIAL, AZORES	(37°N by 28°W) Island in the W central Azores (*q.v.*).
FALKLAND ISLANDS	(Between 51° to 53°S and 57° to 62°W) British colony; island group about 250 miles off SE coast of Argentina, due E of the Strait of Magellan.
FANNING ISLAND, GILBERT AND ELLICE ISLANDS	(4°N by 159°W) Located in the Line Islands, cent. Pacific Ocean, 1000 miles S of Honolulu, Hawaii.
FAYAL	*See* Faial, Azores.
FINNAFJÖRDUR, ICELAND	A fjord in NE Iceland, near Langa Nes Bay (*q.v.*).
FINNMARK, NORWAY	Northernmost county of Norway.
FONUA'LEI ISLAND, TONGA	(18°S by 174°W) Northernmost of Vava'u Island group, S cen. Pacific Ocean.
FORT RUPERT, BRITISH COLUMBIA, CANADA	Was located on Beaver Harbour, NE Vancouver Island, on Queen Charlotte Strait.
FOX ISLANDS, ALASKA	Easternmost group of the Aleutians, extending 300 miles SW from the tip of the Alaskan Peninsula.
FUNNAFJORD	*See* Finnafjördur, Iceland.
GEBE ISLAND, INDONESIA	(0° by 129°E) Located in the Moluccas group, Halmahera Sea, W Pacific Ocean.
GEORGIA, STRAIT OF, BRITISH COLUMBIA, CANADA	A 150-mile-long channel between mainland Canada and Vancouver Island, connecting Queen Charlotte Sound with Puget Sound and Juan de Fuca Strait.
GUADALCANAL, SOLOMON ISLANDS	(10°S by 160°E) A volcanic island in the SW Pacific Ocean.
HAFNARFJÖRDUR, ICELAND	A fjord in SW Iceland, 5 miles S of Reykjavik, the capital.
HOPE ISLAND	*See* Kusaie Island, Carolines group.
JAN MAYEN ISLAND, NORWAY	(71°N by 8°W) Lies in the Arctic Ocean, 400 miles E of Greenland, 500 miles NNE of Iceland, and about 1000 miles W of Norway.

Johnstone Strait, British Columbia, Canada	A 100-mile-long body of water in SW British Columbia, joining Queen Charlotte Strait (*q.v.*) with the Strait of Georgia (*q.v.*), and separating Vancouver Island from the Canadian mainland.
Kaleopolepo Bay, Maui, Hawaii	Probably an obsolete name for Maalaea Bay on the SW side of Maui.
Kamchatka Peninsula, U.S.S.R.	A 750-mile-long land mass jutting S between the Sea of Okhotsk and the Bering Sea in the N Pacific Ocean.
Kerguelen Islands, French Southern and Antarctic Territories	(50°S by 70°E) Island group located in the subantarctic Indian Ocean, about 1400 miles N of the Antarctic mainland and 2300 miles SE of Africa.
Knight Inlet, British Columbia, Canada	A narrow, 75-mile-long arm of Queen Charlotte Strait (*q.v.*), opposite Vancouver Island.
Kolguyev Island, U.S.S.R.	(69°N by 49°E) Lies 50 miles off mainland of NW U.S.S.R., NE of Kanin Peninsula, Barents Sea, Arctic Ocean.
Kusaie Island, Carolines group, U.S. Trust Territory	(5°N by 163°E) Easternmost of the Carolines, W Pacific Ocean.
Langa Nes Bay, Iceland	Situated off NE Iceland about 50 miles S of the Arctic Circle.
Langnaess Bay	*See* Langa Nes Bay, Iceland.
Lofoten Islands, Norway	(Between 67° to 68°N and 12° to 15°W) Archipelago in the Norwegian Sea, lying between 1 to 50 miles off the NW coast of Norway.
Lofotes	*See* Lofoten Islands, Norway.
Madeira	(Between 32° to 33°N and 16° to 18°W) A Portuguese archipelago in the E Atlantic Ocean, lying about 400 miles W of Morocco and 600 miles SW of Lisbon.
Makin, Gilbert and Ellice Islands	(3°N by 173°E) An atoll in the N Gilberts, W cent. Pacific.
Makira, Solomon Islands	(11°S by 162°E) A volcanic island in the

Gazetteer

	SW Pacific Ocean, 40 miles SE of Guadalcanal (*q.v.*)
MARIANA ISLANDS, U.S. TRUST TERRITORY	(Between 13° to 21°N and 145°E) A volcanic island chain situated in Micronesia, W Pacific Ocean, about 1500 miles E of the Philippines.
MAZATLÁN, SINALOA, MEXICO	A seaport town in W Mexico, near the entrance to the Gulf of California.
MOGADOR, MOROCCO	City on SW coast of Morocco, now known as Essaouira.
NANAIMO, BRITISH COLUMBIA, CANADA	City on SE Vancouver Island, lying on the Strait of Georgia (*q.v.*), 40 miles W of Vancouver.
NORDFIORD	*See* Nordurfjördur, Iceland.
NORDURFJÖRDUR, ICELAND	A fjord on the NW coast of Iceland, by the Greenland Sea.
NORTHWEST COAST GROUNDS	(Between 49° to 60° N and 130° to 170°W) Nineteenth century right-whaling area, primarily lying in the vicinity of the Gulf of Alaska.
NOVAYA ZEMLYA, U.S.S.R.	(Between 71° to 77°N and 52° and 69°W) Two large islands lying off the NW coast of the U.S.S.R., between the Barents and Kara seas of the Arctic Ocean.
NOVA ZEMLA	*See* Novaya Zemlya, U.S.S.R.
OCEAN ISLAND, GILBERT AND ELLICE ISLANDS	(1°S by 170°E) A small island in the Gilbert group, W cent. Pacific Ocean, about 60 miles S of the equator.
OKHOTSK, SEA OF, U.S.S.R.	An inlet of the Pacific Ocean, W of the Kamchatka Peninsula (*q.v.*) and Kuril Islands, U.S.S.R.
OLOWALU, MAUI, HAWAII	A coastal settlement about 5 miles S of Lahaina.
PALMYRA ISLAND, FANNING ISLANDS GROUP	(6°N by 162°W) An atoll, administered by Hawaii, in the Line Islands, cent. Pacific, 900 miles SSW of Honolulu.
PATAGONIA, ARGENTINA-CHILE	The southernmost region of S America, extends S to the Strait of Magellan.

Petropavlovsk-Kamchatskiy, U.S.S.R.	A seaport city on the SE coast of the Kamchatka Peninsula (*q.v.*)
Pitts Island	*See* Makin, Gilbert and Ellice Islands.
Queen Charlotte Islands, British Columbia, Canada	Lie about 50 miles off the N coast of British Columbia, separated from the mainland by the Hecate Strait.
Resolution Island, Northwest Territories, Canada	(62°N by 65°W) Situated off the SE tip of Baffin Islands, on the N side of the entrance to Hudson Strait.
Reydarfjördur, Iceland	A fjord located on the E coast of Iceland.
Saint-Augustin Bay, Madagascar (*Malagasy Republic*)	Inlet of the Mozambique Channel on the SW coast of Madagascar.
Saint Catherines	*See* Santa Catarina, Ilha de, Brazil.
Saint Helena Island	(16°S by 6°W) A S Atlantic British colony, about 1200 miles due W of Africa and 1700 miles NW of Cape Town, S Africa.
Saint Lawrence Island, Alaska	(63°N by 170°W) Lies in the Bering Sea, S of the entrance to the Bering Strait.
Saint Matthew Island, Alaska	(61°N by 172°W) Situated in the N cent. Bering Sea, about midway between the U.S.S.R. and Alaska.
San Cristobal	*See* Makira, Solomon Islands.
Santa Catarina, Ilha de, Brazil	An island just off the coast of S Brazil.
Seidisfiord	*See* Seydisfjördur, Iceland.
Serpent's Mouth Strait, West Indies	Lies SW of the island of Trinidad and NE of the coast of Venezuela, S America.
Seydisfjördur, Iceland	A fjord and a town of the same name in NE Iceland.
South Georgia Island	(55°S by 37°W) A British subantarctic island, about 700 miles ESE of the Falkland Islands (*q.v.*).
Spitsbergen (Spitzbergen)	*See* Svalbard (Islands), Norway.
Svalbard (Islands), Norway	(Between 77° to 81°N and 11° to 27°E) An archipelago situated in the Arctic Ocean, about 400 miles N of Norway, between Greenland and Franz Josef Land, U.S.S.R.

Gazetteer

TOBAGO, WEST INDIES   (11°N by 61°W) An island in the Lesser Antilles, Caribbean Sea, about 20 miles NE of Trinidad.

TRISTAN DA CUNHA ISLAND   (37°S by 12°W) A S Atlantic Ocean British colony, lying about halfway between Africa and S America, 1800 miles W of Cape Town and 1600 miles SSW of St. Helena (*q.v.*).

VARDØ, NORWAY   A port at the northernmost part of Norway.

VESTDALS RIVER, ICELAND   Empties into the northern Seydisfjördur in NE Iceland.

VESTDALSEYRI, ICELAND   A village on the N side of the Seydisfjördur in NE Iceland.

VOPNAFJÖRDUR, ICELAND   A fjord and town (at its head) on the NE coast of Iceland.

WEDDELL SEA, ANTARCTICA   An arm of the S Atlantic Ocean, located between the Antarctic Peninsula and Queen Maud Land, Antarctica.

WEYNTON PASSAGE, BRITISH COLUMBIA, CANADA   Located in Johnstone Strait (*q.v.*), between the NE shore of Vancouver Island and the mainland.

ZEELAND, NETHERLANDS   A province in SW Holland.

Index

Academy of Natural Sciences (Philadelphia), 59
Admiralty Court (England), 75
Africa, 3, 74, 93
Alaska, 13, 24, 27, 41, 168, 179–80, 187
Aleutian Islands, Alaska, 23, 27, 42
Amagura Island, *see* Fonua'lei Island, Tonga
America, 144
American Association of Scientific Discovery, 59
Amici, Gaetano, 157, 162
Amsterdam, Netherlands, 91
Andes mountains, South America, 36
Andrews (cooper), 129
Antarctic (region), ix, 4, 18–19, 56, 62, 73, 99, 191–92, 198
Antarctic Ocean, 55, 191–92
Arctic (region), 20, 23, 27, 29, 32–33, 40–41, 46–47, 64, 91, 175, 185, 192, 197–98, 202
Arctic Ocean, 20, 22, 24–25, 27–29, 42, 54, 56, 172, 197
Arctic whaling grounds, ix, 29, 180–81, 197
Arnold, Edward B., 169–70
Atlantic Ocean, 76, 84, 202
Atlantic telegraph cable, 94
Australia, 18, 47–48, 50, 79
Avacha, Bay of, U.S.S.R., 13
Azores islands, Africa, 2, 66, 119, 153

Baffin Bay, North America, 20, 54–55
Baird, John, *see* Fletcher, John Nelson
Baird, Spencer F., 187
Baker, Capt. F. A., 202
Baltimore, Md., 182
Bangor, Maine, 67
Bantry Bay, Ireland, 73

Barbados, West Indies, 74–75
Barbary Coast, San Francisco, 187, 189
Barendsz, Willem, 1
Barents Sea, Arctic, 68
Barkley Sound, British Columbia, 172, 175
Barnes, Capt. Thomas D., 48
Barnes, Capt. W. M., 202
Bassas da India island, Madagascar, 3
Beaufort Sea, Arctic, 27
Beckmann (sailor), 121
Beechey, Capt. F. W., 20
Beluga whale, 26
Bering Sea, Arctic, 19, 23, 27
Bering Strait, Arctic, ix, 19–20, 22, 24, 27, 29, 33, 41, 45, 54–55, 105, 197
Berufjördur, Iceland, 157
Birmingham, England, 70
Biscay, Bay of, Europe, 71
Bishop, Rogers, 71–72
Bistrup, Capt., 118
Bjørn Øya island, Norway, 68
Blair, James, 50
"Blubber Row," Peconic, N.Y., 80–81, 181
Blue whales, 61, 63–64, 66, 68, 70, 73, 78, 100–102, 108, 113, 117, 130, 135, 150, 155, 185–86, 191, 197
Bomb lance, 90
Bonaparte, Napoleon, 142
Bonemill machine, 123–24
Bonin Islands, Pacific, 5, 13
Boston, Mass., 2
Bottemanne, Capt. C. J., ix, 100, 114, 119, 139, 151, 162–67
Bottle-nosed whales, 70
Bowhead whales, ix, 25–27, 29, 41, 45, 54–57, 61, 68, 70, 88, 104, 131, 152, 185, 197

Boxer, Capt. Edward M., 90
Boyd, Benjamin, 47–48, 50
Brand, C. C., 68
Brazil, 10, 153
Bremerhaven, Germany, 75
British Colonist (Victoria), 169–70, 179
British Columbia, 169–70, 172, 174, 179, 199, 202–3
British Isles, 118, 121
Brooklyn, N.Y., 85
Brown, Benjamin, 64, 66–67
Brown, Dr. D. M., 181
Brown, Thomas, 67
Brown's bomb gun, 66
Bryde's whales, 191
"Bunch back" whale, 57
Burgess, Captain, 168
Burrard Inlet, British Columbia, 174

Cabo de São Vicente, Portugal, 75–76
Cadiz, Spain, 76
Calhoun, Capt. Rufus, 176, 179
California, 29, 33, 36–39, 48, 93, 168–69, 180, 184, 186, 202
California Fireworks Co., 189
California Whaling Rocket, 127–28, 181–83, 185–86, 189, 190
Canada, 64, 199
Canary Islands, Spain, 76
Cape Flattery, Wash., 176
Cape Horn, Chile, 11, 19, 36
Cape of Good Hope, South Africa, 4–5
Cape Verde Islands, North Atlantic, 3
Caughill, Capt. James, 185, 202
Central Railroad of New Jersey, 190
Chatham Islands, New Zealand, 10
Chukchi people, 13
Chukchi Sea, U.S.S.R., 27
Church & Co., 184, 189
Civil War (U.S.), 60, 81, 87, 94, 103, 138, 182
Clover Point, Victoria, British Columbia, 172
Clyde River, Scotland, 119
Coahuila, Mexico, 137
Coahuila & Pacific Railroad, 137
Coahuila & Zacatecas Railroad, 137
Cobh (Queenstown), Ireland, 70–71

Cogan, Capt. Bernard, 186, 202
Cold Spring Harbor, N.Y., xi, xii, 20, 23, 26, 33, 46, 197
Cold Spring Harbor Whaling Museum, xi
Columbia University, 93
Confederate States Army, 182
Confederate States Navy, 60, 81
Congreve, Sir William, 73, 91
Congreve rockets, 73, 90–91, 152, 198
Connecticut, 2
Cook, Capt. James, R.N., 51
Cook, Luther D., 4
Cooper, William, 179
Cope, E. D., 59
Copenhagen, Denmark, 104–5, 117, 119–22, 157, 161
Cork, Ireland, 70
Cork *Examiner,* 70
Coston signal rocket, 94
Covill, Capt. George A., 26–27
Crimean War, 90
Cross Sound, Alaska, 179
Crozet Islands whaling grounds, 4–5, 22
Cumberland Inlet, Northwest Territories, 65
Cumshewa, British Columbia, 176
Cunningham & Cogan bomb gun, 186

Dalton, John, 37
Danish Fishery Company, 152, 161–62
Danske Fiskeriselskab, Det, *see* Danish Fishery Company
Darwin, Charles, 51
David City, Neb., 168–69
Davis Strait, North America, 19, 54, 66, 118
Dawson, James, 169
Dawson Whaling Company, 172, 174–76
De Economist, 164
Deep Bay, British Columbia, 173
de Jong, Dr. Cornelis, xi, xii, 109
Denmark, 105, 111, 117, 120–21, 136, 142, 152
Dennis, Captain, 133
"Descriptions of Whales" (Roys ms.), 57, 61, 63, 197
Desolation Islands whaling grounds, 22
Detwiller, Jacob J., 137

INDEX

INDEX

Index

INDEX

BOOKS BY FREDERICK P. SCHMITT

H.M.S. CULLODEN (Donald E. Schmid, coauthor)
Mark Well the Whale!
The Whale's Tale

BOOKS BY CORNELIS DE JONG

Geschiedenis Van de Oude Nederlandse Walvisvaart
A Short History of Old Dutch Whaling